BEATING THE CSET!

Methods and Strategies for Beating CSET Multiple Subjects (Subtests I–III) Elementary Language Arts

BEATING THE CSET!

Methods and Strategies for Beating CSET Multiple Subjects (Subtests I–III) Elementary Language Arts

CHRIS NICHOLAS BOOSALIS

California State University, Stanislaus

Boston ■ New York ■ San Francisco
Mexico City ■ Montreal ■ London ■ Madrid ■ Munich ■ Paris
Hong Kong ■ Singapore ■ Tokyo ■ Cape Town ■ Sydney

Senior Editor: *Aurora Martínez Ramos*
Series Editorial Assistant: *Erin Beatty*
Senior Editorial-Production Administrator: *Beth Houston*
Editorial-Production Service: *Walsh & Associates, Inc.*
Senior Marketing Manager: *Amy Cronin Jordan*
Composition and Prepress Buyer: *Linda Cox*
Manufacturing Buyer: *Andrew Turso*
Cover Administrator: *Joel Gendron*
Electronic Composition: *Omegatype Typography, Inc.*

Between the time Website information is gathered and then published, it is not unusual for some sites to have closed. Also, the transcription of URLs can result in typographical errors. The publisher would appreciate notification where these errors occur so that they may be corrected in subsequent editions.

Disclaimer

This book offers expert and reliable information regarding the exams and content that it covers. It is sold with the understanding that the purchaser/user will verify all of the information about these exams since said information is subject to change. The purchaser/user also recognizes that no promise of success can reasonably accompany the purchase/use of this book. All information about the exams addressed in this text is taken from publicly available materials and materials available as a matter of the public record. The author and publisher specifically disclaim any liability that is incurred from any and all types of use/misuse and/or application/misapplication of the contents herein.

Library of Congress Cataloging-in Publication Data
Boosalis, Chris Nicholas.
    Beating the CSET! : methods and strategies for beating CSET Multiple Subjects
(subtests I-III) elementary language arts / Chris Nicholas Boosalis.
        p. cm.
    Includes bibliographical references.
    ISBN 0-205-43071-6
        1. CSET: Multiple Subjects–Study guides.   2. Language arts
(Elementary)–Examinations–Study guides.   3. Elementary school
teachers–Certification–California.   I. Title.

    LB1766.C74+
    372.112'09794–dc22

                                                                                    2004053527

Printed in the United States of America
10   9   8   7   6   5   4   3   2   08   07   06   05

The term CSET is a registered trademark of National Evaluation Systems, Inc.

This book is dedicated to my wife, Beatriz, who is the finest educator I have ever known and best friend I have ever had—and who also dislikes exams as much as the next person.

CONTENTS

Beating the CSET! offers serious preparation for the CSET Multiple Subjects exams. The methods and strategies covered in this text apply directly to subtests one through three, including the obscure language arts content of subtest one. It is designed to provide comprehensive and in-depth support to test-takers, college instructors, and preparation leaders alike who must pass these exams to receive or retain their teaching credentials in California.

- *Test-Takers.* Preparing for these exams can be challenging and worrisome. There is a lot of information to learn in a very short amount of time, not to mention the daunting format of the subtests. The goal of this text is to ensure that you learn *what to know* before the test so that you understand *what to do* on the day of the test. This will definitely increase your chances of passing on the first attempt. First, *Beating the CSET!* reveals the underlying scores that are *really* required to pass each subtest. Then, you learn how to manage your time whether taking only one exam or all of them at once. Next, you engage the strategies that you need to survive all of the essays and selected multiple choice questions on these tests. In short, this text ensures that you know everything that a candidate should know prior to testing and that a passing score will be well within reach after this essential preparation.
- *College Instructors. Beating the CSET!* offers you a way to ensure that your students have "covered the material" most often tested on the exam. As you know, your class time and autonomy are being consumed by these high-stakes exams, because of their impact on your students' lives and futures. The text offers your students their best opportunity to learn the core content of elementary language arts while you carry out activities and use materials that you know are important for a future teacher to know—but may not be tested on the exam. It also handles material that may not be to your philosophical liking, but that must be covered anyway because "it's on the test." *Beating the CSET!* reduces the burden that these exams place on your shoulders so that you can return to the real profession of preparing future teachers to teach real children, not just to pass state exams.
- *Preparation Leaders.* Test preparation leaders provide an essential link between candidates and their ultimate success on these high-stakes tests. *Beating the CSET!* is written to be immediately practical to candidates and to those charged with preparing them. The examples and explanations are clear and the content can be easily incorporated into any existing framework of preparation. The goal is to help you to help others through time-management models, essential strategies, aligned content, and activities that incorporate state standards for the content areas that will make preparation both comprehensive and easy.

WHAT SUBTESTS DOES THIS BOOK ADDRESS?

Beating the CSET! addresses the *California Subject Exams for Teachers*—Multiple Subjects (Subtests One–Three):

- Subtest One: Language Arts and Social Studies/History.
- Subtest Two: Science and Math.
- Subtest Three: Physical Education, Human Development, and the Arts.

WHAT CONTENT DOES THIS BOOK COVER?

This text covers the core body of language arts content that is tested on all of the exams listed above. Table P.1 below shows the areas that will be covered exhaustively in Chapters Three through Six:

TABLE P.1

DOMAIN ONE: LANGUAGE AND LITERACY CONTENT AREA	
1. Language and Linguistics	Linguistic Terms and Processes
2. Language Development	First/Second Language Acquisition
3. Literacy	Reading Instruction
4. Assessment	Assessment Principles
5. Instruction	Instruction Principles
DOMAIN TWO: CHILDREN'S LITERATURE CONTENT AREA	
6. Genres of Children's Literature	Children's Literature
7. Features of Literature	Elements of Prose and Poetry
8. Interpreting Literature	Responding to Prose and Poetry
DOMAIN THREE: COMMUNICATIONS CONTENT AREA	
9. Writing Applications	Narrative and Expository Writing
10. Writing Process	Prewriting and Drafting Strategies
11. Research Process	Research Strategies
12. Editing Writing	Editing, Polishing, and Publishing Writing
13. Nonwritten Communication	Speech Communications

HOW IS THIS BOOK STRUCTURED?

The structure of *Beating the CSET!* offers comprehensive preparation to candidates. Here is a chapter-by-chapter account of this text:

- Chapter One: You see details about the subtests, how they are scored, and things that you might not have known about them or even considered about them before. Then, you learn the real *underlying scores* required to pass each section and subtest of the exam. Finally, you see how to manage time on each subtest, whether you are taking only one exam or all of them at once.

- Chapter Two: You learn about the major essay formats that appear on each subtest. The essay questions and answers for language arts, history, science, math, and the humanities are dissected for you (eleven essays in all), so that you will know how to handle the written portion of the exam. In addition, you will learn effective strategies for handling multiple choice questions, along with using simple data analysis models to analyze these questions quickly and effectively.

- Chapter Three: This chapter covers English linguistics. You learn about phonology, morphology, syntax, semantics, pragmatics, sociolinguistics, and first and second language acquisition. This chapter prepares you to answer virtually all of the domain one questions on language arts from this chapter that pertain to language, language use, and language acquisition.

- Chapter Four: Literacy is the subject of Chapter Four. The test-maker's view of literacy may be different from what you learned in methods courses, so it presents very essential information. This is important because many of the "wrong" answers on the test may be part of a different literacy paradigm that you may have learned in your methods classes. In addition to understanding the principles of kindergarten through eighth grade literacy, you will also see how one conducts assessment and instruction in the elementary grades.

- Chapter Five: Children's literature is presented in Chapter Five. You learn about types of literature, features of literature, and how to encourage children to respond to literature before, during, and after reading. Most of the multiple-choice questions on literature will ask you to interpret lengthy reading passages, so it is necessary for you to have a good working knowledge of basic literary terms in order to survive these questions. Chapter five provides you with this essential knowledge.

- Chapter Six: The final chapter concerns written and oral language development. Writing and research processes are presented, along with how to edit writing and cite sources. Finally, oral communications are reviewed both in general and for the classroom. The information in this chapter is critical for you to know, because it is very obscure and may not be a part of your normal course of study in education.

IS OUTSIDE READING REQUIRED?

Just like other preparation manuals, we encourage outside reading. That reading can come from methods courses, journals, or from other selected sources. The most valuable information will come from your state standards and any text that your state has adopted to align with them. These items should be easy to locate at any university library for free or maybe even online. Instructors can also place them on reserve for students to use in their preparation. If you do choose to use outside resources, we encourage you to align the materials with the organization of this book. The content of this text is meant to correspond closely to the content that will be assessed on the exam, so outside readings should be adapted to this model.

WHERE IS THE SAMPLE EXAM?

Sample exams are problematic. Our research demonstrates that practicing on contrived sample exams, especially the multiple choice portions, is not only ineffective but also harmful. The items that other manuals include really are nothing more than someone's "best guess" about what the items will be like. Practicing on those items only gives one a false sense of security. Worse, candidates may develop *bad habits* and grow accustomed to reading item formats that won't appear on the actual exam at all. If you do a little online reading about other preparation manuals and what candidates say about them, you will see what we mean in a very short time.

Therefore, the only practice exams that we will endorse at this time and request that you obtain are the ones that come from National Evaluation Systems, Inc. (NES) itself. The study guide for each exam is available online. Visit the California Commission on Teacher Credentialing's website or go directly to NES's official CSET site for information on how to download a full-length sample exam. Additional support may also be found at *http://www.ablongman.com/boosalis*. Please visit the site for more information on state-wide CSET workshops, distance tutoring, and other materials.

WHY PEOPLE FAIL THESE TESTS

People fail these tests for three reasons.

1. No test-management plan.
2. No strategies to tackle the written, constructed-response and multiple choice questions.
3. No knowledge of content.

Problem One: NES Time Management

National Evaluation Systems (NES) exams truly require preparation. The more you know about what to expect on the day of the test, the better you will do. Students who see the test for the first time and have not been prepared for that initial shock may be at a great risk of failure, because CSET Multiple Subjects truly requires test-management plans like no other tests. Mismanaged time and bungled approaches really are a formula for failure. If you enter the exam session without a well-rehearsed battle plan, you can expect to have a difficult experience with the test. Chapter One details specific time-management models that you are sure to find helpful. These time-management models will help you reach the mandatory minimum scores for each subtest. If you follow the time stipulations carefully, completing the exam with time to spare will be a realistic goal for you—and so will passing the exam on the first attempt.

Problem Two: NES Strategies

An effective time-management plan means that you need to have strategies for tackling the written and multiple-choice sections of the test. The written sections must be done in a particular order to maximize your chances of passing. The multiple-choice section, too, has an order that you should follow. The day of the test *is not the time* to begin thinking about what to do on the test and how to do it; instead, you must have considered strategizing well in advance of the test. With a time-management plan and proven strategies to knock out the written and multiple-choice sections, your chances of passing the test have just moved from possible to likely. Chapter Two of this text details those well-researched strategies to beat all of the essay and multiple choice questions on the exam. You will find the information to be invaluable in your preparation and ultimate success.

Problem Three: NES Content

What about content? Knowledge of NES content, while important, appears not to determine success or failure. Clearly, if you do not know the content, you'll have a difficult time with the terms and concepts. Also, you'll probably fail. But ignorance of content does not tell even half of the story of why students don't pass the first time. Candidates who have extensive experience in the content of the test that has been earned in reading-methods classes and through direct experience in elementary classrooms have gone right ahead and failed the test multiple times. The reasons? Numbers one and two. Without a test-management plan that includes solid strategies and goals for reaching the minimum scores, the odds of passing the test on the first attempt are probably worse than flipping a coin (not even 50/50). Because your success depends on how you prepare for the exam and what you do on the day of the test, you are sure to find *Beating the CSET!* the best tool for preparing for the exam.

In summary, *Beating the CSET!* has been carefully crafted to help you to surmount these problems. After studying hard and following the directions offered here, time-management, written responses, multiple-choice questions, and exam content will no longer be an issue for you. Instead, you will learn everything that you must know in the first place—and then you can beat the exam!

ACKNOWLEDGMENTS

I wish to thank my editor, Aurora Martinez, and her assistant, Erin Beatty, for their commitment to this project and for helping me to make it become a reality. I also wish to thank Professor John Mitchell for his help with Haiku. I also appreciate the assistance of Sam Marandos (social studies), Tony Jackson (math), Stefanie Dimiotakis (science), and Leslie Herod (humanities) for their assistance with the essay portions of this text. Thanks also to Carlos Osorio for his work on the graphics. My warm thanks to the reviewers—Zulmara Cline, California State University, San Marcos, and Paula M. Selvester, California State University, Chico—for their time and suggestions for improving this text.

CHAPTER ONE

HOW TO BEAT THE CSET MULTIPLE SUBJECTS EXAM

WHY DO I NEED THIS PREP BOOK?

Beating the CSET provides you with the two essential ingredients for success, including what to know and do to pass each of the subtests of the multiple subjects exam. The information in this book presents all of the information successful candidates knew before they ever sat down to take their exam.

The conditions that surround these exams are always the same. Panicked elementary credential candidates face exams that may deny them a credential or cost them a position if they do not pass it. Their instructors, too, are panicked because their students come to them with many questions, many concerns, and even deep skepticism about how to take and pass the exam. Usually, few resources exist to adequately prepare for the test. The result is this: Test-takers who take and pass the exam often do so without knowing really how or why they did it. "I guess I'm just a good test-taker" is a pretty common response. Similarly, students who are unsuccessful either one or more times respond by saying, "I guess I'm just no good at this"—or worse.

Much has been learned about how to pass—if not outright "beat"—these exams. The most important idea to keep in mind is that there are approaches to these tests that work and that there is also a defined body of content that one can learn in order to pass any one of the exams. This is because all of the exams require you to manage your time carefully, identify questions that are worth answering (some do not count toward your score), and pass each subtest with a particular score. In short, rather than risk passing by chance or failing through a simple lack of test skills, you can actually prepare yourself well for the exam and increase your chances of success on the first attempt. This text will help you to achieve that goal.

WHAT IS THE CSET MULTIPLE SUBJECTS EXAM?

The CSET Multiple Subjects exam exists to ensure that you are a "fully qualified teacher"—or a "fully qualified *test-taker*" as one candidate remarked recently. You face questions on language arts, social studies, science, math, and the humanities (human development, physical education, and the arts), depending on the subtest that you take.

The test is given in a subtest format. There are three subtests that you must pass to be declared "subject matter competent." Each subtest combines two or more content areas, and you must pass a given subtest with a particular score. Here are the subtests and their content-area combinations:

- Subtest One: Language Arts and Social Studies.
- Subtest Two: Science and Math.
- Subtest Three: Human Development, Physical Education, and the Arts.

Each exam session is five hours in length. If you take all three subtests in one session, then you will see 143 multiple-choice questions, and a total of eleven essays (two per each content area within subtests one and two; one per content area within subtest three). Taking only one or two subtests during the five hour session results in a different number of multiple-choice and essay questions. Table 1.1 reflects the number of questions you will see per subtest and the official passing score.

TABLE 1.1   Structure of CSET Multiple Subjects

CSET MULTIPLE SUBJECTS	MULTIPLE CHOICE 70%	ESSAYS 30%	INDEPENDENT SCALED SCORE
Subtest One	**52 items**	**4 Total Essays**	**220**
■ Language Arts	26 items	Two English essays	100–300
■ Social Studies/History	26 items	Two History essays	
Subtest Two	**52 items**	**4 Total Essays**	**220**
■ Science	26 items	Two Science essays	100–300
■ Math	26 items	Two Math essay	
Subtest Three	**39 items**	**3 Total Essays**	**220**
■ Physical Education	13 items	One PE essay	100–300
■ Human Development	13 items	One HD essay	
■ Arts	13 items	One Arts essay	

Source: Data from CSET Registration Bulletin (2003/2004).

Again, you must pass *each* subtest in order to be declared "subject-matter competent," although you do not have to pass all three subtests all at once. This means that you can spend all five hours on only one subtest (passing them one by one over a period of months), or you can register for all three tests and take them in one sitting. The number of times that you can retake a particular subtest is limited by only your budget and your patience.

HOW IS THE CSET MULTIPLE SUBJECTS EXAM SCORED?

The multiple-choice questions are machine scored. You can have them rescanned for a fee if you think they've made a mistake, but you're pretty much stuck with the score that you get. Worse, there are multiple-choice questions that do not count toward your passing score, because they are trying them out on you. These are called "null questions," where the test makers include unscored questions to determine if these questions should be included on future exams based in part on how many people answer them correctly or incorrectly.

The essays, on the other hand, are always scored. There is nothing in the literature to suggest that they will not be scoring your essay, so it is critical that you complete any and all essays that you see on test day. Each essay is rated by two or more people who score it according to a three-point rubric. It is critical that you write these essays in a way that will help the evaluators find what they are looking for—if you don't, you will not earn the points that you need to pass the test.

HOW DO YOU PASS THE CSET MULTIPLE SUBJECTS EXAM?

Very carefully is the trite response; it is also the honest response. You really need an understanding of how the tests work before you sit down to take them. Here are the most important things to know in order to pass the exam:

1. Understand the real passing scores for each subtest.
2. Approach noncompensatory scoring carefully.
3. Compensate for null multiple-choice questions.

Real Scores

NES reports your passing or failing scores on a scale. For example, they tell you that a passing score is 220 on a 100–300 point scale. These numbers are no fun to see, because you don't know exactly how many questions that you have to answer in order to pass each subtest. The rationale for the scale isn't important, but the real passing score is. Imagine this situation: If I tell you that you have to answer seven out of ten questions on a spelling test correctly to keep your job, then you're going to pay very careful attention to what you're doing until you are sure that you've answered seven of them correctly. Anything beyond seven correct questions doesn't matter. The same idea applies to each subtest on CSET Multiple Subjects Exam.

Unfortunately, scaled scores obscure this real passing number; but, luckily for you, this book will demystify those scores for you and offer you a strategy to exploit them. By the end of your reading in this chapter, you will know the real number of questions that you have to answer accurately, so that you can be sure that you reach or surpass that number to increase your chances of passing each subtest.

Noncompensatory Scoring

Noncompensatory scoring means that you cannot use one content area to compensate for another. This information affects both subtest and comprehensive exams. Take a subtest exam like CSET for example. Subtest one pairs language arts and history, and you have to get a **combined** score of 220 in order to pass; however, you cannot get every language arts question correct and completely miss history and still pass the test. That's because there are **mandatory minimums** assigned to each content area within a given subtest. You will learn all about the minimum scores when we address each subtest in the next section.

Null Questions

The final area to consider are the null questions. The test maker uses you as a guinea pig by trying out multiple-choice questions on you, which accounts for the high number of people who leave the test session saying, *"Some of the questions had two right answers!"* That's probably true, because they are most likely the null questions. Though you cannot identify which questions do and do not count, you must learn how to survive the multiple-choice section despite these questions. If you don't, then you will end up spending too much time on questions that do not count toward your score, and you may also end up retaking the test because of these questions. In short, knowing how to handle the null questions figures prominently in how you approach the exam.

IN WHAT ORDER DO THE MULTIPLE-CHOICE QUESTIONS APPEAR ON CSET?

You will see the multiple-choice questions first and the essays last in the booklet. Take subtest one for example: The language arts and social studies questions will be in one section, and the four essays (two from language arts and two from social studies) will immediately follow them.

The order of the multiple-choice question is anyone's guess. They can be by *section, group,* or *jumble.* Ideally, you'll see two **separate sections** of language arts or social studies questions, enabling you to focus on one content area at a time and starting with your strongest area. **Group questions** might alternate five to ten questions: five language arts, five social studies, and so forth. This pattern is more difficult, because you have to shift your train of thought back and forth as you do the test. The worst scenario is the **jumble,** where language arts and social studies questions appear one after another or are simply randomized. This organizational pattern is hard because you really have to be nimble in your approach. Thankfully, we have worked out a plan for you to make any question order survivable through a strategy called *The Tally Strategy.* Once you understand the real score required to pass each content area on each subtest, we will walk you through this very important strategy.

HOW DO I BEAT THE CSET?

First, you have to know the real number of questions that you must answer with care. Second, you have to know how to approach the exam in terms of when you do the multiple-choice questions and when you write the essays. Finally, you have to know how to manage your time on the exam, especially if you're going to take the whole exam at once.

Let's start with the real score that you need to pass the test. Subtest one tests language arts and social studies (history) and contains a total of fifty-two questions and four essays (two for each content area). On subtest two, you face science and math and see a total of fifty-two questions, along with four essays (two for each content area). Finally, on subtest three, you confront the humanities (physical education, child development, and the arts) and a total of thirty-nine items and three essays (one for each content area). The additional challenge is that not all of the multiple-choice questions count, since some of the questions are null. Look at the Table 1.2. Column A shows you the number of questions that you face by subtest and by content area, and column B shows you the estimated number of items that actually count.

TABLE 1.2   Summary of Multiple Choice Items

CSET MULTIPLE SUBJECTS	A MULTIPLE-CHOICE ITEMS THAT YOU'LL SEE	B NUMBER OF ITEMS THAT COUNT
Subtest One	**52 items**	**46 items**
■ Language Arts	26 items	23 items
■ Social Studies/History	26 items	23 items
Subtest Two	**52 items**	**46 items**
■ Science	26 items	23 items
■ Math	26 items	23 items
Subtest Three	**39 items**	**36 items**
■ Physical Education	13 items	12 items
■ Human Development	13 items	12 items
■ Arts	13 items	12 items

Note: Estimates based on similar NES exams.

As you can see in Table 1.2, as many as six questions will be thrown out of any given subtest. In addition, there are minimum passing scores associated with each content area of each subtest. These thresholds were established by the California Commission on Teacher Credentialling (CCTC) and the state legislature. You cannot slip below these thresholds and still pass the test, since it is fully noncompensatory. Column C of the Table 1.3 tells you the official minimum score.

TABLE 1.3   Summary of Minimum Multiple Choice Scores

CSET MULTIPLE SUBJECTS	A MULTIPLE-CHOICE ITEMS THAT YOU'LL SEE	B NUMBER THAT COUNT	C MINIMUM PASSING THRESHOLDS
Subtest One	**52 items**	**46 items**	**26 minimum**
■ Language Arts	26 items	23 items	13
■ Social Studies/History	26 items	23 items	13
Subtest Two	**52 items**	**46 items**	**26 minimum**
■ Science	26 items	23 items	13
■ Math	26 items	23 items	13
Subtest Three	**39 items**	**36 items**	**21 minimum**
■ Physical Education	13 items	12 items	7
■ Human Development	13 items	12 items	7
■ Arts	13 items	12 items	7

Note: Estimates based on similar NES exams.

Column C shows you the minimum scores associated with each content area. Here is an example: To achieve the minimum number of questions required to pass subtest one, you cannot slip below thirteen correct questions on either reading or social studies; therefore, thirteen questions are the threshold on either reading or social studies on **subtest one.** Remember: You cannot simply do really well on language arts and score zero on social studies and still pass the subtest. The same thing is true for the rest of the subtests as the table above shows.

Let's consider the essays now. Unlike the multiple-choice sections, *all of the essays on each subtest exam are scored,* so it is extremely important for you to complete them. Each essay on each subtest will be scored, and each is worth six points each on a three-star scale (two points per star):

★ = 2 points
★★ = 4 points
★★★ = 6 points

Evaluators award points based on your knowledge of content. If you display a minimum amount of knowledge, you will receive two points. The number of stars increase with the level of knowledge that you display on a given topic.

Table 1.4 shows you the number of essays, the minimum number of points you need to earn (in **bold**), and the score that you must average on each essay (in *italics*):

TABLE 1.4   Minimum Essay Scores

SUBTEST ONE	SUBTEST TWO	SUBTEST THREE
Language Arts—2 essays Social Studies/History—2 essays	Science—2 essays Math—2 essays	Physical Education—1 essay Human Development—1 essay Arts—1 essay
24 possible points (6 points per essay)	24 possible points (6 points per essay)	18 possible points (6 points per essay)
14 point minimum	**14 point minimum**	**10 point minimum**
4 points per essay	*4 points per essay*	*4 points per essay*

Note: Estimates based on similar NES exams.

You will see four essays on subtests one and two; three essays appear on subtest three. The essays yield twenty-four possible points on subtests one and two, and eighteen possible points on subtest three (each essay is worth six points). Focus only on either subtests one or two for the moment. As Table 1.4 reveals, you must reach a **fourteen-point minimum from a combined score** of the four essays that you will write for the evaluators. This means that you must average two stars (★★) on each essay, so that you will be awarded an average score of four points. Doing so will ensure that you receive four points for four essays and earn a total of sixteen points—two points more than you need to pass the essay portion of either subtest one or two. To simplify this information further, you cannot score below two ★★ on any of the essays and expect to pass the essay portion of the test.

Look at subtest three now. Eighteen points are possible, because each essay is worth six points. You cannot slip below a score of ten from a combined score on each of the essays. In short, you have to average four points on each essay, so that your combined score from each essay is twelve—two more points than you need to pass the essays on subtest three. Please note that in all cases, you must not leave any essays blank. Blank responses will receive a score of zero. Thus, it is better for you to make an attempt than to risk receiving no score from having written nothing.

The Tally Strategy

Let's put all of this information together now into a strategy that you can apply to each subtest. First, review what you know. Subtests one and two have a total of fifty-two multiple-choice items (twenty-three items per content area) and four essays. You must answer thirteen questions correctly on a given content area (twenty-six total) and reach a total of fourteen points from the four essays in order to pass either subtest one or two. Subtest three has thirty-nine multiple-choice questions (thirteen questions per content area) and three essays. You must answer seven multiple-choice questions correctly (twenty-one total) and earn a combined total of ten points from the essays in order to pass subtest three.

The information that you now know can be turned into an effective strategy to beat the test. It is called the *tally strategy*. Tables 1.5, 1.6, and 1.7 are essential, and you must memorize them in order to make them work for you. Please review each of them now, and notice that the recommended number of correct questions is **higher** than the stated minimum scores to account for the null questions (see Table 1.2).

Here is how to make each of these tables work for you. Memorize each one before test day, and sketch them into your test booklet before you take a subtest. As you answer the multiple choice items, put a "hash mark" into your table for questions that you feel

TABLE 1.5 Tally Table for Subtests One

LANGUAGE ARTS	SOCIAL STUDIES	LANGUAGE ARTS	SOCIAL STUDIES
23 items	*23 items*	*2 essays*	*2 essays*
16 correct	16 correct	4 points per essay	4 points per essay

TABLE 1.6 Tally Table for Subtest Two

SCIENCE	MATH	SCIENCE	MATH
23 items	*23 items*	*2 essays*	*2 essays*
16 correct	16 correct	4 points per essay	4 points per essay

TABLE 1.7 Tally Table for Subtest Three

HUMAN DEVELOPMENT	PHYSICAL EDUCATION	ARTS	HUMAN DEVELOPMENT	PHYSICAL EDUCATION	ARTS
12 items	*12 items*	*12 items*	*1 essay*	*1 essay*	*1 essay*
8 correct	8 correct	8 correct	4 points	4 points	4 points

confident that you have answered correctly. For example, as you complete subtest three, mark off the human development, PE, and arts questions that you're quite certain that you have gotten right. Once you've reached **eight questions** for a content area, you've surpassed the minimum number of seven questions *and have accounted for the null question.* Any additional questions that you answer will either be "money in the bank" or questions that you will just have to guess on because they are simply too hard to answer. NOTE: You should also keep track of the essay questions and how well you think that you did—you will need to write well enough to receive two stars (★★) and earn four points per essay.

In What Order Should I Do a Subtest?

This is a very important question. Since each subtest includes multiple-choice and essay questions, you have to decide on how you will approach each of these areas. You have two basic options. The first option is to do the essays first and then complete the multiple-choice questions. The second option is to outline the essays first, do the multiple-choice questions next, and then finish the essays using any clues to correct answers that you may have gleaned from the multiple-choice questions and answers. Let's look at each option now.

The "One-Pass" Method.   The method is termed "One Pass" because you do the written sections first in a specific order and leave the multiple-choice portion for last. The reason is simple. If you run low on time during the multiple-choice section, you can fill in the bubbles using your favorite letter consistently. Think about it. Getting the written questions out of the way first will allow you to spend more time working the multiple-choice questions strategically. And, if you have to rush through the multiple-choice questions, you can. But if you do the test in the reverse, you won't be able to just "bubble in" the written sections. This may be the biggest mistake that students commit when taking the test the first time—and many people continue to repeat the same error into their sixth and seventh attempts. There is a something to be learned from these unsuccessful experiences, too.

Take subtest one, for example, taken solo during a five-hour period (see Table 1.8).

TABLE 1.8   One-Pass Example

FIRST	SECOND
4 essay questions	*52 multiple-choice questions*
2 hours (30 minutes each)	3 hours

Using "One Pass," you knock out the written sections first. You do them first because you can be sure that the answers will be scored (not the case with the multiple-choice questions). In brief, you would read an essay question, analyze the data, and write the answers. Remember that your essays will most likely count toward your score, so they are much easier to score points on and easier to handle in many ways. Try to spend no more than thirty minutes on each essay question, since you really have to budget your time carefully on NES exams. The remaining time is spent working the multiple-choice section strategically.

The main benefit of "One-Pass" is that it helps you to manage time and to nail the essays to earn points before attempting the multiple-choice section. It is also very straightforward and works best for students who want a simple time-management model to work with. There are some cautions, however. If your knowledge of content is weak or if it appears that you will not have time to prepare for the test, then "One Pass" might not be for you. Instead, you will need to rely on the "Two-Step" method described next, because it is for students who might need additional support during the exam to reach the mandatory minimum score.

The "Two-Step" Method.   The "Two Step" is an alternative method of presentation that is very effective. It is the preferred method for all CSET Multiple Subjects subtests (see Table 1.9).

TABLE 1.9   Two-Step Example

FIRST	SECOND	LAST
Outline all four essays	Do multiple-choice	Finish both essays
Analyze data	Do gimmies and 50/50s	Guess away!

The first step is to survey and outline each of the essays and then do the multiple-choice questions for a defined amount of time (Note: The times will be stated when specific exams are discussed in the last part of this section). After completing as many of the items that you can answer easily, you return to the essays and finish writing them. The multiple-choice questions may be packed with terms and content that will be useful in your essays. Because of the abundance of possible clues that might be contained in the multiple-choice questions, you may be able to actually use the test against itself. This approach is recommended for everyone and proves its effectiveness time and time again. After writing the essays, if you have any time remaining, then you spend it guessing on multiple-choice items that you will never be able to answer, even if you have the best materials available in front of you.

Should I "One Pass" or "Two Step"?   You know yourself best. Here are the criteria for each of these methods and who might benefit from using a particular method over another one. You consider using "One Pass" if both conditions apply to you.

1. You read and write slowly. It is geared for candidates who feel that they might need to stomp their way through the test toward a passing score.
2. Your knowledge of the content seems pretty stable. If you know the content, then use "One Pass." This is because you won't need to try to use the test against itself to answer any of the questions. And, since you know the material, use the easiest method for obtaining your magic score—and that's "One Pass." You'll get a sense of whether you know the content once you have finished reading Chapters Three through Six.

However, the "Two-Step" method is by far the preferred method among the successful test-takers.

1. You manage your time effectively. If you have enough time to learn the time-management strategies for "Two Step," then use it.

2. You find the content particularly baffling or simply don't have enough time to study the content for the test. In this case, you're going to have to get help during the test—and the test itself may be your best partner and study-buddy. By sketching out the written questions first and then attempting to use the multiple-choice questions to supplement terms and activities within each outline, you may increase your chances of passing, even if your knowledge of content is very limited.

The Hybrid Approach.   If you have enough time to prepare for the test, then try to remain as flexible as possible with your time. Review the methods thoroughly, so that you become nimble enough to use a hybrid of these approaches if necessary. A hybrid simply means that you survey the written sections first and either answer or outline the questions. After outlining or answering the written questions, you complete the multiple-choice questions, saving enough time to return to the essays that you still have to complete. The remaining time is spent filling in any written-response outlines with the information that you have "borrowed" from the multiple-choice questions.

You will be on your own to keep track of your progress during the five-hour period (see Table 1.10). Because of the complexity of these subtests, it is recommended that you simply stick to the time-management plans described at the end of this chapter, rather than using the hybrid approach. The choice, as always, is yours.

TABLE 1.10   A "Hybrid" Approach for Subtest One

ESSAY 1	ESSAY 2	ESSAY 3	ESSAY 4	MULTIPLE CHOICE
Spelling	*Metaphor*	*Civil War*	*Constitution*	
Time Spent	Time Spent	Time Spent	Time Spent	Time Spent

Dividing and Conquering the Multiple-Choice Questions

A very important consideration is how to handle the multiple-choice items. Most people simply start with the first question and then work through items one by one. That does not work very well for CSET. When you take the test, you will quickly realize that some of the questions are really obvious and some are quite impossible. You will also note that some the questions are very, very long because they rely on data sets, and others are really short and easy to complete. These facts indicate that you cannot simply start with item one and continue through the questions. Doing the questions in order might mean that you will miss the easiest questions, especially if you are going to take all of the subtest exams at once. You are going to have to employ a different approach that will allow you to move through the test efficiently in order to reach the minimum number of questions required to pass a given subtest.

Divide and conquer is the best approach to the multiple-choice questions. Imagine that you have 100 minutes to complete fifty-two items on subtest one. What you do is divide the questions into five sections, spending no more than twenty minutes per section. Table 1.11 illustrates this approach for you.

TABLE 1.11   **Dividing and Conquering the Multiple Choice**

SECTION 1	SECTION 2	SECTION 3	SECTION 4	SECTION 5
Items 1–10	*Items 10–20*	*Items 20–30*	*Items 30–40*	*Items 40–52*
20 minutes	20 minutes	20 minutes	20 minutes	20 minutes

Dividing a subtest like this will help you to move through the questions effectively. You look at items one through ten first and pick out the easy questions (the gimmies). Do them first. Then, spend time on the ones that are 50/50s (ones that you can get with some effort). Finally, skip the items that are real time wasters and move on to the next section. If you have time at the end, you can go back and work on the time wasters if you want, but you will probably end up guessing on these items.

All of the time-management models use "divide and conquer" because it really is the preferred method for handling the multiple-choice items. Combining this strategy with the tally tables described earlier is the most powerful approach that you can use on the test.

TIME-MANAGEMENT METHODS ILLUSTRATED FOR THE CSET MULTIPLE SUBJECTS EXAM

You have to decide if you are going to take the tests one at a time, two at a time, or all at once. Five time-management plans are offered here:

- Plan A is for taking one subtest only (subtest one or two).
- Plan B is for taking subtest three only.
- Plan C is for taking subtests one and two together.
- Plan D is for taking subtest one or two with subtest three.
- Plan E is for taking all three subtests in one setting.

If this is your first attempt on any of the subtests, then you are advised to register for all of the subtests and to take them at once. In the first place, you may end up finishing—and passing—all of them at once. If not, you will have at least had the opportunity to look ahead at the other subtests to get a sense of what you know and do not know; you can then prepare accordingly. NOTE: *Do not forget to review Tally Tables 1.5, 1.6, and 1.7 and to memorize them for the test! None of the time-management plans below will work for you without the tally tables, so it is critical for you to know them.*

Plan A: Taking Either Subtest One or Two

In this scenario, you elect to take **only one** of the three subtests during a five-hour period. Since the time-management models are the same for both subtests one and two, we will only apply the strategy to subtest one. Please extrapolate the information to subtest two. Table 1.12 shows the content areas, total multiple-choice questions, and essays in subtest one.

TABLE 1.12   Subtest One: Reading, Language, and Literature

SUBTEST ONE	MULTIPLE CHOICE	WRITTEN RESPONSES
Language Arts	26 Questions	Two Language Arts Essays
Social Studies	26 Questions	Two Social Studies Essays
Totals	52 Questions	Four Essays

Tables 1.13 and 1.14 provide two examples of time management for taking Subtest One. Table 1.13 shows you how to approach subtest one **if the test is given by section (e.g., if you see language arts first and social studies second).**

Since you may be free to work on either the reading/literature section first or the history/social studies first, begin with your strongest area. This way, you will be able to work through one test quickly and apply any time saved to your weaker area. As shown in Table 1.13, you may wish to start with the reading/literature section first and outline the essays for about five minutes total. Then, complete the multiple-choice questions using either "divide and conquer" or "seek and destroy." **As you do the multiple-choice items, pull language, content, and ideas out of the items for your essays.** The questions are *content rich* and may give you clues about what to include in each of the essays that you write! You will have eighty minutes to write the essays in this model (twenty minutes each).

Table 1.14 tells you how to spend your time on each of the independent sections. For Language Arts, for example, divide the section into groups of about five questions and spend no more than twenty-one minutes on each group. Repeat the same process for the history section. Since you have about four minutes per question, time should not be an issue.

TABLE 1.13   Section Time Management

START *Language Arts Essays*	SECOND, *Language Arts Multiple Choice*	THIRD, *Social Studies Essays*	LAST, *Social Studies Multiple Choice*
■ Survey essays ■ Outline them **5 minutes**	■ Do multiple choice **105 minutes** ■ Complete Essays **40 minutes total**	■ Survey essays ■ Outline them **5 minutes**	■ Do multiple choice **105 minutes** ■ Complete Essays **40 minutes total**

TABLE 1.14   Language Arts or Social Studies Section

1–5	6–10	11–15	16–20	21–25
21 minutes	21 minutes	21 minutes	21 minutes	21 minutes

26–30	31–37	38–42	43–47	48–52
21 minutes	21 minutes	21 minutes	21 minutes	21 minutes

Jumbled Question Management. Table 1.15 shows you how to handle the test if the items are **jumbled** and not given to you by section. For example, you might not see the Language Arts questions and the Social Studies questions separately; instead, they might be shuffled into fifty-two items with no rhyme or reason.

TABLE 1.15   Jumbled Question Management

Start by outlining *all* of the essays for language arts and social studies.	**Second,** do the multiple-choice items (gimmies only!).	**Third,** write the essays for language arts and social studies.	**Last,** guess on the remaining multiple-choice items.
■ Survey essays ■ Outline them ■ **10 minutes total**	■ Do multiple choice ■ **210 minutes**	■ Write the essays ■ Fill in content ■ **40 minutes total**	■ **30 minutes**

Table 1.16 below shows you how to manage your time on **jumbled** multiple-choice questions. Though you will see Language Arts and Social Studies questions alternately in this scenario (Math or Science in subtest two), you apply the same strategies of divide and conquer. Nail the gimmies first, the 50/50s next, and guess on the time wasters.

TABLE 1.16   Time Management for Jumbled Questions

1–10	11–20	21–30	31–40	41–52
42 minutes	42 minutes	42 minutes	42 minutes	42 minutes

As you do the multiple-choice items, pull language, content, and ideas out of the items for your essays. The questions are *content rich* and may give you clues about what to include in each of the essays that you write. You will have eighty minutes (twenty minutes each) to write the essays in this model.

Plan B: Taking Subtest Three Only

Here, you take only subtest three in five hours. Table 1.17 below shows you how to spend your time if the questions are given to you by section.

TABLE 1.17   Subtest Three Structure

FIRST	SECOND	THIRD
Human Development	*Physical Education*	*Arts*
■ 13 multiple-choice **70 minutes** ■ 1 essay question **30 minutes**	■ 13 multiple-choice **70 minutes** ■ 1 essay question **30 minutes**	■ 13 multiple-choice **70 minutes** ■ 1 essay question **30 minutes**

For each of the three sections of this subtest, you will have under 100 minutes to spend on the multiple-choice and essay questions. A possible course of action is to survey the written question first for less than five minutes, complete the multiple-choice questions in under seventy minutes, and then write the essay for that section in under twenty-five minutes. Repeat this process for each section. The essays here are brief, so you should have more than enough time to write good quality essays.

Jumbled Question Management.   Table 1.18 shows you how to manage time if the questions on subtest three are jumbled.

TABLE 1.18   Jumbled Questions on Subtest Three

Start by outlining *all* of the essays.	**Second,** do the multiple-choice items (gimmies only).	**Third,** write the essays.	**Last,** guess on the remaining multiple-choice items.
■ Survey essays ■ Outline them ■ **10 minutes total**	■ Do multiple choice ■ **200 minutes**	■ Write the essays ■ Fill in content ■ **30 minutes each**	■ **15 minutes** ■ Check grammar

Table 1.19 shows you how to manage your time on **jumbled** multiple-choice questions. Though you will see Human Development, Physical Education, and Arts questions alternately in this scenario, you apply the same strategies of divide and conquer. Nail the gimmies first, the 50/50s next, and guess on the time wasters.

TABLE 1.19   Subtest Three Divide and Conquer

1–5	6–10	11–15	16–20	21–25	26–30	31–39
28 minutes	28 minutes	28 minutes	28 minutes	28 minutes	28 minutes	28 minutes

As you do the multiple-choice items, pull language, content, and ideas out of the items for your essays. The questions are *content rich* and may give you clues about what to include in each of the essays that you write! You will have eighty minutes (twenty minutes each) to write the essays in this model.

Plan C: Taking Both Subtests One and Two

In this scenario, you elect to take two subtests together that are parallel in structure (e.g., subtest one and subtest two). Table 1.20 below shows a time-management plan for both subtests *if they are given in sections.* The order presented is arbitrary, since you will probably want to begin with your strongest content area first and that may not be reading/literature.

In this scenario, you budget your time among the sections, leaving yourself 150 minutes per subtest. You may wish to order the exams from best to worst and complete your

TABLE 1.20   Taking Subtests One and Two Together

FIRST, *Survey the Essays*	SECOND, *Language Arts Multiple Choice*	THIRD, *Social Studies Multiple Choice*	FOURTH, *Write the Essays*
■ Survey essays ■ Outline them **10 minutes**	■ Do multiple choice **50 minutes**	■ Do multiple choice **50 minutes**	■ Language Arts **20 minutes total** ■ Social Studies **20 minutes total**
FIFTH, *Survey the Essays*	SIXTH, *Science Multiple Choice*	SEVENTH, *Math Multiple Choice*	LAST, *Write the Essays*
■ Survey essays ■ Outline them **10 minutes**	■ Do multiple choice **50 minutes**	■ Do multiple choice **50 minutes**	■ Science essays **20 minutes total** ■ Math essays **20 minutes total**

strongest areas of knowledge first. For example, if Language Arts is your strongest area, start with subtest one and with that content area. Doing so may allow you to spend more time on your weaker areas, since you will complete your strongest section more quickly. For each of the two subtests, you will have only about two minutes per question and only ten minutes for each essay. You will have to work very efficiently through both the multiple-choice and written response questions if you are to finish in time (see Table 1.21).

TABLE 1.21   Time Management for Sectioned Multiple-Choice Questions

1–5	6–10	11–15	16–20	21–26
10 minutes	10 minutes	10 minutes	10 minutes	10 minutes

27–32	33–37	38–42	43–47	48–52
10 minutes	10 minutes	10 minutes	10 minutes	10 minutes

Jumbled Question Management.   Table 1.22 shows you how to handle the test if the items are **jumbled.** Because you are taking subtests one and two, your time is much shorter to complete each section of the exam. In this scenario, start with your strongest suit, meaning the subtest on which you believe you will have the most success. Stick to the times in Table 1.22 and repeat the process on the next subtest once you are finished.

Start with your strongest subtest and outline the four essays. Then, spend 100 minutes on the fifty-two questions, keeping in mind that they will alternate from one content area to another. After nailing the minimum number of questions, complete the essays, spending no more than twenty minutes on them. Remember to pull any content that you can from the multiple-choice questions into your essays. Any remaining time should be spent either completing or guessing on the multiple-choice items that you could not finish earlier. You will have 150 minutes remaining to apply the same strategy to the next subtest.

TABLE 1.22   Jumbled Question Time Management

Start with your strongest subtest and outline its essays.	Second, do the multiple choice (gimmies and 50/50s).	Third, write the four essays utilizing content from the multiple choice.	Last, guess on the remaining multiple-choice items. REPEAT ON NEXT SUBTEST!

▪ Survey essays
▪ Outline them
  10 minutes total
	▪ Multiple choice
	  100 minutes
		▪ Write four essays
		  40 minutes total
			Remaining time

Table 1.23 shows you how to manage your time on **jumbled** multiple-choice questions.

TABLE 1.23   Multiple Choice Time Management

1–10	11–20	21–30	31–40	41–52
20 minutes	20 minutes	20 minutes	20 minutes	20 minutes

Plan D: Taking Either Subtest One or Two with Subtest Three

In this plan, you take either subtest one or two with subtest three. The example utilizes subtest one with subtest three. If it is a section test, divide your five hours among the sections as shown in Table 1.24:

TABLE 1.24   Time Management for Adding Subtest Three

FIRST, *Survey Subtest Essays*	SECOND, *Language Arts* *Multiple Choice*	THIRD, *Social Studies* *Multiple Choice*	FOURTH, *Write the Essays*

▪ Survey essays
▪ Outline them
  10 minutes
	▪ Do multiple choice
	  50 minutes
		▪ Do multiple choice
		  50 minutes
			▪ Language Arts
			▪ Social Studies
			  40 minutes total

FIFTH, *Survey Subtest* *Three Essays*	**SIXTH,** *Subtest Three* *Multiple Choice*	**SEVENTH,** *Write the Essays*	**LAST,** *Guess Away*

▪ Outline essays
  10 minutes
	▪ Do PE, CD, Arts
	▪ 39 questions
	  70 minutes total
		▪ PE essay
		▪ CD essay
		▪ Arts essay
		  30 minutes total
			▪ Finish any
			  remaining items
			  30 minutes total

You have 150 minutes per subtest. Here, begin with your strongest. Table 1.25 shows what time management will look like if you begin with either subtest one or two and leave subtest three for last. Ten minutes are spent outlining the essays, leaving 100 minutes for both the language arts and social studies questions. You will have a total of forty minutes to write the four essays on the first subtest and to import any content that you can pull from the multiple-choice questions into your essays. Turning to subtest three, you outline the essays for ten minutes and then complete the multiple-choice questions for seventy minutes. Doing so will leave thirty minutes to complete the three essays on physical education (PE), child development (CD), and the arts. Using this plan, you will have thirty minutes remaining for any multiple-choice items that you could not get. Review Table 1.23 for how to manage time on either subtest one or two.

TABLE 1.25 Managing Time on Subtest Three

1–5	6–10	11–15	16–20	21–25	26–30	31–39
10 minutes	10 minutes	10 minutes	10 minutes	10 minutes	10 minutes	10 minutes

Jumbled Question Management. If the questions in each subtest are jumbled, then apply the time management model shown in Table 1.26:

TABLE 1.26 Jumbled Question Management

FIRST, *Outline the Essays.*	SECOND, *Do the Multiple Choice (gimmies and 50/50s).*	THIRD, *Write the Four Essays Utilizing Content from the Multiple Choice.*	FOURTH, *Guess on the Remaining Multiple-Choice Items.*
■ Survey essays ■ Outline them **10 minutes total**	■ Multiple choice **100 minutes**	■ Write four essays **40 minutes total**	**Remaining time**
FIFTH, *Survey Subtest Three Essays.*	SIXTH, *Multiple Choice.*	SEVENTH, *Write the Essays.*	LAST, *Guess Away.*
■ Outline three essays **10 minutes**	■ Do PE, CD, Arts ■ 39 questions **70 minutes**	■ PE essay ■ CD essay ■ Arts essay **30 minutes total**	■ Finish any remaining items **30 minutes total**

See Tables 1.23 and 1.25 for how to manage time on the multiple-choice questions in this model.

Plan E: Taking All Three Subtests

You may also choose to take all three subtests at once. **Taking all exams at once is really recommended if you are taking CSET Multiple Subjects for the first time.** Doing so will allow you to (maybe) pass all of the exams at once or (at the very least) get you a solid idea of what the rest of the exam is like.

You have 120 minutes to spend on subtests one and two and sixty minutes left for subtest three. If the multiple-choice questions in each subtest appear in **sections,** then follow Table 1.27.

TABLE 1.27   How to Take All Three Subtests at Once

SUBTEST ONE	
First	*Second*
Reading, Language, Literature Survey all essays 26 questions (40 min.) Two essays (20 min. total)	*History and Social Studies* Survey all essays 26 questions (40 min.) Two essays (20 min.)

SUBTEST TWO	
Third	*Fourth*
Science Survey all essays 26 questions (40 min.) Two short essays (20 min. total)	*Math* Survey the essays 26 questions (40 Min.) Two short essays (20 min. total)

SUBTEST THREE		
Fifth	*Sixth*	*Last*
Physical Education 13 questions (15 min.) 1 short essay (5 min.)	*Human Development* 13 questions (15 min.) 1 short essay (5 min.)	*Visual and Performing Arts* 13 questions (15 min.) 1 short essay (5 min.)

Order the exams by difficulty and first finish the exam that you believe is your strongest area. Begin each subtest by outlining the essays and then completing the multiple-choice questions. Locate the questions that are required to pass the subtest and complete the tally table. Turn to the essays and fill in the outlines with information that you have pulled from the multiple-choice questions. Doing so will put you in the best position to pass the exam. Table 1.28 shows you how to spend your time on each section of the subtest.

TABLE 1.28   Time Management for Each Content Area of Subtests One and Two

1–5	6–10	11–15	16–20	21–26
8 minutes	8 minutes	8 minutes	8 minutes	8 minutes
	1–13	14–26	27–39	
	15 minutes	15 minutes	15 minutes	

Jumbled Question Management. If the questions on each of the three subtests are **jumbled,** then follow Table 1.29.

TABLE 1.29   Jumbled Question Management

SUBTEST ONE	
First	*Second*
Survey the essays (5 min.) 52 questions (75 min.)	Complete the four essays (40 minutes total).

SUBTEST TWO	
Third	*Fourth*
Survey the essays (5 min.) 52 questions (75 min.)	Complete the four essays (40 minutes total).

SUBTEST THREE	
Fifth	*Last*
Outline the essays (5 min.) 39 questions (40 min.)	Complete three essays (15 minutes total).

Manage the multiple-choice questions using Tables 1.30 and 1.31:

TABLE 1.30   75-Minute Model

1–10	11–20	21–30	31–40	41–52
15 minutes	15 minutes	15 minutes	15 minutes	15 minutes

TABLE 1.31   40-Minute Model

1–5	6–10	11–15	16–20	21–25	26–30	31–39
5 minutes	5 minutes	5 minutes	5 minutes	5 minutes	5 minutes	5 minutes

Needless to say, the time is very tight. You will have to be very judicious in your choice of which questions to answer and which to skip in this model.

CONCLUSION

This chapter covered a great deal of important information. You have learned about the real scores underlying each subtest and how to use those scores to your advantage. For example, you know that the minimum scores for subtests one and two are thirteen questions per content area, and seven questions for subtest three. You also understand that there are null questions that you have to account for, meaning that you must answer a minimum of sixteen questions correctly on subtests one and two and eight questions on each content area of subtest three. In addition, you have seen how to approach each subtest, regardless of whether you choose to do one, two, or all three subtests at once. You know how to spend your time on any combination of tests, regardless of whether the questions appear nicely in sections or in a more challenging jumble.

In the next chapter, you will learn about how to complete the eleven essays that will appear on the CSET Multiple Subjects exam, starting with the major essay formulas that you must memorize to have the best opportunity to beat them. There are definable outlines and approaches that you must know before you take the test, so that you can outline the questions before you write them. Also, there are strategies for the multiple-choice questions that you need to understand, so that you can make the most of those sections and pull content from them into your outlines.

Before we turn to the essays and multiple-choice questions in the next chapter, please take one more look at the tally tables required for each of the subtests (see Table 1.32). Take the time to commit these to memory.

TABLE 1.32 Complete CSET Tally Tables

LANGUAGE ARTS MULTIPLE CHOICE	SOCIAL STUDIES MULTIPLE CHOICE	LANGUAGE ARTS ESSAYS	SOCIAL STUDIES ESSAYS
16 questions correct	16 questions correct	2 essays	2 essays

SCIENCE MULTIPLE CHOICE	MATH MULTIPLE CHOICE	SCIENCE ESSAYS	MATH ESSAYS
16 questions correct	16 questions correct	2 essays	2 essays

PHYSICAL EDUCATION MULTIPLE CHOICE	HUMAN DEVELOPMENT MULTIPLE CHOICE	ARTS MULTIPLE CHOICE	PHYSICAL EDUCATION ESSAYS	HUMAN DEVELOPMENT ESSAYS	ARTS ESSAYS
8 correct	8 correct	8 correct	1 essay	1 essay	1 essay

CHAPTER TWO

BEATING ALL ESSAY AND MULTIPLE-CHOICE ITEMS

This chapter is divided into two sections. The first section presents the major essay formats you need to know for the test, and the second section presents the multiple-choice strategies essential to passing the test. Remember that your score depends upon your performance in both of these areas, so it is essential that you learn how to handle them.

In the case of the essays, it is extremely important for you to complete all of them and *leave no essay behind*. This is because all of them will be scored and you should earn points for writing something. For the multiple-choice questions, there are tricks to doing the questions effectively; you will see how to apply such strategies to make the questions work for you rather than against you. You will have the opportunity to perform a diagnostic test in Language Arts, and you will learn about the common problems that candidates have on this part of the exam. Then, you will learn how to avoid those problems and to make the most of your time on the test.

Remember, too, that these essays will be read by as many as three people and that the evaluators read the answers for very specific information. Therefore, you must learn how to organize the answers so that the evaluators can find what they are looking for, thus enabling you to receive all the points that you have coming to you.

Let's first look at how to write effective essays on CSET Multiple Subjects exam. You will see eleven essays across each of the content areas, and you will learn how to write appropriately for the evaluators.

EFFECTIVE WRITTEN-RESPONSE OUTLINES

In this section, you will see the major essay forms that you should memorize for the written portion of the test. These formats will allow you to write answers to the questions very quickly, and they will also help you to understand the information in the rest of this chapter. The principle behind these formats is pure application: By memorizing them, you can sketch the formats into the answer book, so that your answers will be as focused as possible and you will have a guide for your writing.

Please look at each of the formats common to each of the subtests (see Table 2.1). A description of each format immediately follows the summary table.

TABLE 2.1   Essay Formats across Subtests

SUBTEST ONE		SUBTEST TWO		SUBTEST THREE
Definition	*Cause/Effect*	*Comparison*	*Proof*	*Discussion*
¶ Definition	¶ Cause(s)	¶ Central Idea(s)	¶ Formula	¶ Principle(s)
¶ Example	¶ Elaboration	¶ Comparison	¶ First Proof	¶ Observation
¶ Conclusion	¶ Effect(s)	¶ Conclusion	¶ Second Proof	¶ Observation

Types of Formats

Definition Essays.   The format of the definition essay includes a definition in the first paragraph, an example to support the definition in the second paragraph, and a conclusion in the final paragraph. The types of questions to prepare for include descriptions of linguistic elements or processes, acquisition orders, the writing and revising process, and the features of prose or poetry. Two examples, a spelling question and a question about metaphor, will be analyzed for you.

Cause/Effect.   The format of the cause and effect essay includes a statement of either causes or effects (or both) in the first paragraph, an elaboration of one of the items from the first paragraph, and an a major effect in the final paragraph. The format may appear across the subtests (like the descriptive essay), though you really need to prepare for them as part of the Social Studies/History portion of the test. You will see two questions in the analysis of cause and effect questions, including one on U.S. conflicts and another on medieval history.

Comparison.   Comparative essays have the following formula: Paragraph one presents the central idea or ideas, paragraph two offers the comparison, and paragraph three posits the conclusion. Like the previous formats, it may appear across all of the exams. You will see this format applied to the Science portion of subtest two, where one question about the validity of a scientific claim is evaluated and another question about plant and animal physiology is analyzed.

Proofs.   Proofs may appear on the math portion of subtest two. You will be traveling back in time to seventh- and eight-grade algebra and geometry to remember how to write up proofs of algebraic equations in addition to maybe calculating linear equations. The format of the proof includes the formula you will be using in the first paragraph, the first part of the proof in the second paragraph, and the second part of the proof in the final paragraph (if it is a two-part question).

Discussions.   Discussion essays populate subtest three, though they can also appear across all of the previous subtests. The format presents a principle in the first paragraph (of human development, for example) and observations of the effects of the principle in the final two paragraphs. You may be asked to discuss a particular physical education activity, for example, and how it might impact the children who participate in it. The same is true for questions about human development or art. We will present and analyze three questions that utilize this format from each of the content areas in subtest three.

Before looking at each of the formats in action, please note that the essays included in this chapter are very short. Essay length was kept brief on purpose to ensure that you write original material on the exam. The essay lengths will have to be increased through examples and additional explanations that you will supply. These essays are of approximately fifty to seventy-five words; you should expect to increase that length by a minimum of one hundred words. The next sections of this chapter dissect example essays and answers from each of the subtests, so that you can see the formats in action.

Language Arts and Social Studies

In this section, you will learn how to write essays for subtest one: Language Arts and Social Studies.

Question One: Spelling Development.   The first question that we will explore with you targets literacy development, a major content area on the exam. In this case, you will see writing data and a question on spelling.

A third-grade student is asked to write about his favorite memory in class. Printed below is his essay response.

MY FAVORITE MEMORY

My best memery are about last chrismas. When I got a brant new bicicle. I rode it every day. When the snow melted. I saw it at ericks bike shop it was really cool, like the one that evel kenevels got. its biger than my old bike. My freind mike jumped it at taft park and he skined his knee. My dad told me that I'd havto be real carefull on my bike cause santa isn't enshured. I wanto jump my bike real high to like evel. Thats why I like this memery the best.

Write a response in which you describe one aspect of the student's writing development and an area of need. Make sure to cite specific examples to support your conclusions.

Step One: Identify the Question.   The question asks you for two important things. First, you have to **define** the one aspect of the student's current level of writing development, along with an example that supports your contention. As you will learn in Chapter Six (content area twelve), there are three areas that you could consider: paragraph organization, grammar, or word formations. In Chapter Four, you will learn about spelling development as part of content area three, so let's arbitrarily choose that area for this essay (see Table 2.2).

Analyzing the data should be rather easy, since you can immediately recognize whether there are prephonetic, phonetic, transitional, and/or conventional spellings in the data. If the terminology does not immediately jump out at you, don't worry; we will cover spelling development in depth in Chapter Four.

TABLE 2.2   Spelling Development

PRE-PHONETIC	PHONETIC	TRANSITIONAL	CONVENTIONAL
⟨scribble⟩	t r	Tre	*tree*

Step Two: Analyze the Data.   The student's spelling lies somewhere between transitional and conventional for many of the words. You must further analyze the data looking for the **strengths** and **needs** present in the data. You can accomplish this identification by looking at the correct spellings and the errors in Table 2.3:

TABLE 2.3   Spelling Strengths and Needs

Sight words (*about, when, got*)	Capitalizing proper nouns
Some contractions (*I'd, isn't*)	Final sounds in words (*brant*)
Blends and digraphs in initial and final positions	Doubling consonants (*biger, skined*)
	Phonetic spellings (*havto, wanto, enshured, memery*)

Step Three: Write It Up.   Following the format of definition essays, you write your answer in a way that will enable evaluators to find what they are looking for quickly and unmistakably.

DEFINITION

This student's development is at the transitional level for many words, as he needs instruction beyond a word's phonology for spelling. Some words are transitionally spelled (*biger, skined*).

EXAMPLE

One sees the phonetic stage reflected in spellings of *brant* for *brand, havto* for *have to, wanto* for *want to, enshured* for *insured,* and *memery* for *memory.* A need to understand consonant doubling to preserve short vowel sounds is demonstrated in the words *biger* and *skined.* There are other spelling mistakes in capitalizing proper nouns, like *erick's bike shop, santa,* and *evel knievel.* Finally, the student needs work in spelling certain contractions of words correctly: *its* and *thats.*

CONCLUSION

This student could build up a better understanding of the correct spelling of words through direct instruction in spelling patterns (doubling consonants), capitalization, and forming contractions.

Question Two: Metaphors.   Question Two moves away from language use to literature, another potential target of essay questions in this section of the test. This hypothetical question on Language Arts tests your knowledge of literary devices.

Metaphors are common features of novels, short stories, poems—even film. For example, Alfred Hitchcock used many visual metaphors to comment on the human condition. In *North by Northwest,* for example, the main characters walk atop the sculptured heads on

Mount Rushmore—much like head lice—perhaps conveying the *auteur's* sentiments about humanity and our position in the world.

> Using your knowledge of literary conventions, write a response in which you describe the use of metaphor in literature. Be sure to cite specific evidence from the text that you select for your discussion.

Step One: Identify the Question. The question is asking you for two important things. First, you have to **define** what a metaphor is and then support your contention. To do that effectively, you must draw on your own knowledge of metaphor from literature and provide an adequate answer to the question. You will learn about such devices in Chapter Three when we describe **metaphor** for you as a an implied comparison between story elements and ideas outside the story through symbols.

Step Two: Analyze the Data. Begin with your definition and apply this understanding to a story that may employ metaphor, the *Old Man and the Sea* for example (see Figure 2.1):

FIGURE 2.1 "Old Man and the Sea"

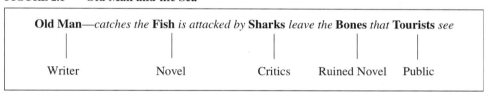

Using this example as an guide, you simply write the essay following the format of a discussion essay.

Step Three: Write It Up. Just like before, you write your answer in a way that will enable evaluators to find what they are looking for quickly and unmistakably.

DEFINITION

Metaphors are an implied comparison between the characters, the setting, or the themes in a story and "real life" accomplished by way of symbols.

EXAMPLE

Hemingway's *The Old Man and the Sea* provides an example. In the story, the old man catches the fish of a lifetime. While making the long journey back to shore, he winds up eating from his prize—worse, it is later destroyed by sharks. At the end of the story, only the bones are left. Tourists, who know nothing of the old man's struggles, comment that a storm must have blown the carcass ashore.

CONCLUSION

Metaphorically, Hemingway might be commenting on the human condition, though he himself said that it "was just a fish story." The Old Man could symbolize Hemingway; the prized fish could symbolize his novel. The sharks (humorously) might be critics, while the tourists represent we, the public, who only see what's left of the shredded novel. Extending the metaphor is easy: All human beings have trials that no one (only ourselves) can understand or appreciate—all that is seen is what is left of us, perhaps damaged and destroyed, once the struggle is over.

Question Three: U.S. Conflicts.   Cause and effect essays are the next format to be covered. These essays may emphasize either cause or effect or both, depending on the format of the question. Let's apply the form to questions from the History and Social Studies portion of subtest one, both of which require you to state causes and effects.

Using your knowledge of American History, select a war or conflict and:

1. Cite two causes of the conflict.
2. Elaborate upon the causes in detail.
3. State its conclusion and the effects it brought upon our nation.

Step One: Identify the Question.   In this question, you are asked to identify a conflict from U.S. history, elaborate upon one of the causes, and then state its effects.

Step Two: Outline It.   The outline that you will create will help you to answer the question (see Figure 2.2).

FIGURE 2.2   Conflict Causes and Elaboration

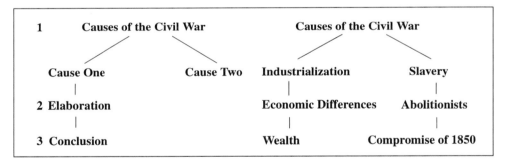

Step Three: Write It Up.   Follow the format and write up the outline that you created to answer the question.

CAUSES

The Civil War figures prominently in U.S. history. One major cause of the Civil War was the industrialization taking place in the North while the South remained an agricultural region. Another major cause was the rift between the North and the South over the question of slavery.

ELABORATION

The first of these causes was significant because the North got an advantage over the South in terms of wealth and of continued growth of its population. The North was able to build factories and mass produce manufactured goods. The stream of new immigrants provided the workers necessary to keep up with its ever expanding economy. The South, on the other hand, remained agricultural with its dependence on tobacco and cotton. Very few immigrants came to the South and workers were few. This caused the South to become more and more dependent upon slave labor.

EFFECTS

These differences were at the heart of the conflict between the North and the South. Industrialization caused the North to become more wealthy, its economy was ever expanding and growing, and its population kept growing by leaps and bounds. The population growth also gave the North the political advantage of having more representation in the House of Representatives and also more votes in the Electoral College. The South's dependence upon slavery made it necessary for Southerners to try to expand their lands into the new territories of the West. However, the Compromise of 1850 put a damper in their efforts because it called for settlers of that territory to vote whether they wanted to be a free state or a slave state. In the case of Kansas, many Northerners and abolitionists moved to Kansas in order to make sure that they had more votes to make Kansas a free rather than a slave state. This caused a rift between the two sides and blood was shed. Abolitionists also had been attacking the practice of slavery in the South through newspaper stories and the Underground Railroad. For these reasons, the Southerners went on the defensive and felt that they had to fight for their way of life.

Question Four: Medieval History. Another question from social studies might involve a **comparison** of one aspect of history with another one.

Read the question below to get a sense of the question and its required compare/contrast format.

> Using your knowledge of medieval history, write a response where you,
>
> • Identify and analyze movements within this time period.
> • Select one area and describe its contributions to later historical periods.

Step One: Identify the Question. The format of the question asks you to identify periods of medieval history. The Age of Enlightenment and the later Renaissance would serve this purpose. Here, you are to present their similarities and differences and then select one movement and outline its contributions. Let's look at how to accomplish this goal.

Step Two: Outline It. The first thing to do is to sketch an outline of the question. Since it is a compare/contrast question that also asks you to dissect one movement in detail, your outline should look like the one shown in Figure 2.3.

Step Three: Write It Up. Based on the outline, you write up your answer, organizing it so that evaluators can find the information quickly and unmistakably.

COMPARE AND CONTRAST

The Renaissance and Age of Enlightenment share a focus on advancing human development and improving the human condition. Also, both movements help to advance other significant changes in human history. In the former, the Renaissance influenced the Age of Enlightenment; whereas in the latter, the Age of Enlightenment influenced the development

FIGURE 2.3   Outline Sketch

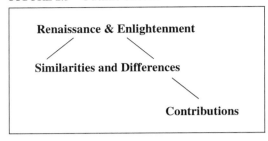

of the modern-day West. Each movement differs in that the Renaissance was a fourteenth-century Italian movement that focused on reviving Greek and Roman culture, and the Age of Enlightenment was most concerned with the application of the scientific method to all aspects of human life and advancing humanity through reason.

CONTRIBUTIONS OF THE RENAISSANCE

With its focus on the scientific method and reason, the Age of Enlightenment centered on improving government, education, and law. It also produced thinkers who believed strongly in natural rights and liberties that no government could deny to its citizens. Undoubtedly, these ideas influenced the authors of the Declaration of Independence, which declared that all people were entitled to natural rights and freedoms. This idea has its roots in the Age of Enlightenment.

Science and Math

The next essays concern Science and Math (subtest two). **Comparative essays** are common for Science essays. These questions will ask you to compare theories, physiological features, or other processes. Proofs and solving linear equations are common for mathematics.

Question Five: Astronomy

A major change in scientific thought occurred when we moved from a geocentric universe to a heliocentric one. Using your knowledge of astronomy, briefly describe both ideas and cite one reason that one theory supplanted the other.

Step One: Identify the Question.   In this case, you evaluate the validity of an argument. Here, you are asked to compare and contrast two competing theories in astronomy, though that fact might not be immediately visible to you. In deciding how to write the essay, you must first identify each theory and then state why one theory is preferable to another theory.

- Ptolemy's position on our solar system.
- Copernicus' position on our solar system.
- Role of Galileo's invention of the telescope.

Step Two: Outline It.   Given the above, your outline might look like that shown in Figure 2.4.

FIGURE 2.4   Outline Sketch

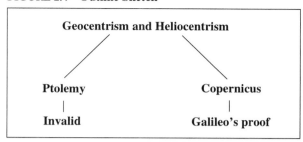

Step Three: Write It Up.   The next step is to write up the outline using the content of science to do so.

PTOLEMY'S POSITION

Geocentrism was the belief that all the universe, the moon, sun, and five ancient planets, circled the Earth. This idea was concocted by Ptolemy in 140 A.D. He believed the planets exhibited a retrograde motion. He also believed that the planets and other objects in the universe that circled Earth were attached to epicycles that explained the brightness seen on Earth. The belief at this time was that a prime mover had control over everything in the universe and the Earth was supposed to be the middle of the universe by divine right.

COPERNICUS'S POSITION

Heliocentrism is the belief that all objects in the universe are measured with the sun at the center. This idea was theorized by Copernicus in 1543. He believed that the sun was in the center of the universe and that the planets orbited the sun. He also believed that the moon orbited Earth and all of the planets had a circular orbiting pattern that they followed. His observations conflicted greatly with those of Ptolemy's, and Copernicus's predictions were more accurate using this heliocentric model.

HELIOCENTRISM WINS

Why heliocentrism over geocentrism? With the invention of the telescope, Galileo was able to disprove Ptolemy's theory of geocentrism. Galileo was able to see that Jupiter had moons. This meant that not all objects in the universe circled the Earth. He was also able to see the imperfections in the sun and moon. With the progression of time and the invention of more powerful telescopes, scientists have been able to show that Copernicus' theory of heliocentrism is correct.

Question Six: Human and Plant Cells.   This question **compares** plant and animal cells to reveal their similarities and differences. Many of the questions and answers may be as brief as the one below.

> Plants and animals share common characteristics and important differences. Using your knowledge of plant and animal cells, write a response in which you state the similarities and differences.

Step One: Identify the Question.   In this question, you are asked to state similarities and differences. Your outline will compare and contrast plant and animal cells.

Step Two: Outline It.   Your outline might look like that shown in Figure 2.5.

FIGURE 2.5   Outline Sketch

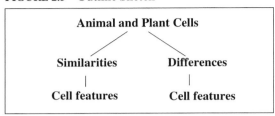

Step Three: Write It Up.

CENTRAL IDEA

Similarities and differences in plant and animal cells can be seen in their features and processes.

COMPARISON (SIMILARITIES)

A cell has a plasma membrane to protect it from the outside environment and to regulate the movement of water, nutrients, and wastes. Each cell also has a nucleus that contains the genetic code, along with organelles: ribosome, mitochondrion, and lysosomes.

COMPARISON (DIFFERENCES)

One major difference between plant and animal cells is the cell wall. The cell wall in plants is a cellulose structure outside of the cell membrane. This wall gives the plant cell its shape and enables it to support individual parts of the plant. Plant cells also have an organelle called the chloroplast that animal cells do not have. The chloroplast is responsible for harvesting energy from sunlight.

Question Seven: Geometry and the Pythagorean Theorem.   The next set of essays will require *writing* answers to math problems. You will be required to write **proofs** as part of the essays in subtest three. The basic format of the proof is to state the formula in the first part of the essay, state the first proof in the second paragraph, and include any transformation of that proof in the final paragraph. You may also have to draw diagrams or "show your work" directly on the test. Following are two questions for geometry and algebra.

Given the drawing and the information below, prove that the triangle formed in the circle is a right triangle and then calculate the length of side *AC*.

Given

AC is a diameter of the circle.

An inscribed angle is equal to ½ of its included arc.

Figure *ABC* is a triangle.

Line *AB* = 6

Line *BC* = 8

Using your knowledge of geometric proofs, complete each of the following tasks:

A. Write a geometric proof that demonstrates that *ABC* is a right triangle.

B. Write an essay that demonstrates how to calculate the length of side *AC* using the Pythagorean Theorem.

To receive full credit on this essay, you have two tasks. First, you must write a formal geometric proof to prove that triangle *ABC* is a right triangle. Second, you must write an essay that explains how to calculate the length of *AC* using the Pythagorean Theorem. Let's do each item one step at a time, beginning with Item A from the exercise above.

ITEM A: The Geometric Proof of Triangle ABC.   You're going to write the geometric proof first. To determine that *ABC* is a right triangle, you have to demonstrate that one of the angles is of ninety degrees. This will satisfy Item *A* and enable you to answer Item *B*, applying the Pythagorean Theorem (you can only apply the Pythagorean Theorem to a right triangle). Here are the steps for writing a geometric proof that demonstrates that *ABC* is a right triangle.

Step One: State the Given Information from the Sample Problem.   First, look at the "given" information in the sample problem. "Given" in geometry means that the statements are assumed to be true for the purposes of the question. Simply transfer this information from the problem to the first part of your proof as shown in Table 2.4:

TABLE 2.4

STATEMENT	REASON
AC is a diameter of the circle.	Given.
An inscribed angle is equal to ½ of its included arc.	Given.
Figure ABC is a triangle.	Given.
Line *AB* = 6	Given.
Line *BC* = 8	Given.

Yes, it is just a matter of copying the information. You would probably get a score of two or one ★ for just having known that you must copy the information.

Step Two: State Any Information that Is Not Given.   Remember that you are trying to prove that triangle *ABC* is a right triangle. The next thing that you must do is state the information that will help you to accomplish this task. Look at the drawing shown in the exercise and note that the triangle is inscribed inside of a circle. You should know that circles have 360 degrees (see Figure 2.6):

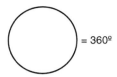

FIGURE 2.6

You also know that diameters (here: line *AC*) divide circles into two equal parts and that line AC is part of triangle ABC (see Figure 2.7).

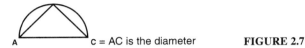

c = AC is the diameter   **FIGURE 2.7**

You should also know that semicircles have 180 degrees, one-half of the circle itself and that arc *AC* is 180 degrees as shown in Figure 2.8.

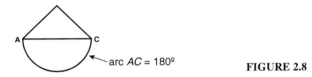

arc *AC* = 180°   **FIGURE 2.8**

Table 2.5 provides basic geometric definitions that, although unstated in the sample question, will never change. Write them down in your proof.

TABLE 2.5

A circle contains 360 degrees.	Definition of a circle.
A diameter divides a circle into two equal parts.	Definition of a diameter.
Arc *AC* is a semicircle equal to 180 degrees.	Definition of semicircle.

Step Three: Prove That ABC Is a Right Triangle.   Since right triangles contain an angle of 90 degrees, you have to find a right angle to prove that triangle *ABC* is in fact a right triangle. Here is how you do that. Since arc *AC* is a semicircle equal to 180 degrees, one-half of it is equal to 90 degrees. Do you see angle *B* in the graphic below? Its angle includes the 180 degree arc *AC*, so half of the arc is equal to 90 degrees (see Figure 2.9).

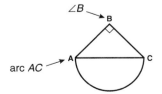

FIGURE 2.9

Therefore, you simply write

TABLE 2.6

$\angle B = 90°$	An angle is equal to ½ of its included arc.

At last! You have found your right angle! This means that triangle *ABC* is a right triangle. Finish your proof by stating the obvious (see Table 2.7).

TABLE 2.7

Angle *B* is a right angle.	Definition of a right angle.
Triangle *ABC* is a right triangle.	Definition of a right triangle.

ITEM B: The Essay on the Pythagorean Theorem.   Recall that you have a second task here. Your first task was to write a complete proof for triangle *ABC*. Now, your second task is to answer item B:

Write an essay that demonstrates how to calculate the length of side *AC* using the Pythagorean Theorem.

This must be written in essay form. You will use three steps to complete this item.

Step One: Import the Information from Your Proof.   Remember that the Pythagorean Theorem is used to calculate the lengths of the sides of right triangles. If it doesn't have a right angle, then you can't use the Pythagorean Theorem. Since you are writing an essay, start to sketch it out on your scratch paper. See Table 2.8 for information that you have just proved:

TABLE 2.8

Angle *B* is a right angle.	Definition of a right angle.
Triangle *ABC* is a right triangle.	Definition of a right triangle.

This information will be essential to your written response to the question, and you cannot forget to include it when you write your essay.

Step Two: Perform the Calculation.   The next step is to perform the calculation by hand on your scratch paper before you write the essay. First, write the Theorem down:

$$a^2 + b^2 = c^2$$

Second, substitute the length of each side of the triangle for *a*, *b*, and *c*, recalling that *c* is always the hypotenuse.

$$AB^2 + BC^2 = AC^2$$

Now, substitute the numerical lengths of each side into the equation. Note that we have to use a variable for the hypotenuse (side *AC*), because we don't know it:

$$6^2 + 8^2 = c^2$$

Now, solve for c^2.

$$36 + 64 = c^2$$

$$100 = c^2$$

$$\sqrt{100} = \sqrt{c^2}$$

$$10 = c$$

Therefore, line $AC = 10$

Step Three: Write It Up.   Your final task now is to write the essay for using the Pythagorean Theorem to calculate the length of line AC. Here is what each part of the paragraph should contain.

1. State the Given that you wrote down on your scratch paper: *Angle B contains 90 degrees, which is a right angle.* A right triangle is described as a one that contains a right angle. Therefore, triangle ABC is a right triangle.

2. State the definition that enables you to use the Pythagorean Theorem: *Since triangle, ABC is a right triangle the Pythagorean Theorem ($a^2 + b^2 = c^2$) may be applied to it.*

3. Logically lay out, step by step, what happens and your reasons for it: *Angle B contains 90 degrees, which is a right angle.* A right triangle is described as a one that contains a right angle. Therefore, triangle ABC is a right triangle. Since triangle ABC is a right triangle, the Pythagorean Theorem ($a^2 + b^2 = c^2$) may be applied to it. Using substitution, we can restate the Pythagorean Theorem as $AB^2 + BC^2 = AC^2$. Substituting for a second time, the values for each side can be added to the equation $6^2 + 8^2 = c^2$. The square of 6 is 36 and the square of 8 is 64. Their addition results in $100 = c^2$. To find c, one must take the square root of c^2. Whatever operation is done to one side of the equation must be done to the other or equality will be lost. The square root of 100 is 10.

4. State the length of line AC: *Therefore, line AC has a length of 10.*

Table 2.9 shows the answer to the question in its entirety.

Question Eight: Graphing Equations.   Some **proofs** may ask you to develop an equation, display data, and explain it in writing. Consider the following problem. It discusses the prices of belonging to a gym and what is the most economical for an athlete to consider. Observe how the information is developed and the answer displayed.

An athlete can join a gym in two different ways:

Option 1:   A one time membership fee of $250 and a $20 per month maintenance fee.
            OR
Option 2:   Pay no membership fee and pay $50 per month.

Using your knowledge of equations, find the point at which one of the options would be more beneficial to the athlete than the other. In your response you should:

• Develop equations to fit the situation.
• Display a data table.

- Graph each option.
- Show which option has the best savings over one year.

Show all work and reasoning you used in your analysis of the problem and your methods of solution.

TABLE 2.9

ITEM A: THE GEOMETRIC PROOF OF TRIANGLE *ABC*

Statement	*Reason*
AC is a diameter of the circle.	Given.
An inscribed angle is equal to ½ of its included arc.	Given.
Figure *ABC* is a triangle.	Given.
Line *AB* = 6	Given.
Line *BC* = 8	Given.
A circle contains 360 degrees.	Definition of a circle.
A diameter divides a circle into 2 equal parts.	Definition of a diameter.
Arc *AC* is a semicircle equal to 180 degrees.	Definition of semicircle.
$\angle B = 90°$	An angle is equal to ½ of its included arc.
Angle *B* is a right angle.	Definition of a right angle.
Triangle *ABC* is a right triangle.	Definition of a right triangle.

ITEM B: THE ESSAY ON THE PYTHAGOREAN THEOREM

Since triangle *ABC* is a right triangle, the Pythagorean Theorem ($a^2 + b^2 = c^2$) may be applied to it. Using substitution, we can restate the Pythagorean Theorem as $AB^2 + BC^2 = AC^2$. Substituting for a second time the values for each side can be added to the equation $6^2 + 8^2 = c^2$. The square of 6 is 36 and the square of 8 is 64. Their addition results in $100 = c^2$. To find *c*, one must take the square root of c^2. Whatever operation is done to one side of the equation must be done to the other or equality will be lost. The square root of 100 is 10. Therefore, line *AC* has a length of 10.

To adequately develop a response, first evaluate what is being asked and the steps that you must take to work to that solution. This sort of problem is very straightforward and asks you to develop the equations, display the data in tables, graph the data and locate the breakeven point, and discuss how you arrived at the solution. NOTE: You will be provided with a basic four-function calculator during the exam. Please check the registration bulletin for the most up-to-date information on the type of calculator in use.

Step One: Develop the Equation.   Examine option 1 and option 2. They tell you prices but not the number of months. The first price is $20 per month plus a $250 fee. The second price is $50 per month with no fee. Since you don't know the number of months, this is the variable. We'll call it *m*. Now, you must develop two independent equations as shown in Table 2.10 using the unknown number of months:

TABLE 2.10

OPTION 1	OPTION 2
20m + 250	50m

In option 1 $20 is multiplied times the *m* along with the $250 fee added to it. In option 2, you simply multiply the $50 fee times the *m*. Table 2.11 shows what you would write in your essay:

TABLE 2.11

LET M = THE NUMBER OF MONTHS OF MEMBERSHIP

Option 1:	20m + 250
Option 2:	50m

Step Two: Develop the Data Tables.   In this step, you simply create data tables for each option that show how much the athlete will spend over a twelve-month period. In option 1, you begin with the first month and plug in 1 for *m* in the option one formula:

$$20(1) + 250$$

This gives you 270. Move on to the second month. Substitute 2 for *m* and you get 290. Repeat the process for the remaining months. You would do the same procedure for option two by substituting the month for *m* and multiplying that by 50. Table 2.12 shows the information that you would write on your test:

TABLE 2.12

THE DATA TABLES BELOW REPRESENT THE INFORMATION FOR OPTION 1 AND OPTION 2 OVER A 12-MONTH PERIOD.

OPTION 1:   **20M + 250**

Months	1	2	3	4	5	6	7	8	9	10	11	12
Dollars	270	290	310	330	350	370	390	410	430	450	470	490

OPTION 2:   **50M**

Months	1	2	3	4	5	6	7	8	9	10	11	12
Dollars	50	100	150	200	250	300	350	400	450	500	550	600

Step Three: Graph Your Results.   As you can see, option one is the better deal, since it is cheaper over a twelve-month period. Your next step is to graph the data. Set up the graph with an *x*- axis and a *y*- axis. The *x*- axis will be the number of months (twelve in this case), and the *y*-axis will be the amount of money the athlete will pay over time.

Figure 2.10 shows what you would display in the form of a graph. Options 1 and 2 can be graphed on a coordination grid as shown.

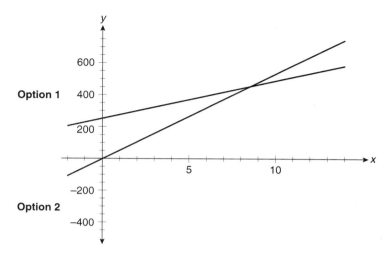

FIGURE 2.10

Step Four: Defend Your Conclusion. Now, it is time for you to explain how you arrived at the conclusion that option 1 is the best option of all. Simply examine your equation, tables, and graph and explain what they tell the reader. Your response should look like this:

> Using m to indicate the number of months, option 1 increases at a constant rate of 20m + 250 and option 2 increases at 50m. Both of these equations are linear functions since the graph each creates is a straight line. At the point of intersection, options 1 and 2 are even. For all months before this point, option 2 represents the greatest savings for the athlete. **However,** after the tenth month, option 1 will provide the athlete with the greatest benefit over at twelve-month period.

Note how the answer followed the steps posed in the question and how the information was displayed in an orderly manner.

Physical Education, Child Development, and Arts

The following questions provide examples of essays in areas including physical education, child development, and the arts.

Question Nine: Physical Education

Aerobic and anaerobic exercises play important roles in one's physical conditioning. Using your knowledge of the principles of physical education, write a response in which you describe activities associated with both types of training and the related benefits each activity brings to a person's health.

Step One: Identify the Question. This question asks you for simple **definitions** and for benefits of two different kinds of physical activities. The associated questions are:

- What are examples of aerobic exercises and their benefits?
- What are examples of anaerobic exercises and their benefits?

The question can be answered in two complete paragraphs, one on each type of physical activity.

Step Two: Outline It.   The outline is straightforward: You simply identify different activities and **discuss** their attendant benefits (see Figure 2.11).

FIGURE 2.11   Outline Sketch

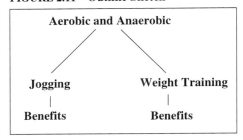

Step Three: Write It Up.

PARAGRAPH ONE: AEROBIC EXERCISES AND BENEFITS

Aerobic exercises are activities such as walking, running, jogging, and riding a bicycle. These activities are termed *aerobic* because they not only increase the heart rate, but also sustain that increase over a long period of time (aerobic exercises last at least twenty minutes). People consume more oxygen when they perform aerobic activities, and that increase in oxygen helps to burn fat that the body has stored. In addition, the elevated heart rate strengthens one's cardiovascular system. Finally, aerobic exercise is also good for relieving stress, a major factor in coronary heart disease.

PARAGRAPH TWO: ANAEROBIC EXERCISES AND BENEFITS

Anaerobic exercises are activities such as lifting weights, doing pullups, and stretching out. These activities are of a short but very intense duration, where one exerts energy and then rests for a period of time. Stronger muscles are the reward of anaerobic exercise, though one does not burn as much stored fat because the heart rate is not elevated for a long enough period of time. There are, however, positive metabolic effects, because stronger and bigger muscles consume more calories. In addition, anaerobic activities are also helpful in stress relief, so there is some additional benefit of reducing coronary heart disease through anaerobic exercise, too.

Question Ten: Human Development.   Human development questions can also follow the **discussion** format that you have just seen in PE. Consider the following question.

Researchers of psycholinguistic development posit that children learn language in stages and through hypothesis testing during language acquisition. Using your understanding of child development, describe one aspect of language acquisition that reflects these psycholinguistic elements and include how they do so.

Step One: Identify the Question. Here, you are asked to trace an element of psycholinguistic development and **discuss** both stages and hypothesis testing during language acquisition:

- Provide evidence of a stage of language development.
- Provide evidence of hypothesis testing.
- State how they illustrate psycholinguistic language acquisition.

Step Two: Outline It. Sketch an outline of the question as shown in Figure 2.12.

FIGURE 2.12   Outline Sketch

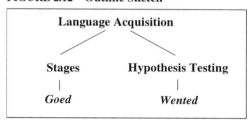

Step Three: Write It Up.

PARAGRAPH ONE: LANGUAGE ACQUISITION STAGES

Psycholinguistic development shows that children learn aspects of their first language in definable and recognizable stages. After acquiring the past tense inflectional morpheme -ed, children tend to learn how to apply it appropriately in stages of acquisition. On their way to producing the correct form for many verbs that have irregular past tense conjugations, many children pass through these steps:

Stage One: I goed to the story yesterday.
Stage Two: I wented to the store yesterday.
Stage Three: I went to the store yesterday.

It is important to note that corrections during stages one and two often do not take; and even if they do, the child continues to produce the incorrect forms for a while.

PARAGRAPH TWO: HYPOTHESIS TESTING

Each stage that precedes the correct formation of the past tense at stage three is the result of hypothesis testing. Hypothesis testing means that the child believes he or she is actually producing the correct form when making the error. At first, the child simply overextends the inflectional morpheme -ed to any verb to make it a past tense verb, because many of our verbs in English are formed this way. At stage two, the child overgeneralizes this inflectional ending to include the correct irregular forms of the verb (*wented, runned, boughted*). The child hypothesizes that both forms must work together somehow to properly form the past tense, so combining both elements seems like a very safe bet.

PARAGRAPH THREE: PSYCHOLINGUISTIC ASPECTS OF LANGUAGE ACQUISITION

Developmental stages and hypothesis testing clearly illustrate psycholinguistic processes clearly because it is unlikely that the child's linguistic environment offers him or her the incorrect forms that the child produces. For example, very few other people around them, with the exception of other young language learners, will probably produce *goed* and *wented*, yet children produce these forms anyway. The most likely explanation of these phenomena are the psycholinguistic processes that children use to structure language in their minds.

Question Eleven: Art History.   Different periods of history reflect different forms of artistic expression (and vice versa). Using your knowledge of art history, describe the characteristics one finds in Impressionism versus Expressionism. Then select one of these art forms to describe in terms of its historical context.

Step One: Identify the Question.   In this question, your task is to **compare and contrast** two forms of artistic expression, then select one form and offer a sketch of the historical context surrounding its development.

- State the characteristics of Impressionism.
- Contrast those characteristics with Expressionism.
- Select one of the two forms of expression and describe its historical context.

Step Two: Outline It.   Here, you are asked to draw distinctions between Impressionism and Expressionism. You can use two paragraphs for that task and reserve the second paragraph for the discussion of the historical contexts for one of them (Impressionism, in this case) as shown in Figure 2.13.

FIGURE 2.13   Outline Sketch

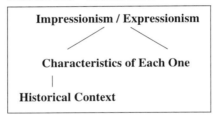

Step Three: Write It Up.

PARAGRAPH ONE: IMPRESSIONISM

Impressionism is a late nineteenth-century French movement that features studies of light in the composition of the work. Claude Monet is a famous impressionist artist. His pieces, sometimes bright, others soft, feature portraits of the natural world. When one views Monet's work, it is almost as if one is looking at the world at a distance or through a softly focused lens. Although the features of the landscape that figures in them are discernable, degrees of light and color are the clear subjects of study that preoccupy his style.

PARAGRAPH TWO: EXPRESSIONISM

Expressionism is an early twentieth-century style with German roots. Expressionist works differ from the Impressionist style in two fundamental ways. First, although light and also color are featured in Expressionism, they can be severe and overwhelming—nearly drowning out any discernable features or forms the artist captures. Secondly, Expressionism is a highly subjective style, because mood and introspection dominate this style where the artists paint their inner perception of the external world.

PARAGRAPH THREE: IMPRESSIONISM'S HISTORICAL CONTEXT

Impressionism precedes Expressionism chronologically and can be seen as an initial step away from formalistic and traditional painting that emphasized form over more elemental studies of light and color. Although Impressionism might be less subjective in its presentation (the features of the subjects and the setting are still discernable), it is still a clear departure from more rigid styles of artistic expression.

Conclusion

In this section of Chapter Two, you learned about the major essay formats and saw sample questions dissected for you. Since 30 percent of your score comes from essays, it is extremely important for you to learn how to handle them. This is especially true of the math proofs, if it has been a long time since you've written any math essays (if you have ever written any).

EFFECTIVE MULTIPLE-CHOICE STRATEGIES

This section will teach you tricks to surviving the multiple-choice questions that appear on the exam. Before you learn the short cuts, you need to find out just how strong your multiple-choice skills really are. You'll be asked to take a diagnostic test to find that out for yourself.

Diagnostic Test

In a moment, you will begin a diagnostic test. You will see that *how* you do the test is just as important as *what* you do on the exam. You have only two minutes per question, so please time yourself on this portion of the test. Get in the habit of checking your watch as you do the test—you may even want to write down your start time and end time to get an exact idea of how long it takes you to do questions like these. Turn the page and try out some questions from elementary Language Arts. Give yourself only eight minutes to do these questions.

Read the traditional poem below and answer the two questions that follow.

PADDY WEST'S

E're years before in London Town
I come to Paddy West's house.
He gave me a dish of American Hash
and he called it Liverpool Scouse.
He said, "There's a ship that's wantin' hands
and on her you'd quickly climb
The mate is a jackel the boatswain's worse,
but she will suit you fine."

Take off yer dungaree jacket,
and let me tell the rest,
Let's think of them cold nor'westers[1]
that we had at Paddy West's.

Now when I'd had a feed me, boys,
the wind began to blow.
Ol' Paddy sent me up to the attic,
the main royal[2] for to stow.
But when I got up in the attic,
No main royal could I find—
So I turned myself to the window and I furled the
    window blind.

Now Paddy he piped "all hands on deck!"
their stations for to man
His wife stood in the doorway with a bucket
    in her hand.
And Paddy he cries, "Now let her rip," and she
flung the water my way, crying
"Clue in the fore t'gan'sl, boys,
she's taken in a spray!"

Now seeing she's bound for the south'ard
oh to Frisco she was bound,
Paddy he takes a length of rope
and he lays it on the ground.
We both stepped over and back again
and Paddy he said, "That's fine.
And if they ask was you ever at sea
you can say you've crossed the line[3]."

"There's just one thing for you to do
before you sail away. That's to step around the
table where the bullocks underlay. And when
they ask was you ever at sea you can say ten
times round the horn[4] and by gracious you're an
old sailor since the day that you was born."

"Put on y'er dungaree jacket,
And walk out looking yer best,
And tell'em you're an old sailor man
That's come from Paddy West's."

1. Very cold ocean winds.
2. The main sail on a ship.
3. Crossed the equator in a ship.
4. Rounded the African continent in a ship.

---

1. In the poem, Paddy West's house is analogous
   to:
   A. A training facility.
   B. A diploma mill.
   C. A house of ill-repute.
   D. An apprentice's shop.

2. The narrator of the poem is best described as:
   I.   A neophyte in search of training
   II. An experienced sailor reflecting on his
        past.
   III. Feeling bitter about having been tricked
        by Paddy West.
   IV. Waxing nostalgic for Paddy West and his
        experiences there.

   A. I only.
   B. I and IV.
   C. III and IV.
   D. II and IV.

3. A first-grade teacher is planning a big book activity for her students. First, she selects the text and gathers the materials that will be required for the activity. She decides to use an easel and a pointer for the activity. Since the students have been working on big book readings for several weeks now, she decides to let the children take a direct role in the activity. After deciding to have the children take turns identifying the parts of a book, including the cover, the title, and the author's name, she considers what to do next. Which of the following items best reflects what the students could do next?

A. React and comment on specific parts of the text that the teacher will pre-select.
B. Review the story's components (setting, purpose, etc.) after it has been read.
C. Demonstrate their knowledge of the correct direction in which to read.
D. Discuss the type of text that was read.

4. A kindergarten teacher writes the following sentence on the board:

Today is Friday, January 29, 2005.

She then reads the passage to the students, pointing to each word as she reads. Next, she reads the passage aloud with the children, pointing to each word as the group reads together. Using your knowledge of early reading activities, which response best represents the skill that the teacher is targeting?

A. Reading text with proper intonation and fluency.
B. Understanding that individual letters represents individual sounds.
C. Recognizing that days of the week should be capitalized.
D. Understanding the direction in which text is read in English.

Answers. The answers are as follows: 1. B, 2. D, 3. C, 4. D.

Self-Assessment. What you did to answer the questions is just as important as whether you got any of the questions correct. See if you fell victim to any of the following traps.

1. You did the questions in order, starting with the first question and ending with the fourth question.
2. You spent longer than two minutes per question.
3. You read the "Paddy West" poem first before reading the question items.
4. You couldn't do the question with the Roman numerals in it quickly—or at all.
5. You didn't do question number four first.
6. You didn't write on the test.

If any of the above items were true for you, then you have habits that need to be changed. In the first place, doing the questions in order and spending longer than two minutes per question may be traps that many unsuccessful students fall into. This is because you might lose valuable opportunities to do easy questions and questions that are actually scored. Remember that not all of the multiple-choice questions count on the test. Just imagine if items 1–3 on the diagnostic test were the ones to be thrown out—basically, you spent all of that time reading the poem and answering the questions for nothing.

Do not expect to do the questions in order; instead, know the raw score required to pass the test and skip through the exam effectively on your way to a passing score. If your test has subtests and you are going to take more than one of them, manage your time carefully as you work throughout the exam. Think back to your approach to the test: If you spent longer than two minutes per question, you might want to reconsider your approach. Time probably evaporated, because you spent time reading the poem first before reading the questions. Reading the test items first is really important, because you can decide immediately whether you are going to attempt the question, skip it for now, or guess on it later. If you do decide to attempt the question, at least you'll know what you're reading the passage for. If you read the poem first, then you're reading for pleasure—and that's not how to approach a test.

If the Roman numeral question gave you trouble, then you probably need to learn the strategies to beat them. Roman numeral questions may or may not appear on the test. They are used on many NES exams, so you might as well learn how to do them just in case. Besides, the odds are that you will have to complete some pretty weird-looking questions anyway. Plus, all of the questions will require some degree of "figuring," so learning how to do these questions will give you some insight about how to do other kinds of odd questions. You'll learn how to do them a bit later.

At this point, think about how you really performed on the four questions. If you got all of them correct—great! Nonetheless, please think about the strategies that you used to arrive at those correct answers, since better ones may be available.

Multiple-Choice Strategies

This section contains strategies that show you how to make the multiple-choice questions work for you. First, we will present the "tally strategy." Since all the exams have a certain number of questions that do not count, there is an important approach that you ought to employ on your way to earning the raw score required to pass the test.

Read the Questions First.   Read the questions first. Recall the sample test. Reading the poem "Paddy West's House" first before reading the questions themselves was not the best approach. If you think back to that passage and the questions, it should be apparent that it might have made the task of understanding the poem easier if you had read the questions first. Doing so will enable you to decide whether you are going to do the question now, later, or not at all. You will of course be answering every single question, but some can be answered with just a simple bubble.

Do the Easy Ones First.   In order to reach the raw score required to pass the test, you really should focus your time by first finding and answering the easy questions. I would have done the last question on the diagnostic test first, for example, because it is short and easy to understand. "Paddy West's" is a question that I would have skipped and answered much later, since it takes time and effort to read the poem and then figure out how each question applies to it.

Do the "Unattached" Questions First.   Attached questions are ones that are tied to data sets. For example, you will see something like the "Paddy West" passage with three to four questions attached to it. Then, there are questions that are not attached to a big piece of data. Which should you do first? The answer is obvious: Do the unattached questions before the attached questions. The reason is that the unattached questions can be answered much, much faster than the attached ones, since you won't have to try to read and digest a whole passage of information.

food

Strategies for the Weird Ones. Do the weird-looking questions strategically. Roman numeral questions, like question number two in the diagnostic test, require strategies. Reread that question below.

The narrator of the poem is best described as:

I. A neophyte in search of training.
II. An experienced sailor reflecting on his past.
III. Feeling bitter about having been tricked by Paddy West.
IV. Waxing nostalgic for Paddy West and his experiences there.

    A. I only.
    B. II and III.
    C. I, II and IV.
    D. II and IV.

The best approach is to look at the Roman numeral items first and shorten them as follows:

I. A **neophyte** in search of training.
II. An **experienced sailor** reflecting on his past.
III. **Feeling bitter** about having been tricked by Paddy West.
IV. **Waxing nostalgic** for Paddy West and his experiences there.

Next, apply the shortened items to the passage. Since the narrator is obviously not a neophyte (beginner) and is not expressing bitterness, items one and three are out.

I. ~~A **neophyte** in search of training.~~
II. An **experienced sailor** reflecting on his past.
III. ~~**Feeling bitter** about having been tricked by Paddy West.~~
IV. **Waxing nostalgic** for Paddy West and his experiences there.

Turn now to the answers and eliminate any item with a one or a three in it:

    A. ~~I only.~~
    B. ~~II and III.~~
    C. ~~I, II and IV.~~
    D. II and IV.

A, B, and C are eliminated because they contain the items eliminated from the Roman numeral items. This leaves D as the only correct response.

Guess Strategically. By now, you should be familiar with the process of elimination by virtue of having done hundreds of multiple-choice exams throughout your career. The way that you should approach the balance of the exam after first having answered every one of the easy questions would be to find the questions that you think you can do with some effort. That might require doing the questions strategically as explained earlier or simply trying to eliminate as many wrong answers as possible before guessing on the remaining possibilities. For questions that you know you will never be able to answer, consider just picking the same letter each time. For example, if you have five questions left, use either *B* or *C* on all of them. The old "high school" approach that you might be familiar with entails guessing *A* on one item *C* on another item and *B* on another item (because the next one must be *D*). That's a pretty weak approach. You are far more likely to pick up one or two correct answers by using the same letter throughout the items that you know you'll have to just guess on, rather than relying on ESP to arrive at the correct answers telepathically.

Don't Forget the Null Questions and Time Wasters.   Consider the following question from the arts.

> The Mellonville Stomp and the Lindeyville Hop have what steps in common?
>
> A. Left, Right, Left, Left, Stomp.
> B. Right, Right, Left, Left, Hop.
> C. Left, Hop, Right, Stomp.
> D. Stomp, Stomp, Stomp, Stomp.

The odds are that you will see several of these kinds of questions. You are recommended to treat it as you would **any** time waster: **guess away.** The question is either a null question or a piece of trivial nonsense. Either way, you cannot become shocked and panicked when you see questions like this one. Just acknowledge the question and move on.

Using the Content of Chapters Three through Six

In these content chapters, you will see many tables that organize the information for you. They are meant to be immediately applicable to the multiple-choice questions. Let's look at two questions that draw upon what you will learn in these chapters. You will see one question on the difference between phonemic awareness and phonics instruction and another question on second language acquisition. You will see that the easiest way to manage these questions is to have the content in mind, along with knowing the elements of that content. Let's start with phonemic awareness and phonics.

One important area that you will learn about in Chapter Four is the difference between phonemic awareness and phonics. *Phonemic awareness* is the awareness of individual sounds in the language, and *phonics* is the understanding that sounds attach to letters that we decode when we read. The activities that one uses to develop both of these essential skills are different. Further, phonemic awareness comes before phonics. Table 2.13 below captures these elements.

TABLE 2.13

PHONEMIC AWARENESS	PHONICS
Oral Language is used.	Printed language is used.
Pictures are used but not text.	Letters, word families, and text are used.
Segmenting sounds are goals.	Fluent decoding of print is the goal.

An important part of your learning the content will be in how you apply your knowledge to the test. Basically, you must have the content organized in your mind as seen in the Table 2.13 in order to answer questions like this:

> The key feature of an effective phonemic awareness activity includes:
>
> A. Letter–sound associations.
> B. Whether the child can track print.

    C. Picture–sound associations.
    D. Whether the child knows where to start reading.

Using the content, it is easy to see and understand why *C* is the best response. Differentiating phonemic awareness from phonics is part of the domain and content area descriptions for this test, so it is an important area for you to know. Again, the content has been captured to the greatest extent possible to ease your study and application of Chapter Two.

    The content from Chapter Three will also be helpful to you if you are asked about second-language acquisition. For example, you will learn about something called *interlanguage* and how it includes two kinds of learner errors: *transfer errors* and *developmental errors*. Knowing the definitions is not enough, because you have to understand the underlying elements as shown in Table 2.14:

TABLE 2.14

INTERLANGUAGE

Transfer	Development

"House White" shows influence from Spanish where adjectives follow nouns. In Spanish, one literally says "house white" rather than "white house"	*Wh-* questions develop in stages like this:
	  Stage One: Where cat?
	  Stage Two: Where the cat is?
	  Stage Three: Where is the cat?

Now consider the following question.

    A second-language learner writes the following sentence during a Language Experience Activity.

    Where Chris is today?

    Which of the following best reflects the child's current stage of interlanguage?

        A. Transfer–influence.
        B. Orthographic.
        C. Developmentally ordered.
        D. Transitional.

After reading the data set and considering the content, it is easy to see that answer *C* is the correct one. The first answer, transfer–influenced, is incorrect because the word reversal is not influenced by the first language. The remaining items, orthographic and transitional, pertain to spelling and not to this example. Once again, knowing the content will help you make the multiple-choice questions work for you and not against you.

Conclusion

Below are some final thoughts about how to handle the multiple-choice sections on NES exams.

1. Remember the minimum thresholds.
2. Remember that the test is noncompensatory.
3. Keep track of your tally.

4. Remember the null questions.

5. Apply the strategies to the exam.

Each exam, whether it is subtest format or a comprehensive format, has mandatory minimum thresholds for each section. You must reach a minimum number of correct answers to be declared "subject matter qualified" on any of the content areas. That is because the test is noncompensatory, meaning that you cannot use one content area in place of another—by doing really well at Math, for example, and very poorly on Science.

Because you must reach these mandatory minimums, you are advised to carefully tally the number of questions you have answered. The tally tables will help guide you as you answer questions, so that you have a clear idea of how many questions you're answering on your way toward meeting the minimum score. In addition, they help you surpass the null questions that are present on all of these exams.

Do not forget about the null questions. You are going to see repeated items and, even worse, items where two answers seem to be correct. That's because *two answers actually can count.* Furthermore, you are going to pass by some pretty bizarre items that probably no one could answer correctly, unless they are as insane as the question itself. At any rate, you cannot predict which questions are real and which questions are not, but you can at least not get thrown off by any really weird questions.

CHAPTER THREE

ENGLISH LINGUISTICS

The Language Arts content applicable to CSET Subtest One will be taught to you in four chapters. This chapter covers English linguistics, Chapter Four presents literacy, Chapter Five describes language arts, and Chapter Six details written and oral communications. These areas are very broad, so you will only learn the major elements from each of these content areas. Ideally, the information in this chapter should only be a review for you, since you have already completed coursework in these areas. Please rely on your own judgment as you read the chapter: If the content seems completely unfamiliar to you, then you are encouraged to seek outside resources and assistance. Space will only permit an informed discussion of each subject in these chapters.

A NOTE ON THE CONTENT

The content of each chapter will help you immensely on the both the essay and multiple-choice portions of the exam. Many of the questions will ask you about what to do "first" and "next" when planning or delivering classroom lessons. Consider this example about the writing process.

A fifth grade teacher wishes to implement the process approach to writing in her classroom. Which of the following statements best represents the action that the teacher should take first?

A. Consider the grammar points that the students know already and the ones that they will need to learn through the activity.

B. Plan to have the students brainstorm topics that they might like to write about before attempting the first draft.

C. Prepare the students to work together to develop a rubric so that they can participate in how the writing project will be scored.

D. Demonstrate each step of the writing process for the students first and then work with them to carry out the steps together.

The answer is *D*, and that might be hard to understand because all of the answers look equally valid. In short, you need to model the writing process for the students first, because the teacher plans to *implement* the process in the classroom. The remaining statements are valid but do not constitute the *best* first step in the process of planning instruction in the classroom. The content presented here will be taught to you in a particular order with particular principles so that you can get through questions like this one. In short, your success on the test will depend on how well you understand the test maker's position on the content, no matter how valid other ideas may be in the "real world." Remember that you're validating "test reality" not "real reality" here.

THE DOMAINS AND CONTENT AREAS OF ELEMENTARY LANGUAGE ARTS

The test makers organize language arts content into domains and content areas. Domains are the major areas you need to know for the test and the content areas are the subareas that are targets of the exam. There are three domains of knowledge that you have to learn for the test—linguistics, literature, and communications—and they are organized as shown in Table 3.1.

TABLE 3.1

DOMAIN ONE: LANGUAGE AND LINGUISTICS	DOMAIN TWO: NONWRITTEN/ WRITTEN COMMUNICATION	DOMAIN THREE: TEXTS
1.1 Language and Linguistics	2.1 Language Conventions	3.1 Concepts and Conventions
1.2 Language Development	2.2 Writing Strategies	3.2 Genres
1.3 Literacy	2.3 Writing Applications	3.3 Interpretation of Texts
1.4 Assessment	2.4 Oral Communications	
	2.5 Research Strategies	

Unfortunately, none of the domain and content area descriptions lend themselves to self-study because the structure is not transparent. Domain two, for example, presents oral communications (2.4) before research strategies (2.5), and that is not an easy way to learn the material. The content has been reorganized for you as shown in Table 3.2 to make the learning process easier.

This order is much, much easier to understand. Plus, what you will learn in each domain and content area will be immediately applicable to the written and multiple-choice questions on the test. Each domain and its content area is presented to you in table format to make both learning, applying, and writing the information easy through dedicated study. Let's look at the principles of the first domain, English linguistics, before looking at first- and second-language acquisition. Doing so will prepare you for learning about literacy (Chapter Four), language arts (Chapter Five), and communications (Chapter Six).

DOMAIN ONE: ENGLISH LINGUISTICS

Let's turn now to the first major area of the exam, English linguistics, and learn about its major areas, from the most micro level (phonology) to the most macro level (sociolinguistics). The major content areas of this domain include the terms and processes of English

TABLE 3.2

CHAPTER THREE

Domain One: Linguistics	*Content Area*
1 English Linguistics	Linguistic terms and processes
2 Language Acquisition	First and Second Language Acquisition

CHAPTER FOUR:

Domain One (continued)	*Content Area*
3 Literacy	Reading Instruction
4 Assessment	Assessment Principles
5 Instruction	Instruction Principles

CHAPTER FIVE

Domain Two: Language Arts	*Content Area*
6 Genres of Children's Literature	Narratives, Poems, and Plays
7 Features of Literature	Elements of Prose and Poetry
8 Interpreting Literature	Responding to Prose and Poetry

CHAPTER SIX

Domain Three: Communications	*Content Area*
9 Writing Applications	Narrative and Expository Writing
10 Writing Process	Pre-Writing and Drafting Strategies
11 Research Process	Research Strategies
12 Editing Writing	Editing, Polishing, and Publishing Writing
13 Nonwritten Communication	Speech Communications

linguistics (content area one), along with how children and adolescents acquire English as a first and as a second language (content area two).

Content Area One: Linguistics Terms and Processes

This content area is vast. Table 3.3 on page 52 presents the terms and concepts at a glance. Familiarize yourself with the terms and some simple examples first, before reading further and trying to learn the content in depth.

Table 3.3 captures the elements of linguistics. **Phonology** is the study of sound units and functions, like consonant and vowel sounds in English. **Morphology** is the study of how sounds come together to make meaning, as in how we tell the difference in meaning between a collection of sounds like /bat/ and /pat/. **Syntax** is about grammar and how we structure sentences in speaking and writing to make meaning. **Semantics** is the study of meaning itself, where one studies the fine shades of meaning between words like *need* and *want*. Finally, **pragmatics** looks at very large language practices, like the act of apologizing or refusing, or how we use language differently when negotiating a transaction at a bank or when buying fruit at the store. The following few sections will explain each of these areas in greater detail to assist you in learning what you need to know for the test.

TABLE 3.3   Linguistic Elements

	PHONOLOGY	**MORPHOLOGY**	**SYNTAX**	**SEMANTICS**	**PRAGMATICS**
TERMS	The Study of Sound Units	The Study of Units of Meaning	Lexical/Nonlexical Categories, Grammar	Word/Sentence Meaning	Speech Acts, Discourse Theory
EXAMPLE	Consonant and Vowel Sounds in English	Tense Markers like *-ed* or *-ing,* or whole words like *cat*	Parts of Speech, Sentence Types	The difference in meaning between the auxiliary verbs *need* and *want.*	Apologizing, refusing, or interacting "at the bank" or "at the store."

Phonology.   Let's begin with English phonology. The most important areas on which to focus in this section are the phonological processes that affect the sounds of the English language. You will be treated to background information that is necessary for you to understand phonological processes, but it may not be tested directly on the exam. Therefore, do not let the amount of information intimidate you; focus instead on the larger concepts in this section.

Phonology describes the study of speech sounds (phonemes) in languages, including sounds in the English language, intonation patterns, and stress patterns (Carr, 1993). When studying speech sounds, linguists represent speech sounds between two forward slashes: /s/ and /z/. Please note that these representations are no longer the letter names "es" and "zee." They are the sound equivalents of "sssss" and "zzzzz." Here's a helpful example. Say the words *cats* and *cars* aloud to yourself and pay careful attention to the final sounds in each word. Here is what you should have said:

/kats/   /karz/

When these words are written, both of them have the letter *s* at the end; however, when they are spoken, these words have a different final sound. Why? Because the consonant sounds /t/ and /r/ affect what /s/ sounds like though a process of **devoicing** and **voicing** (to be explained shortly). In short, **phonology** is not only the study of individual sounds, but also the **linguistic processes** that affect what we hear in words when they are spoken. In the next sections, you will learn about consonant and vowel sounds, along with the major linguistic processes that affect them.

Consonant and Vowel Sounds.   Consonant and vowel sounds differ. For the test, you need to know why they are different. Let's stay with our first example, /cats/ and /cars/. The first sounds in each word are /k/ and /a/. As if you didn't know, the former is a consonant sound and the latter is vowel sound. But *why are they different*? They are different because consonant sounds are made through high degrees of friction and obstruction, and vowels are made with the mouth open and the tongue in a different position. To get a sense of this difference, say the following sounds to yourself:

Consonant Sounds: /p/ /b/ /t/ /d/ /k/ /g/ (puh, buh, tuh, duh, kuh, guh)

Long Vowel Sounds: /A/ /E/ /I/ /O/ /U/ (letter names)

Here is what you should notice. In the consonant line, you make the sounds using different combinations of your lips, teeth, tongue, and throat; whereas, in the vowel line, you made the sounds by altering the position of your tongue in your mouth and the shape of your mouth. In short, some consonant sounds are made by stopping the air that comes out of your mouth, and vowel sounds are formed without obstructing the air coming out. That's the nature of the difference. What you need to understand for the test is more complicated, however, since you have to know much about the terms **voicing, place of articulation,** and **manner of articulation,** and how they apply to both vowel and consonant sounds.

Voiced and Voiceless Consonants.   Say the consonant sounds again from the previous example, but this time, place your hand gently across your throat.

Consonant Sounds: /p/ /b/ /t/ /d/ /k/ /g/ (puh, buh, tuh, duh, kuh, guh)

You should notice that some of the consonant sounds made your throat vibrate but others did not. Here is what the pairings look like:

Voiceless: /p/ /t/ /k/

Voiced: /b/ /d/ /g/

If you try the pairs again, you should notice that each pair of sounds is made in exactly the same place in your mouth and in the same way; however, one sound makes your throat vibrate but another does not. You may not care much about that, but think about the impact voicing makes on what we understand. Say /pat/ and /bat/ to yourself. The only difference between how the sounds in these words are made is voicing—and that affects what we understand. If this difference did not exist, then there would be no difference in the spoken sentences: "*Hand me the bat.*" or "*Hand me the pat.*" Our understanding of the spoken sentences hinges on whether the initial consonant sound is voiced.

Since you have some understanding of voiced and unvoiced consonants, let's now learn about our first linguistic processes: **voicing** and **devoicing.** Recall that the /s/ at the ends of *cats* and *cars* has two possible sounds: /s/ or /z/. This is because the consonant that comes before the /s/ will affect whether it sounds like /s/ or /z/. Here is the rule for voicing and devoicing /s/:

- If /s/ follows /t/ or /k/, it is **unvoiced** as in *cats* and *trucks.*
- If /s/ follows any **voiced consonant,** then it sounds like /z/ as in *cars, goes,* and *runs.*
- If /s/ follows /sh/ or /ch/, then it sounds like /ez/, as in *washes* and *churches.*

These possible sounds for /s/, including /s/, /z/, and /ez/, are called **allophones,** because they are related to one another and emerge depending on the environment in which they are found.

Now, try saying the long vowel sounds again, this time with your hand on your throat.

Long Vowel Sounds: /A/ /E/ /I/ /O/ /U/ (letter names)

In each case, your throat vibrated because **all vowel sounds are voiced**—there is no unvoiced counterpart. Instead, there are short vowel counterparts for each of the long vowels:

Short Vowel Sounds: /a/ /e/ /i/ /o/ /u/ (ah, eh, ih, oh, oo)

Let's move from voiced and unvoiced sounds to descriptions of *where sounds are made in the mouth* (**place of articulation**) and the *characteristics of sounds* (**manner of articulation**).

Place and Manner of Articulation (Consonants).   You need to learn the terminology associated with where sounds are made in the mouth and how to describe the characteristics of the sounds we make (beyond mere voiced and voiceless sounds). We will start with **place of articulation.** Table 3.4 shows the terms associated with where sounds are made in the mouth:

TABLE 3.4   Places of Articulation (Consonants)

LABIAL	INTERDENTAL	ALVEOLAR	PALATAL	VELAR	GLOTTAL
With the lips	*Between the teeth*	*Right behind the teeth*	*With roof of mouth*	*With soft palate*	*In the throat*

Nothing demands an example more than does Table 3.5. Say the sounds within each category and note what happens to your lips, teeth, and tongue as you say them:

TABLE 3.5   Examples of Articulated Consonants

LABIAL	INTERDENTAL	ALVEOLAR	PALATAL	VELAR	GLOTTAL
With the lips	*Between the teeth*	*Right behind the teeth*	*With roof of mouth*	*With soft palate*	*In the throat*
/b/	/th/	/t/	/sh/	/k/	/h/

You should notice that different combinations of your teeth, tongue, and lips are used to make these sounds. Below is a summary of each type of place of articulation. Please say the sounds so that you can associate them with different places in your mouth. Pay particular attention to your lips, the shape of your tongue, and different places in your mouth as you learn the sounds associated with the terms listed below (Anderson, 1985).

- **Labials** are made with your lips, like /b/, /p/, /f/, /v/, /m/, /w/.
- **Interdentals** are made between the teeth, like /th/ in "thin") and /th/ in "these."
- **Alveolars** are made right behind your teeth, like /t/, /d/, /s/, /z/, /n/, /l/, /r/.
- **Palatals** are made with the roof of your mouth, like /sh/ (ship), /zsh/ (azure), /tsh/ (witch), /dz/ (gym).
- **Velars** are made with your soft palate, like /k/, /g/, /ing/.
- **Glottals** are made in the back of your throat, like /h/.

You will need to memorize these terms. Using a combination of note cards, sound associations, and oral practice making the sounds will help you. You need to learn the terms associated with the different quality of the sounds, before putting both **place** and **manner of articulation** together.

Manner of Articulation (Consonants). The major **manners of articulation** appear in Table 3.6. Remember that "manner" refers to the **characteristic and quality** of the sound. Try to associate the definition with the **sounds** listed in the table.

TABLE 3.6   Manners of Articulated Consonants

STOPS	FRICATIVES	NASALS	LIQUIDS	GLIDES
Stops the air	*Vibrates the air*	*Out the nose*	*Fluid air*	*Evaporating air*
/p/ /b/ /t/ /d/ /k/ /g/	/f/ /v/ /th/ /s/ /z/ /sh/ /tsh/ /h/	/m/ /n/	/l/ /r/	/w/

We describe the sounds in Table 3.6 based on their characteristics. **Stops,** for example, stop the air coming out of the mouth. Say *pat, bat, tap, dog, king,* and *go,* and you have the idea. **Fricatives** make the air vibrate. Try *fat, valley, thin, that, sat, zap, ship, witch,* and *hat* for illustration. The nasal sounds, both of which are in *man,* send the air out the nose, whereas **liquids** sound very fluid and "liquidy." Say "luscious" and "lugubrious" a few times to get an idea. Finally, **glides** have a quality that sounds like the air evaporates after it leaves your mouth. Try just the sound /w/ (e.g., "wuh, wuh, wuh") and that description should make sense to you.

In short, **place of articulation** and **manner of articulation** describe where in your mouth the sounds are made (**place**) along with the quality of the sound produced (**manner**). Now let's put it all together.

Place, Manner, and Voicing of Consonants. Table 3.7 sums up place, manner, and voicing for you. You should try copying the table outline and filling it in with the information until it is memorized. **Note:** The voiced consonants are in **bold** and appear right below their unvoiced counterparts.

Vowel Place and Manner of Articulation. Vowels are different from consonants because they pass out of the mouth and/or nose with very little obstruction. Say the letter names A,

TABLE 3.7   Summary of Place, Manner, and Voicing of English Consonants

MANNER	PLACE OF ARTICULATION					
	Labial	*Inter-dental*	*Alveolar*	*Palatal*	*Velar*	*Glottal*
Stops	p **b**		t **d**		k **g**	
Fricatives	f **v**	th (thin) **th (this)**	s **z**	sh **dsh**		h
Nasals	**m**		**n**		**ing**	
Liquids			l r			
Glides	**w**			y (yellow)		

E, I, O, and U aloud, and you should notice how your tongue and oral cavity form different shapes to make the sounds. Thus, the position of your lips and tongue cause minute changes that cause different vowel sounds to emerge. Table 3.8 shows the place and manner of articulation of some common short and long vowels. Note: Long vowels say their name and are shown in capital letters in the table.

TABLE 3.8   Place of Articulation (Vowels)

		POSITION OF TONGUE IN MOUTH		
Tip of Tongue	*Front of Mouth*	*Middle of Mouth*		*Back of Mouth*
High	feet /E/			shoot /oo/
Mid	mate /A/	but /u/	should	coat /O/
Low	let /e/		caught	
	mat /a/	cot /aw/		

The place of articulation of vowel sounds depends on where the tongue itself is placed (position of the tongue) and where the tip of the tongue is pointing (high, midway, or low). Try saying the words again and note the position of your tongue in your mouth.

Manner of Articulation (Vowels).   The sound quality of vowels is described as being **tense and diphthongized** or **lax. Tense vowels** include some vowel names, like the /o/ in *coat.* You can also hear **tense, dipthongized** sounds like the /oi/ in *boy* and the /ow/ in *cow.* **Diphthongs** are easy to identify because there are two sounds heard when you say them. Say *boy* and *cow* again, and you should hear two vowel sounds in each word. There are even **triphthongs** in English where three separate vowel sounds are heard in words: *loyal, liar, power.* **Lax vowels** are all of your short vowels: /a/—*pat,* /e/—*pet,* /i/—*bit,* /o/—*hot,* and /u/—*but.*

LINGUISTIC PROCESSES.   What happens to sounds after we make them? Different **combinations** of sounds affect what we hear when we listen to spoken words or words in sentences. You have already learned about one process called **voicing** and **devoicing.** There are other rules to know for the exam. Now let's learn about **flapping** and **aspirating.**

Flapping is a common process in U.S. English. For example, say the word *butter,* first slowly then quickly. Try it a couple of times. If you pay careful attention to the way that you probably pronounced each word, then you should have noticed the following:

Slow Speech Nonflapping	Rapid Speech Flapping
butter—/buter/	*butter—/buder/*

In the case of *butter,* rapid speech affects the phonemes we hear in the word. The linguistic process where the voiceless stop /t/ becomes a voiced stop /d/ in rapid speech is called **flapping.**

Aspiration is another common linguistic process. Hold a piece of paper against your lips and try saying this pair of words: *pit* and *spit.* Pay attention to how far the paper moves away from your lips as you say the words. You should notice that the paper moved *away* from your lips when you said *pit* but hardly moved at all when you said *spit.* Why? Because the combination of phonemes in each words affects how they are pronounced:

Aspirated	Non-Aspirated
pit—/pʰit/	*spit—/spit/*

In the word *pit,* for example, you make an "explosive" sound when the voiceless stop /p/ heads the word. *But when the phoneme /p/ follows a voiceless phoneme like /s/, then it is not aspirated.*

These minor processes affect pronunciation and accents in English. For example, it is easy to identify a speaker of British English because he or she tends not to flap their stops; instead, the speaker aspirates them.

U.S. English	British English
butter—/buder/	*butter—buthʰah/*

Other languages (neither British nor U.S. English) tell the difference between words based on aspiration. As a Khmer speaker explained in class one day, aspiration in her language differentiates words that would sound exactly the same to a monolingual English audience. In her language, /pong/ and /pʰong/ mean different things. The former means "wish" and the latter means "also." When she pronounced these words for us, they sounded exactly the same to all monolingual English speakers.

The student added that it was difficult for her to learn English in the beginning because she kept hearing all of our aspirated consonants in English (/p/, /t/, /k/) and wondered what was happening!

In addition to aspiration and flapping, there are six linguistic processes that you should know for the test. These are called **assimilation, deletion, devoicing, epenthesis, metathesis,** and **palatization.** They are common processes and are easy to identify (Anderson, 1985; Hyman, 1975; Wolfram & Johnson, 1982).

- **Assimilation.** In rapid speech, many words that we say sound different than they do in slow speech. The example of **flapping** in the word *butter* is an example of assimilation. Here, one sound becomes absorbed into another in rapid speech. The phonemes /t/ and /d/ are the most commonly assimilated sounds. Say the words *water, rotting,* and *putting,* first carefully then very rapidly, and you can see the process of assimilating /t/ into the 'flapped' /d/ at work.
- **Deletion.** In rapid speech, we sometimes delete entire phonemes or syllables in spoken words. This explains how *contractions* are formed in written languages. The spoken verb phrase *I am* said rapidly sounds like */im/.* Here, we deleted the short vowel /a/ from the phrase in rapid speech. To the unease of many grammarians and college professors, we have inducted this form into written English. Deletion also explains the mismatch between what we write and what we say. The name of the fourth day of the week is spelled *Wednesday,* but is usually pronounced /wensday/. In this case, we have completely deleted a part of the syllable in the word that was once pronounced /owdensday/ named after the Saxon god of war, Odin. The linguistic process of deletion in spoken speech, then, accounts for many of the odd spelling patterns found in English as well as the difficulties in learning how to spell many

words. There is often a great mismatch between what we say and what we write. Deletion is responsible.

■ **Devoicing.** You have already learned about how consonants that precede /s/ can affect whether it sounds like /s/ or /z/. The phoneme /t/ is either voiced or unvoiced depending on the whether the consonants that it follows are voiced or unvoiced. Say *runned* and then *worked* to yourself. You should have said /rund/ and /werkt/. In the former, the /t/ sounds like /d/ because /n/ is a voiced consonant; in the latter, /t/ sounds like /t/, because the /k/ sound is unvoiced.

■ **Epenthesis.** Just as we delete many phonemes and syllables in words when we speak rapidly, we also insert sounds that are not normally there. Say the words *something, warmth,* and *length* slowly and then rapidly. You may have said the following during rapid speech (not everyone does this): /sumpthing/, /warmpth/, and /lenkth/. If your slow and rapid speech shows differences, then you are guilty of **epenthesis,** where you insert other sounds where they are not normally heard in slow speech. Again, this affects how children spell words in the beginning: Since they tend to spell by words based on what they say, these words may often be seen as *sumpthing, warmpth,* and *lenkth* in the early stages of spelling development. Misspelling of words like *athelete* are also the result of epenthesis.

■ **Metathesis.** In some regional variations of English in the United States, **metathesis** is common. If you have ever heard a speaker pronounce *asks* as /aks/ (e.g., *I need to aks you a question*), what you are hearing is the linguistic process of metathesis. Put simply, the final phonemes /s/ and /k/ are "swapped' one for the other, creating an identifiable regional accent when one hears a speaker **metathesizing** sounds in speech.

■ **Palatalization.** Some spoken words shift sounds in regional speech. *Williams* can be heard as /weyams/, where the liquid /l/ becomes a palatal /y/ sound.

In summary, these linguistic processes affect what we hear in slow and rapid speech, and they can affect how we spell and the regional accents that we have. Let's now move from simple speech sounds and their processes to a higher level of how we make meaning with words in English.

Morphology.   Morphology is the study of the smallest units of meaning in a word (Katamba, 1993). Just as there are phonemes in each language (individual sound units), there are also morphemes (individual units of meaning). Sometimes, morphemes can be as small as one sound. Take /s/ for example. This phoneme also functions as a morpheme in English, because it makes words plural (cars) and possessive (Chris's). Not all sounds or letters are morphemes by themselves. The letters p, e, l, h, n, and t do not mean anything all by themselves; however, if you arrange them differently and add a few more letters to the combination, you get a singular morpheme: *elephant.* If you add the letter "s" to this singular morpheme, you get **two morphemes:** *elephants* (*elephant* + *s*). To understand these concepts fully, let's learn about free and bound morphemes next.

Free and Bound Morphemes.   There are two types of morphemes to know for the test. They are called free and bound. Here is a summary in Table 3.9 to help you remember the difference.

TABLE 3.9   Free and Bound Morphemes

FREE MORPHEMES	BOUND MORPHEMES
■ Stand-alone words	■ Attached to stand-alone words.
■ Cat	■ Inflectional suffixes like -s, -'s, and -ed.
■ Chris	■ Derivations like -tion, -ize, and -al.
■ Run	■ Root words like *tele* and *form.*

When you think of free morphemes, just imagine any combination of letters or sounds that can stand alone and have meaning. Free morphemes appear in the examples above. The words *car, Chris,* and *run* are free morphemes, because they can stand all by themselves and have individual meaning. Bound morphemes, on the other hand, cannot stand alone and have meaning. The morpheme, -s, for example, only makes sense when functioning as a plural marker (car**s**) or as a possessive indicator (Chris**'s**) or as an indicator of third person singular for verbs (**runs**). It has no meaning when it is all by itself, however. It must be attached to some word in order to have meaning. For the test, you may have to be able to tell the difference between very particular types of bound morphemes called *inflections, derivations,* and *root words* as they appear in Table 3.9. You will learn about them in a moment after seeing how to count morphemes in words.

Counting Morphemes.   Since you may be asked to count free and bound morphemes in words, let's begin with a simple example. The word *duck,* represents one morpheme. When spelled, it has four letters in it (d, u, c, k), but when spoken, it has three phonemes: /d/, /u/, /k/. Together, these sounds and letters combine to make **one morpheme,** even though it has four letters (graphemes) and three phonemes.

The word *ducks* has two morphemes in it: One is free and the other is bound. See if you can identify them before reading further.

ducks

You should have identified *duck* as the free morpheme and the plural marker *-s* as the bound morpheme, because the former can stand alone and the latter cannot. Try the same thing with the words below:

cars   Chris's   works   working   worked

The bound morphemes are *-s,'s, -s, -ing,* and *-ed.* The words *car, Chris,* and *work* are all free.

Let's now consider a different combination of letters. Say *ptffs* aloud. *Ptffs* represents **no morphemes,** because this combination of letters means absolutely **nothing** in English. There is nothing **free** or **bound** about the word. The plural marker *-s* doesn't mean anything either in this case, because the **base word,** *pttfs,* doesn't mean anything.

In summary, one way to count morphemes in words is to look for the base word and for any endings that might represent separate morphemes. This leads us to the next discussion of different kinds of **morphological affixes,** called inflectional and derivational affixes.

Affixes are either prefixes or suffixes and can be counted as **morphemes.** There are two major groups of affixes that you need to understand for the test. As shown in Table 3.10, the first group of countable affixes are called **inflectional suffixes;** the second special group is called **derivations affixes** (both prefixes and suffixes) (Wysocki & Jenkins, 1987).

TABLE 3.10   Common Inflectional and Derivational Affixes

AFFIXES	
Inflectional	*Derivational*
■ Plurals: books, cars, wishes ■ Possessives: Mike's, Chris's ■ Comparative: bigger ■ Superlative: biggest ■ Verb tense: walks, walked, walking, chosen ■ Third singular: He runs, walks, stops	■ Prefixes: un-, re-, inter-, de- ■ Suffixes: -able, -tion, -al, -ize, -ment

Let's look at the first type of affix: the inflection. Inflections make nouns plural or possessive; they make adjectives comparative or superlative; and they make different tenses and mark subject/verb agreement. What they do not do is radically change the meaning of a word or its grammatical category, because that is the job of the **derivational prefix or suffix.**

Read the sentence below and pay careful attention to the word in bold.

The speaker was rebuked for his position on **internationalization.**

In the word, *internationalization,* there are five morphemes. One of them is the **base word** *nation* and the rest are **derivational prefixes** and **suffixes** (see Table 3.11). Let's count all of the **morphemes** in *internationalization.* In addition, watch as the meaning of the word and its grammatical category change as prefixes and suffixes are added to the word.

The process of counting derivational morphemes and analyzing their meaning in words is called **structural analysis.** In this example, *internationalization* has a number of important derivational affixes in it that radically alter the meaning and grammatical category of the free morpheme *nation:*

- *Nation* to *national* (noun to adjective).
- *National* to *nationalize* (adjective to verb).
- *Nationalize* to *nationalization* (verb back to noun).
- *Nationalization* to *internationalization* (national unity to international unity).

A final important note about derivational affixes is that they tend to retain the same meaning across words. The meaning of the prefix *re-* is stable across a variety of words, includ-

TABLE 3.11   Applied Structural Analysis

1	2	3	4	5
Prefix	*Base Word*	*Suffix*	*Suffix*	*Suffix*
inter- between	nation state	al adjective marker	ize verb marker	ation noun marker

ing *rewrite, reread, rethink,* and so forth. Some affixes, however, can be **both** inflectional and derivational. The suffix *-er* in the word bigg**er** is an inflectional suffix because it makes the adjective *big* the comparative adjective *bigger*. However, in the word teach**er,** *-er* is a derivational suffix because it changes the verb *teach* into a noun meaning "one who teaches."

In summary, derivational affixes are far more powerful than simple inflectional suffixes. Derivations can change a words meaning or its grammatical category, but inflections can only make nouns plural or possessive or verbs past or present. Let's turn now to the final kind of bound morpheme: the root word.

Root words are similar to derivational affixes, in that they are all bound morphemes. They cannot stand alone and mean anything. But unlike prefixes and suffixes, they *carry the meaning of a word by themselves* and *other letters attach to them to convey meaning* (prefixes and suffixes are like leeches, since they attach themselves to words and alter them *parasitically*). Consider the root word *ann* (from the Latin, meaning "year") and *tele* (from the Greek, meaning "to send").

- **Ann-** **ann**ual, **ann**iversary, **ann**um, **ann**uity
- **Tele-** **tele**vise, **tele**x, **tele**port

In each case, *ann* and *tele* function as root words, because they carry the meaning of the word, even though they are **bound (derivational affixes** are not this powerful) they can *alter* meaning (e.g., *retelevise)* and alter a word's grammatical category, but they do not carry most of a word's meaning like a root word does. In addition, when looking for root words within words, you are actually studying a word's *etymology*—its history, meaning, and origin.

One caution is required when counting both root words and derivational affixes. Some syllables in words may look like either root words or derivational affixes, when they are in fact neither. Consider *chimpanzee.* If we divide *chimpanzee* into syllables: chim / pan / zee, you might be tempted to count the syllable *pan* as the derivational morpheme *pan* (meaning, "across"). You would be wrong in doing so, because this syllable within *chimpanzee* does not function as a **bound morpheme,** since the entire word represents **one free morpheme.**

Syntax. The next major area you need to understand is English syntax. Syntax describes the grammar of any language, and we will cover the major things you should know regarding this topic.

For the test, you need to know that there is a distinction between **descriptive grammar** and **prescriptive grammar.** Descriptive grammar describes a language the way that people use it without judging whether the utterance is correct or incorrect. Descriptive grammarians, for example, are less interested in whether *Who should I say is calling?* or *Whom shall I say is calling?* is the correct form, but are more preoccupied with how one transforms *I shall say who is calling* into the question form. Prescriptive grammarians, however, are concerned with correct usage, and that is why we will review the **eight parts of speech, phrases, clauses,** and **sentences** with you just in case you are asked questions on traditional English grammar.

Let's learn about descriptive grammar first. Since descriptive grammar will probably amount to only one question on the test, we will not spend a great deal of time on it. Descriptive grammar uses two key terms that you should know for the test: deep structure and surface structure. *Surface structures* are the sentences that we produce; *deep structures* are the underlying sentences that we use to make our utterances. Consider the following utterance.

Whom are you addressing?

Wh- questions, like the one above, represent a surface structure, because they are what one says to ask the question. The utterance has a deep, beginning structure that starts out like this:

You are addressing whom.

This deep structure has an order: Subject / Verb / Object, as shown in Table 3.12.

TABLE 3.12

SUBJECT	VERB	OBJECT
You	are addressing	whom

To arrive at the surface wh- question, one moves through a number of **grammatical transformations.** In Table 3.13, the utterance moves from deep to surface structure (Walsh, 1996):

TABLE 3.13   *Wh-* Movement

Deep Structure	**You are addressing whom.**
Wh- Movement	**Whom** you are addressing _____.
Inversion	Whom *are you* addressing.
Surface Structure	Whom are you addressing**?**

This pattern holds across all interrogatives (*who, what, where, why,* and *when*). The point of this discussion is that descriptive grammar and deep structures appear across languages, and there are some interesting commonalties that hold across languages. For example, there are nouns, verbs, adjectives, and adverbs across languages, so that any idea that can be expressed in one language can also be expressed in another language.

Another important notion is that some deep structures appear to be part of a "universal grammar" because they are found cross-linguistically. The subject / verb / object pattern is one that is found in many languages and may be part of a universal deep structure that all of us as learners of language arrive on Earth predisposed to use. Consider an utterance in English and then in Spanish as shown in Table 3.14:

TABLE 3.14

	SUBJECT	VERB	OBJECT
English:	I	have	a dog.
Spanish:	Yo	tengo	un perro.

Since this subject/verb/object pattern is very stable in English and in other European and Romance languages, it seems to be a reliable deep structure that is shared across many languages. Therefore, the structure could be said to be part of a universal grammar (White, 1989).

Recognizing the Eight Parts of Speech.   Since the bulk of your questions about English grammar will be of the prescriptive kind, let's spend some time reviewing traditional grammar, starting with the eight parts of speech.

For the test, you may be asked to identify any number of grammatical terms or to identify the parts of speech within written sentences. Page length will not permit a full review of English grammar, but we will present the major areas that you need to know for the exam. There are eight parts of speech that you need to recall: **nouns, pronouns, verbs, adjectives, adverbs, prepositions, conjunctions,** and **interjections.** Let's review each one for the test.

NOUNS.   Nouns name persons, places, things, ideas, animals, qualities, and sometimes actions that we perform (e.g., **Swimming** is fun).

Below are the major terms and example associated with nouns; they are ideal candidates for flashcards.

- **Common nouns** name unspecific persons, places, things, ideas, and so forth. For example, men, cars, and policies are all unspecific, common nouns.
- **Proper nouns** name specific persons, places, things, and so forth and are usually capitalized. For example, Chris Boosalis is a proper name, so it is capitalized, as is his place of birth (Minnesota), ethnicity (Greek), and title of the book he is writing (*Beating The CSET!*).
- **Concrete nouns** name things that we can see, feel, taste, touch, and/or smell and can be either common or proper. For example, the word *car* is a concrete, common noun, whereas Colgate, the brand of toothpaste, is a concrete, proper noun.
- **Abstract nouns** name things that we cannot experience through the five senses. They can also be common or proper. The feeling *love* is a common, concrete noun, but Einstein's Theory of Relativity is not only proper but also *very* abstract.
- **Collective nouns** name groups of people or collections of things. For example, a **team** refers to a group of people, while **herd** refers to a group of animals.
- **Compound nouns** are made up of two words, like heating duct, air horn, or Batman.
- **Singular nouns** name individual people, places, or things, but **plural nouns** name more than one noun.

One important note concerns spelling plural nouns. There are rules that you should remember for the test when spelling some nouns in the plural. Fortunately, you can often make a noun plural by just adding the **inflectional ending** *-s* to the end of the word, like *cars, bats, trucks*. Here are more spelling patterns that you should be aware of:

- Some nouns take *-es* if they end in *s, x, z, ch,* or *sh,* like *basses, axes, fezzes, churches, wishes.* This is also true for many words that end in *-o*, like *potatoes* and *tomatoes;* however, there are enough exceptions to this rule for words that end in *-o* that you should probably consult a dictionary to be sure on the spelling (*pianos, radios,* etc.).

- Other nouns change their spelling when adding -*s*. For example, some words that end with a consonant + *y* add -*ies* to form the plural (*harmony* → *harmonies*), unless the word ends with a vowel + *y* (*monkey* → *monkeys*).
- Most nouns that end with the letter *f* simply take -*s* to form the plural (*tiff* → *tiffs*), though there are exceptions (*wife* → *wives*, *leaf* → *leaves*).
- Some nouns take *ablaut* forms in the plural, where they change their internal spelling. *Mouse* → *mice, foot* → *feet,* and *goose* → *geese* are examples.
- We preserve the etymology of some words that we spell in English. For example, *thesis* in the plural is *theses, medium* is *media* (like *print media*), *datum* is *data,* and *analysis* is *analyses.*
- Possessive nouns are formed by adding *'s* or *s',* depending on whether it describes individual or group ownership. To show that one person has possession of a book, one writes *Chris's book;* however, if there were multiple authors with the first name Chris, then one would write *Chris' book,* since **the book belongs to all of the authors named Chris.**
- **Gerunds** are verbs with the inflectional affix -*ing* attached to them. They are used as nouns to describe activities that we like or dislike to perform. For example, ***Thinking is my favorite thing*** to do or *I hate **running*** are two examples of gerunds functioning as nouns.

Having described nouns and the terms associated with them, let's move now to pronouns, words that are used to replace nouns in sentences.

Pronouns.   Like regular nouns, pronouns name people, places, things, both concrete and abstract, but they are used to replace nouns to help eliminate redundancy. Consider the following paragraph without pronouns.

> **Isaac Eziquial Montague Williams** worked at the post office. **Isaac Eziquial Montague Williams** enjoyed working at the post office. **Isaac Eziquial Montague Williams** retired from working at the post office when **Isaac Eziquial Montague** turned 65.

Pronouns eliminate the need to say nouns over and over again. They are sensitive to the position they occupy in sentences, the number of things they are replacing, and the function they are performing. Pronouns must also have an **antecedent,** the person or thing that defines what the pronoun in a sentence or paragraph means:

> **Isaac Eziquial Montague Williams** worked at the post office, and **he** enjoyed it.

In the sentence above, the pronoun **he** is used to replace the rather lengthy name **Isaac Eziquial Montague Williams.** Thus, the **antecedent** Isaac Eziquial Montague Williams defines who **he** refers to in the example sentence above. Without clear antecedents, sentences can be confusing, as the next sentences is meant to illustrate to you.

> The **man** walked the **dog,** and **he** was happy.

Who is happy? The man? The dog? Because **he** might refer to either potential antecedent, one cannot say for sure. This is also called structural ambiguity, because you cannot immediately tell to whom the pronoun *he* is referring.

Table 3.15 captures the major categories of pronouns that you need to know for the exam, and explanations follow the table.

TABLE 3.15   Pronouns

Pronouns replace nouns and require an antecedent.

Antecedent Number	Subjective	Objective	Possessive		Reflexive
			Subjective	Objective	
Singular	I	me	my	mine	myself
Singular	you	you	your	yours	yourself
Plural	we	us	our	ours	ourselves
Plural	they	them	their	theirs	themselves
Singular	he	him	his	his	himself
	she	her	her	hers	herself
	it	it	its	its	itself

Antecedent number simply means that you must ensure that your pronouns agree in number with whatever noun they are replacing. For example, singular, first-person pronouns include *I, me, my, mine,* and *myself.* Singular, second-person pronouns are *you, your, yours,* and *yourself.* Plural, first-person pronouns (if you're included in a group) include *we, us, our, ours,* and *ourselves.* Plural, third-person pronouns (if you're not included in a group) include *they, them, their, theirs,* and *themselves.*

To understand pronouns, you need to understand **subjective** and **objective** positions in sentences. When a pronoun acts as the subject of a sentence (the thing performing an action or under description) it uses the subjective case:

- I am here.
- You are here.
- They are here.

Subjective case pronouns must agree with their antecedents both numerically and conceptually. Consider the following absurd sentences:

- The **team** is here, and **he** is happy.
- The **idea** is a good one, so **she** should be carried out immediately.

Each of the sentences above is problematic. In the first sentence, the antecedent and pronoun do not agree in number, while the second sentence simply sounds ridiculous.

If the pronoun receives the action (direct object) or benefits from it (indirect object), its form sometimes changes:

- He called me. (not *I*)
- He called you. (no change)
- He called them. (not *they*)

The same thing happens with **possessive pronouns.** They change depending on their position in the sentence as shown in Table 3.16.

TABLE 3.16   Possessive Pronoun Cases

SUBJECTIVE	OBJECTIVE
My book is taking too long to write.	That book is **min·**
Our work is hard.	That book is **our**:

Reflexive pronouns direct actions or descriptions bac]

- I tend to keep things to myself.
- The dishwasher works by itself.

Table 3.17 shows other types of pronouns that you nee

TABLE 3.17   Other Types of Pronouns

INTERROGATIVE	DEMONSTRATIVE	INDEFINITE	
who/whose/whom	this/that	everyone	each other
what	these/those	everybody	one another
which		nobody	
		no one	

Interrogative pronouns usually head sentences that ask questions:

- Who are those people?
- Whose dog is that?
- Whom is she speaking to?
- What are they doing?
- Which one should I buy?

Demonstrative pronouns indicate which person or object is being described and its distance from the speaker:

- That is a nice suit.
- This is a nice suit.
- These are fine shoes
- Those are fine shoes.

That and this do have subtle differences. *That is a nice suit* and *This is a nice suit* reflect potential differences in distance: That indicates that the speaker is a greater distance from what he or she describes, whereas *this* indicates a closer proximity. The same idea is true for *these* and *those*. In actual speech, these differences are pretty much arbitrary and moot, since many speakers use them interchangeably.

Indefinite pronouns refer to things and people in a general and collective sense:

- Everyone is here.
- Everybody is here.
- No one is here.
- Nobody is here.

There is virtually no difference between *everyone/everybody* and *no one/nobody.* Note that all of these pronouns are singular.

Reciprocal pronouns refer to actions or descriptions that apply to plural and collective groups of people and things.

- We must love **one another.**
- Be kind to **each other.**

The difference between *one another* and *each other* is very subtle: *One another* seems more general than *each other,* because *each other* seems to include the speaker and whomever he or she is speaking to in the statement. Once again, the distinction seems pretty arbitrary in actual speech.

VERBS   Time to move into *action,* as we discuss verbs. Types of verbs are shown in Table 3.18.

TABLE 3.18   Types of Verbs

VERBS MAKE STATEMENTS, ASK A QUESTIONS, OR GIVE A COMMANDS OR DIRECTIONS.

Being	Action	Auxiliary	Transitive	Intransitive	Infinitive
is, am, seems, feel	run, walk, stand, feel	has, have, had, be, am, is, are, will	take, make, bring	run, walk, sleep	to be, to run, to walk, to stand

The first distinction to make is between **being** and **action verbs.** Being verbs describe or qualify the subject of a sentence:

Chris **is** a 34-year-old male teacher.

In this sentence, no action is taken; instead, Chris, the subject of the sentence, is described in terms of being: age, gender, and profession. Contrast this sentence with the next one that describes action:

Chris **walks** his dog, Krusty, in the morning.

Here, Chris undertakes the act of walking his dog. It is a concrete action. There are also abstract actions, like *Chris* **swears** *to tell the truth, the whole truth, and nothing but the truth.* Note that some verbs can be **both being and action verbs.** Compare the next two sentences:

- Chris **feels** sick.
- Chris **feels** his dog for ticks.

In the first sentence, **feels** functions as a being verb, since one cannot physically touch the adjective following the verb (sick). The use of **feels** in the second sentence is an action verb because a physical act is taking place (touching the dog to find ticks).

Auxiliary verbs clarify when an action takes place, took place, or will take place. In other words, they tell us present, past, and future, along with really fine shades and degrees of time (the progressive and perfect tenses). We will deal with these tenses in greater detail in a moment. For now, just consider this sentence.

Chris **will** walk his dog in the morning, and Krusty **will** be happy.

In the sentence above, the auxiliary verb, **will,** tells us that an action will take place in the future (walking the dog), in addition to the resulting, future effect on the dog (happiness).

Transitive and intransitive verbs may also appear on the exam. Here is how to identify and describe them. Transitive verbs require an object in order to make sense. A **direct object** is a something that benefits from the action performed in the sentence:

Chris **writes books** in the morning.

In this case, the act of writing produces something—in this case, a book. Here, *writes* is a transitive verb because it acts upon something (a direct object) and the sentence makes sense when it is read. Transitive verbs may also take things called **indirect objects,** something that benefits from the action being performed:

Chris writes a letter **to Beatriz.**

The act of writing in the sentence above produces a direct object (letter). The beneficiary of the letter is the one who receives the product (Beatriz), making her the indirect object of the action.

We can easily contrast transitive verbs with intransitive verbs. Intransitive verbs need no objects to make sense. Consider each column of sentences in Table 3.19, and ask yourself which ones make sense and which ones do not:

TABLE 3.19

A	B
I take.	I run.
I make.	I walk.
I bring.	I sleep.

The statements in Column A make no sense to you because the verbs have no objects after them; however, the sentence in Column B make perfect sense, since they can stand all by themselves without objects. Please note that **run** and **walk** from Column B can also be transitive if you want them to be transitive. Simply add an object to them:

- I run machines for a living.
- I walk my dog in the morning.

Sleep, on the other hand, cannot be transitive because no object will make sense in the object position.

- I sleep sharks.
- I sleep raisins.
- I sleep coconuts.

The last item in Table 3.18 are the infinitive forms of verbs. You will learn more about **infinitive verbs** later in the section on phrases. For now, simply understand that infinitives are the **pure, unconjugated** form of the verb (see Table 3.20):

TABLE 3.20

INFINITIVE FORM	BARE INFINITIVE
to be	be
to walk	walk
to see	see

Infinitives appear after many verbs, like **need** and **like:**

- I need **to work** today.
- I like **to work** on writing.

Bare infinities appear after other verbs, like **must** and **shall:**

- I must **work** today.
- I shall **work** today.

We move now from this general discussion of verbs to something more specific: tense.

Verb tenses in English are important to know for the test (just in case), and there are plenty of them. Learn the simple ones first: past, present, and future as shown in Table 3.21:

TABLE 3.21   The Simple Tenses

	PAST	PRESENT	FUTURE
Regular	I walk.	I walked.	I will walk.
Irregular	I was here.	I am here.	I will be here.

Conjugating present, past, and future tenses of verbs depends, first, on number of persons undertaking the action or being described. Second, conjugation depends on whether the verb is regular or irregular. Space will not permit us to present every conjugation available for regular and irregular verbs, but free lists do exist on the internet. Tables 3.22 through 3.24 provide very brief examples of person and regular and irregular conjugations in the present, past, and future tenses.

TABLE 3.22

PRESENT TENSE	REGULAR	IRREGULAR
first person	I walk.	I am here.
second person	You walk.	You are here.
third person	He, she, or it walks.	He, she, or it is here.
first-person plural	We walk.	We are here.
third-person plural	They walk.	They are here.

For regular, present tense verbs, only third-person singular varies, since you must add the inflectional suffix -*s*. On the other hand, the irregular verb *to be* varies wildly according to person (see Table 3.23).

TABLE 3.23

PAST TENSE	REGULAR	IRREGULAR
first person	I walked.	I was here.
second person	You walked.	You were here.
third person	He, she, or it walked.	He, she, or it was here.
first-person plural	We walked.	We were here.
third-person plural	They walked.	They were here.

The past tense for regular verbs is accomplished by a simple addition of the inflectional suffix *-ed*. Once again, the irregular verb *to be* varies depending on the number of persons in question (see Table 3.23).

TABLE 3.24

FUTURE TENSE	REGULAR	IRREGULAR
first person	I will walk.	I will be here.
second person	You will walk.	You will be here.
third person	He, she, or it will walk.	He, she, or it will be here.
first-person plural	We will walk.	We will be here.
third-person plural	They will walk.	They will be here.

We represent the future tense in English through the auxiliary verb *will*. For both regular and irregular verbs, one simply adds the auxiliary plus the bare infinitive form of the verb. For example, the sentences above look like this: *will + (to) walk* or *will + (to) be*.

Participles are formed in two ways: by adding *-ing* or *-ed*. The *-ing* form describes the progressive tense (to be described next), and the *-ed* form makes the past tense.

I am work**ing**.   I have work**ed** here before.

There are irregular forms of past tense participles, too. Consider **wear:**

I have worn that suit several times before.

Both present and past participles can function as adjectives (see Table 3.25).

TABLE 3.25

What a **tiring** job it is to write. (Tiring describes the job.)	The **worn** dress looks horrible on her. (Worn describes the dress.)
This job is **tiring.** (Tiring is a predicate adjective.)	That dress is **worn.** (Worn is a predicate adjective).

The final type of participle is the perfect participle. Its form is easy to recognize, because it uses *having* and the past participle form of a verb:

- Having typed for four hours, my fingers hurt.
- Having worn these shoes for two days, my feet hurt.

We will have even more to say about participles when we discuss phrases toward the end of this section on syntax.

Progressive tenses describe actions that began in the past and are either (a) happening now, (b) finished completely, or (c) starting at some point in the future as shown in Table 3.26.

TABLE 3.26

PRESENT PROGRESSIVE	PAST PROGRESSIVE	FUTURE PROGRESSIVE
I am walking.	I was walking.	I will be walking.

The difference between the simple and progressive tenses are subtle but important. To say, *I walk,* means that you are capable of walking or that is one of your means of transportation. *I am walking,* on the other hand, means that you are now, at this moment, walking.

Perfect tenses describe actions that were completed in the past and may or may not happen again (see Table 3.27).

TABLE 3.27

PRESENT PERFECT	PAST PERFECT	FUTURE PERFECT
I have walked here before. (and I'm doing it now)	I had walked there before. (but not now/any more)	I will have walked for four hours when I get there.

The perfect tenses, particularly present and past perfect, vary in speech. You will hear many speakers use them interchangeable, saying *I have walked here before* and *I had walked there before* with no distinction in meaning.

The **perfect progressives** are the most complicated of all and describe the past, present, and future as shown in Table 3.28.

TABLE 3.28

PRESENT PERFECT PROGRESSIVE	PAST PERFECT PROGRESSIVE	FUTURE PERFECT PROGRESSIVE
I have been walking now for four hours.	I had been walking there before. (but not now/any more)	I will have been walking for four hours when I get there.

ADJECTIVES AND ADVERBS.   Let's now look at the next parts of speech, adjectives and adverbs, that further qualify and clarify the parts of speech we have just learned about.

Adjectives modify or qualify both nouns and pronouns.

Adjectives perform the function of modifying nouns and pronouns. **Modify** simply means describing nouns in the following terms:

- Color: *The **blue** car is here.*
- Condition: *The **dirty** blue car is here.*
- Number: ***Three** dirty blue cars are here.*
- Comparative: *That car is **dirtier** than that one.*
- Superlative: That is the **dirtiest** car I have ever seen.

Note the final two examples, comparative and superlative. Comparative adjectives are formed by adding the inflectional ending -*er* to the end of the adjective, and superlatives are formed by adding -*est*. There is an exception to this rule: If the word has more than two syllables, then the adverbs (to be discussed next) **more** and **most** are used instead of the inflectional affixes -*er* and -*ing* as shown in Table 3.29. NOTE: The incorrect statements are notated by an *.

TABLE 3.29

COMPARATIVE WITH MORE

*The first test was challenginger than the second one.
The first test was more challenging than the second one.

SUPERLATIVE WITH MOST

*It was the terrificest play I've seen.
The was the most terrific play I've seen.

When adjectives follow being verbs, they are called **predicate nominatives:**

- He looks **sick.**
- He seems **tired.**
- She is **joyful.**
- She is **nice.**

Determiners are another type of adjective. **A, the,** and **that** are the most common types of determiners. They tell us whether a noun is specific or nonspecific:

- A car hit a man. (nonspecific)
- The car hit the man. (more specific)
- That car hit that man. (very specific)

Some determiners must agree with the nouns they modify. Your choice of using **a** and **an,** for example, depends on whether the noun that follows it has a vowel sound at the beginning or not.

- a car, a bike, a rock
- an apple, an orange, an omelet

In short, adjectives modify nouns and pronouns; adverbs, the subject of our next discussion, modify everything else.

> **Adverbs** define, qualify, or limit verbs, adjectives,
> other adverbs, phrases, clauses, or whole sentences.

As you can see from the definition, adverbs do a lot of modifying. Here they are in action:

- Verb: I wrote *quickly.*
- Adjective: I have a *very* small dog.
- Adverbs: I see *very* well.
- Phrases: The book is *right by the door.*
- Clauses: *Since* you didn't complete the work, I cannot pay you.
- Sentences: I like pizza; *however,* the doctor said I can't have it.

Here are the functions they perform in various sentences.

- Location (here, there): The cat runs **here** and **there.**
- Manner (sloppily, neatly): I painted the house **neatly,** but mowed the lawn **sloppily.**
- Degree (very, hardly): I am **very** happy, though I am **hardly** surprised.
- Time (now, later): I want the project finished **now** rather than **later.**
- Negation (not): I'm **not** going there, and I'm **not** coming here.

PREPOSITIONS.

> **Prepositions** show relationship between a noun
> and its object to other words in a sentence.

Propositions tell us where things are (*at, above, near, far*). Prepositional phrases tell us when things will happen (*in the morning, at noon*), and describe nouns in greater detail (in the red car, in the green shirt). Here are ten common prepositions: in, on, near, far, before, after, for, to, with, without. *NOTE: In* describes both where and when.

Prepositions require a noun to have meaning. The noun is called the **object of the preposition,** as in:

- In **the car.**
- On **the floor.**
- Near **my house.**

Together, the preposition and its noun are called a **prepositional phrase. Prepositional phrases** can perform the functions of **adverbs** and **adjectives** depending on what they are describing or qualifying.

- **Adverbial Prepositional Phrases:** Turn **to the left.** (indicates in which direction one must turn)
- **Adjectival Prepositional Phrases:** The man **in the blue shirt** is holding a gun. (specifies which man among others is holding a gun)

The easiest way to distinguish between both types of prepositional phrases is to decide whether the prepositional phrase is modifying or qualifying a noun or a verb. If it modifies a noun, then it is adjectival; however, if it modifies a verb, then it is adverbial.

The preposition **to** is a special case. In English, **to** can be a preposition or it can act as an **infinitive marker.** Here is how to tell the difference:

A. I went to the store.
B. I like to dance.

In sentence A, **to** is a preposition. You know this is true, because of the noun phrase **the store** (that is the object of the preposition). In sentence B, on the other hand, **to** is an infinitive marker, since *like* takes infinitive phrases and because *to* is attached to a verb (dance).

CONJUNCTIONS.   **Conjunctions** link words, phrases, or clauses together. Conjunctions may connect individual words as well as phrases and clauses. Table 3.30 shows the three types of conjunctions that you should know for the test.

TABLE 3.30   Common Conjunctions

COORDINATING	CORRELATING	SUBORDINATING
and, but, nor, for, or	either/or both/and neither/nor	when since because

Coordinating conjunctions balance words, phrases, or clauses together:

- Words: *Chris* **and** *Mike* are here.
- Phrases: Chris and Mike ran *in the park* **and** *in the field.*
- Clauses: *Chris and Mike ran in the park,* **and** *they swam in the lake.*

Each of the sentences above uses a conjunction to join words, phrases, and clauses together. Your selection of the correct conjunctions depends on what you're trying to express:

- Balance: Chris and Mike.
- Choice: Chris or Mike.
- Exclusion: Not Chris but Mike.

Correlating conjunctions show positive or negative relationships between words, phrases, or clauses.

- Words: Either Chris or Mike will do the work.
  Neither Chris nor Mike will do the work.
- Phrases: Neither working at the store nor saving all my coupons helps.

Correlating conjunctions require **parallelism. Parallelism** simply means that whatever words or phrases or clauses that the conjunctions are correlating must be in the same form.

- Not Parallel: Swimming and to run are my favorite activities. (incorrect)
- Parallel: Swimming and running are my favorite activities. (correct)

Subordinate Conjunctions, like **when, since,** and **because,** show orders and contingencies, where one thing or idea depends upon some other, superior idea. **Subordinate conjunc-**

tions are easy to identify: Although they look like independent sentences, they make no sense if they are by themselves. In the list below, the subordinate clauses are in bold; the independent clauses (the ones that can stand alone) are italicized.

- **When I get home,** *I will eat.*
- **Since you didn't come to work,** *you going to be fired.*
- **Because you didn't come to work,** *you're fired.*

In summary, conjunctions exist to link words, phrases, and clauses together in a coherent way.

INTERJECTIONS. Let's turn now to the shortest part of speech that we have: the interjection.

Interjections show emotion (surprise, awe, disappointment, excitement, etc.).

Interjections capture emotion—*any* emotion. They are short and use a comma if the expression is matter-of-fact or an exclamation point if the expression is emphatic.

- Pain: **Ouch!**
- Joy: **Yea!**
- Interruption: **Oh,** pardon me.

Phrases. To this point, you have reviewed the eight parts of speech: nouns, pronouns, verbs, adjective, adverbs, prepositions, conjunctions, and interjections. You will now learn about how these words become organized into **phrases, clauses,** and, finally, **whole sentences.**

Phrases are groups of words that do not stand as sentences by themselves. We can describe phrases in terms of their simplicity or complexity.

SIMPLE PHRASES. **Simple phrases** are called noun phrases, verb phrases, and prepositional phrases (see Table 3.31).

TABLE 3.31 Simple Phrases

NOUN PHRASES	PREPOSITIONAL PHRASE	VERB PHRASES
The man in *the blue hat…*	The man *in the blue hat…*	I *ran very, very, very quickly to the store.*

The there are two **noun phrases** in Table 3.31. The first noun phrase is *the man* and the second one is found in the prepositional phrase *in the blue hat.* In brief, noun phrases contain the **central noun** (*hat*) and all of the articles (*the*) and adjectives (*blue*) used to describe it. Now, look at the prepositional phrase again. The phrase, *in the blue hat,* is **adjectival** because it describes the noun *the man.* **Verb phrases,** like **noun phrases,** contain the **verb** and all of the **adverbs** and **prepositional phrases** used to describe it. The **verb phrase** *ran very, very, quickly* describes not only what action took place (*ran*) but also how the action was carried out (*very, very quickly*) and in which direction (*to the store*). Direction is conveyed through an adverbial prepositional phrase, because it describes the action further.

A note on noun phrases: Noun phrases perform many, many functions as shown in Table 3.32. We have already seen how they can be objects of prepositions (**in** *the blue hat* and **to** *the store*), but there are a few more ways that they can exist in sentences:

TABLE 3.32   Noun Phrases and Functions

Subjects	The man who is standing right here wrote the book.	The entire noun phrase, including the words that describe where the man is standing, is the subject.
Predicate Nominative	Bob is *the man who is standing right here.*	The noun phrase in italics is a predicate nominative that functions as a descriptor that further qualifies the subject, *Bob.*
Direct Objects	I brought *a really delicious pumpkin pie.*	The noun phrase is part of the predicate and is a direct object that tells us what I brought.
Indirect Objects	I brought a really delicious pumpkin pie to *my sick friend.*	The noun phrase, *my sick friend,* is the object of the preposition *(to).* The prepositional phrase functions as an indirect object telling us to whom I brought the pumpkin pie.

COMPLEX PHRASES.   The other variety of phrases are more complex and perform a variety of functions as shown in Table 3.33.

TABLE 3.33   Complex Phrases

PARTICIPIAL PHRASE	GERUND PHRASE	INFINITIVE PHRASE	APPOSITIVE PHRASE
The man **wearing the blue suit**...	**Running in the morning with my wife**...	**To run in the morning**...	The teacher, **Mr. Johnson,** is here.

Participles are the progressive and past tense forms of verbs. As you learned earlier, they are formed using the inflectional affix *-ing* (if it is progressive) and *-ed* if it is past tense (unless it is an irregular verb). We discussed how participles function as an adjective (*the* **driving** *rain*) or as a predicate nominative (*The day was* **tiring**). Participles can also function as whole phrases that function as adjectives to further describe nouns.

- The man **wearing the blue suit** is mysterious. (The present participle further describes the man.)
- **Agitated by her co-worker's lack of work,** she considered alternatives. (The participial phrase in above further describe Chris's state of mind.)

One additional example of a participial phrase is the perfect form. You can usually spot them because they begin with *having:*

Having thought about your plan, I have decided against it.

This perfect participial phrase further describes the subject's state of mind.

Gerunds are the *-ing* forms of nouns. They function as subjects and convey a sense of action at the same time. The sentence ***Running*** *is my favorite activity* shows how gerunds can function as subjects. You may be asked to tell the difference between a gerund phrase and a participial phrase. To do so, ask yourself if the *-ing* form of the verb functions as a noun or as an adjective. If it is a noun, then it is a gerund; if it is an adjective, then it is a participle:

- *Running in the morning with my wife and small dog* is the best part of my day. (The gerund phrase acts as a complete subject of the sentence.)
- *Running out of control,* the robot became dangerous. (The participial phrase describes the robot more adjectivally.)

Infinitive phrases are marked with *to + verb,* as in *To run in the morning* is fun. Infinitive phrases act as parts of speech (nouns, adjectives, and adverbs) as sentence subjects, objects, predicate nominatives, and adverbial/adjectival modifies. They come in two varieties: present and perfect. Here they are in action:

The following list shows examples of present infinitives:

- *To run in the morning* is fun. (subject)
- I like *to run in the morning.* (direct object)
- My goal is *to create life in this jar. (*predicate nominative—it follows a being verb)
- The worst way *to do* things is the hard way. (adjective describing *things*)
- I was happy *to see* you. (adverb qualifying the adjective *happy*)

Perfect infinitives are more nebulous; they describe things that took place before the action in the sentence:

(A) I appear *to need a different brain for this task.*
(B) I am sorry *to have forgotten my pants.*

If you are asked to identify perfect infinitives, just ask yourself if the infinitive phrase describes an action happening prior to whatever is being described in the sentence. For example, *sentence* A describes the need for a past condition to complete a present task; *sentence* B describes a past act of forgetting that now affects a present situation.

Appositive phrases are easy to identify, because they are offset with commas and function as adjectives to further describe nouns:

- The teacher, *Mr. Dobbs,* is here.
- The car, *a brand new Toyota Solara,* is what I want for my birthday.

Sentence Clauses.   Sentence clauses are much larger than phrases. They have a subject and verb and can be mistaken for sentences sometimes because of these features. Clauses can either stand independently or be dependent upon other clauses in the sentence. Another type of clause, the relative clause, is termed restricted or nonrestricted depending on whether the information it adds to the sentences is essential or nonessential to the meaning of the sentence. Let's now look at each type of clause.

INDEPENDENT CLAUSES.   This is part of a sentence that can stand all by itself and has a subject, verb, and maybe an object or predicate nominative. You can identify an independent clause because it makes sense all by itself. You will see an example of and independent clause when we discuss dependent clauses.

DEPENDENT CLAUSES.   This part of a sentence cannot stand all by itself, even though it has a subject, verb, and maybe an object or predicate nominative. You can identify a dependent clause because it does not make sense all by itself; instead, it must be clarified through another, independent class. They are introduced by a subordinating conjunction, like: *because, when, if, since, when,* and *so.*

Below is an example of an independent and dependent clause. Note that their order is arbitrary. The dependent clause is shown in **bold.**

- I could not work today, **because I was sick.**
- **Because I was sick,** I could not work today.

In each of the examples above, the dependent clause cannot stand by itself. It makes no sense to say: *Because I was sick (period).* This results in a sentence fragment. You may be asked to identify problems in writing, and this is certainly one of them. Just read the data and look for any incomplete-sounding ideas. When you find them, they will probably be due to a lonely dependent clause that lacks an independent clause for meaning.

RELATIVE CLAUSES.   These clauses provide more information about nouns and use *that, which, who, and whom.* Like dependent clauses, relative clauses cannot stand alone. The relative clauses are shown in **bold.**

- The man **that I know from school** is here.
- The man **who I know from school** is here.

Note that the difference between a subordinate clause and a relative clause is the word used to introduce it (subordinating conjunctions introduce dependent clauses, and words like *that* and *who* introduce relative clauses).

You may also be asked about restricted and nonrestricted relative clauses. If the clause is restricted, you offset the clause with commas; if it is nonrestricted, you do not use commas. Restricted simply means that the information is essential to one's understanding of the sentence.

- Restricted Clauses: The girl who came in first won the race.
- Nonrestricted Clauses: The boy, who is next to Bob, won the race.

The relative clause, *who came in first,* is essential information in the restricted clause example above. No commas are used to offset the information because it is essential to the meaning of the sentence. The relative clause, *who is next to Bob,* in the non-restricted example is offset with commas because it is incidental information. In both cases, the relative clauses simply add more information about the nouns to which they are attached, yet their degree of purpose affects whether they are treated as being restricting or nonrestricting in their function.

Sentence Types.   You may also be asked to identify four different types of sentences on the exam: simple sentences, compound sentences, complex sentences, and compound–complex sentences. Table 3.34 below captures each of these types of sentences. NOTE:

TABLE 3.34 Sentence Types

SENTENCE TYPE	EXAMPLE
Simple Sentences: One Subject + One Predicate.	Simple sentences are straightforward.
Compound Sentences: Two Main Clauses.	One sentence contains a subject and verb, and the second sentence contains another subject and verb.
Complex Sentences: Subordinate Clause + Main Claus.	If the sentence has a main clause and a subordinate clause, it is complex.
Compound–Complex Sentences: Two or More Main Clauses and a Subordinate Clause.	If the sentence has two main clauses and a subordinate clause, it is compound and it is complex.

Subjects and main clauses are underlined once; predicates and subordinate clauses are underlined twice.

Please keep in mind that some sentences have only compound subjects or predicates in them, which does **not** make them compound sentences.

- **Chris and Mike** are here. (compound subject)
- Chris and Mike **ran and jumped.** (compound predicate)

KERNEL SENTENCES.   The final area of syntax to know is the kernel sentence. There are five major categories of kernel sentences to know for the exam. They include declaratives, interrogatives, exclamatories, conditionals, and imperatives. Examples of each are shown in Table 3.35.

TABLE 3.35   Kernal Sentences

Declarative	Today is a very nice day.
Interrogative	Where are you going? Do you need a ride?
Exclamatory	You're late again!
Conditional	If you don't work hard, you won't finish.
Imperative	(You) Shut up.

Each of the examples should be obvious to you. **Declarative** sentences make simple statements of fact, and **interrogatives** pose questions using a wh- or do form. **Exclamatory** sentences make emphatic observations or statements and use an exclamation point. **Conditionals** pose contingencies that will either be satisfied or not satisfied. Finally, **imperatives** make commands and use the understood *you* for the subject.

Semantics.   Having been given a tour of English syntax, you now need to learn about the next major area of linguistics: the study of how we make meaning in English.

Language is arbitrary. Why do we call a frog a frog and a rose a rose? There is no reason beyond our mutual agreement that *that is what we are going to call those things.* Semantics is the study of these assigned labels that we attach to everything in the English language and how we assign meaning to things (Kemporson, 1977). The areas of semantics to know for the exam include denotation, connotation, structural meanings, etymology, and the effect of context.

Denotative Meanings.   *Denotative* meanings of words are their dictionary definitions. Consider the denotative meaning of the word *cool*. The literal meaning of this word that one might encounter in any dictionary is "below room or body temperature."

Connotative Meanings.   The *connotative* meanings associated with *cool* are beyond this narrow definition:

- He is very cool.(Hip)
- She is cool to the idea.(Feels negative)
- The officer cooled the thief.(Knocked unconscious)

Connotative meanings are all of the other assigned meanings to the word that move beyond the literal definition of the word. Many words in English acquire these other meanings through use.

Structural Meanings.   Meaning is built into many words through their internal structures. You learned about this earlier when we discussed morphology and how derivational affixes and root words contribute to a word's meaning. Certain derivational prefixes can drastically change the meaning of a word. Recall the base word *nationalization*. Its meaning will change depending on the prefix we assign to it:

- Denationalization
- Internationalization

The addition of *de-* and *inter-* to *nationalization* radically alters the meaning of this base word. Prefixes do not have to alter the meaning so drastically though. Some prefixes offer very subtle changes to a word's meaning:

- It was so dark that his features were *undistinguishable.*
- Janet is *indistinguishable* from her twin Christine.

The prefixes *un-* and *in-* provide very subtle distinctions for how we use *distinguish* in certain sentences. Please note that this discussion does not mean that we can attach prefixes and suffices to words any way that we want, because some constructions are quite *unpossible,* like:

- inspectabulatious
- preremarkablinglouser

Structural analysis is used to teach children vocabulary using prefixes, suffixes, roots, and base words. Table 3.36 shows an example the process of structural word analysis applied to the word *antidisestablishmentarianism:*

TABLE 3.36   Semantics and Structural Analysis

PREFIX	PREFIX	BASE WORD	SUFFIX	SUFFIX	SUFFIX
anti-	*dis-*	*establish*	*ment*	*-arian*	*-ism*
opposed to	the removal of	the state		believers of	a philosophical position

Word Types.   You may also be asked about four different kinds of words, including homophones, homographs, synonyms, and antonyms. Following are selected examples of each type of word:

- Homophones: site, cite, sight.
- Homographs: subjéct and súbject.
- Synonyms: happy, joyful, merry.
- Antonyms: happy versus sad; calm versus stressed

Homophones are words that sound the same but their spellings indicate the differences in their meanings and how they are used in sentences. Homographs are words that are *orthographically* (e.g., written) the same way but are pronounced differently. The examples reflect two sets of words whose meanings change, depending on whether the medial vowel is long or short (*lead* v. *lead*) or whether the stress is placed on the first syllable or the second (*subjéct* and *súbject*). Synonyms and antonyms are words that are related to one another either by meaning roughly the same thing or by having meanings that are in opposition to one another.

Many synonyms, like *sloppy, messy, dirty, disorganized, disarrayed,* and *disheveled,* can be analyzed for their fine shades of meaning. Table 3.27 below shows an analysis of semantic features, a common classroom activity for vocabulary (Peregoy and Boyle, 1993).

TABLE 3.37   Semantic Features Analysis

	DISORGANIZED	DISARRAYED	DISHEVELED
Characterizes a person's behavior.	X		
Characterizes a person's appearance.			X
Characterizes the order of objects. Describes the condition of a location.	X	X	

Contextual Meaning.   Context plays a role in which words we select for reading, and this is especially true of homographs (Carr, Dewitz, & Patberg, 1989). Consider the following:

- He **leads** a group of scouts through the forest.
- He needs a number two **lead** pencil for the test.

Context determines whether you read *lead* with a long or short vowel. When *lead* is a verb, the vowel sound is long; when it is a noun or adjective, it is short. The same is true for homographs that involve stress shift:

- Give me a **minute** while I think of the answer.
- I looked at a very **minute** sample under the microscope.

Context determines whether the stress is on the first or second syllable: on the first syllable, *minute* means "a moment in time"; on the second syllable, it means "very small."

In multiple-meaning words, context also tells you how to interpret the word either denotatively or connotatively:

- He hammered the nail into the board.
- He got really hammered last night.

Clearly, the meanings of the word *hammer* in each sentence above are different, and that difference is determined by sentence context.

Pragmatics.   Pragmatics is the study of language use in social situations (Levinson, 1983). Linguistics look at use at the micro and macro levels. At the micro level, one looks at speech acts, styles, and registers. At the macro level, linguists analyze discourse (conversation) within social contexts (language used in the classroom, at the bank, etc.). The registration bulletins for all of the exams list only a few descriptors for this area of linguistics, so we will only present the major areas for you.

Speech Acts.   Speech acts include requests, commands, statements, and any other functional kind of utterance that you can think of. Linguists discuss all utterances in three ways: illocution, locution, and percolation. Illocution is the kind of speech at that the utterance happens to be (a command, warning, refusal, apology). Locution refers to the surface meaning of the utterance. Percolation is the underlying effect of the utterance. Here are these levels applied to an example utterance:

If you don't stop following me, I'll call the police.

- Illocution: Warning.
- Locution: Leave me alone.
- Percolation: There will be trouble if my condition isn't met.

Style.   Speech acts get much of their illocutionary, locutionary, and percolationary effect from the phonology, morphology, and semantics we select when speaking. This is because we vary our styles when we communicate, particularly in the level of informality or formality (Cohen, 1996). Consider these examples at face value:

Gimme the pencil!	*Would you please lend me a pencil?*
- Illocution: Command.	- Illocution: Request.
- Locution: I need a pencil.	- Locution: I need a pencil.
- Percolation: Hurry up!	- Percolation: Formal, polite request.

Although both of these utterances have the same locution (*I need a pencil*), they accomplish the goal of satisfying the locution differently. *Gimme a pencil!* is a command with the effect of hurrying the holder-of-the-pencil. It is also **informal,** because the phonology and syntax are reduced ("give me" becomes "gimme"), and it is said as an imperative (exclamatory) sentence. Conversely, the second sentence, *Would you please lend me a pencil?*, is a **formal** request. The phonology is not reduced and grammatically correct forms are used (*Would you* and *lend*). The entire request is modified by *please,* marking it as a polite request.

Registers.   Informal and formal styles are part of registers (Joos, 1967). Registers are appropriate speech styles that we use in different social situations and vary depending on formality. We vary our phonology, morphology, syntax, and semantics depending on with whom we are speaking and in what situation. There are four registers to consider:

- Intimate: Couples' speech. (*baby cakes, lover, sweetie pie*)
- Casual: Speaking among friends and family. (*Gimme the pencil.*)

- Formal: Speaking among unfamiliar co-workers, employers, etc. (*Would you please…*)
- Frozen: Languages used on signs and in ceremonies. (*Dearly beloved…*)

These registers affect the choices we make when speaking. For example, the way that we speak to an intimate partner is probably different from the way that we might address a principal or school administrator. Look at the utterances in Table 3.38 and consider how the utterances vary linguistically:

TABLE 3.38   Common Register Variations

	PHONOLOGY	MORPHOLOGY	SYNTAX	SEMANTICS
Casual	I like runnin'.	It ain't unpossible.	She goin' home.	He fly an' phat.
Formal	I like to run.	It is impossible.	She went home.	He is quite acculturated and rather attractive.

The casual and formal registers affect all of the elements of linguistics. Casual speech permits phonological reductions (*to run* becomes *runnin'*), questionable morphology (*impossible* becomes *unpossible*), grammatical reductions (*she went* becomes *she goin'*), and casual semantic lingo (using *fly* and *phat*). These casual speech characteristics are not found (usually) in formal speech styles.

Social Contexts.   Speech acts, registers, and styles all vary according to **genre.** Genres are social situations that require particular speech acts, registers, and styles (Halliday, 1978). Table 3.39 shows common genres and offers some comparisons of the register and vocabulary found therein.

TABLE 3.39   Common Genres

GENRE	AT A SHOWER	AT A FUNERAL	AT BURGERWORLD	AT THE INTERVIEW
Register	*Casual*	*Formal*	*Casual*	*Formal*
VOCABULARY	all things baby (first steps, remembrances)	dearly departed; this great man/woman/cat	burger, fries, coke	experience, abilities, salary
SPEECH ACTS	declarations and expressions	declarations and expressions	requests and refusals	requests and explanations

Each genre uses different styles, registers, and speech acts, not to mention vocabulary. If we are native speakers of English, then we probably have expectations for each of these areas. Our knowledge of the appropriate use of language in a variety of social genres is called *communicative competence.* As defined by Hymes (1972), communicative competence is something that we acquire through experience (e.g., the language of the home, workplace, school, etc.). Using the wrong register, style, or speech act during a formal job interview (calling the interviewer *sweetie*) can reveal one's communicative *incompetence.* Communicative competence and knowledge of social genres will be more of an issue when you learn about the needs of English language learners in content area two.

Sociolinguistics.   Sociolinguistics is the study of register and genre variation within a culture and between cultures (Fasold, 1984; 1990). Intraculturally speaking, consider the language that brain surgeons use when betting on a putt at the local golf course versus the language that they use when separating conjoined twins in the operating room. Clearly, the registers will vary sociolinguistically, given the linguistic demands that these activities present: The registers, styles, and speech acts will be very different indeed.

In the *inter*cultural sense, we can look at sociolinguistic differences across cultures (Barnlund, 1989). Doing business in Japan versus the United States is an oft-cited example of the differences in styles between two cultures, especially in the way that refusals are conveyed. In the United States, the phrase, *We'll think about it,* might actually mean just that: *We will consider the offer and get back to you on it.* For the Japanese, this phrase usually is a flat and firm refusal. Cross-cultural communications are very important, given the different ways that speech acts can be carried out across cultures.

Face is another sociolinguistic consideration. Some cultures value harmony to a great degree, such that ensuring that members do not lose face (e.g., become publicly shamed) is highly valued. In *Top of the World* (Ruesch, 1991), a novel about Inuit Alaskans, a common confrontation might sound something like this: "*Someone* had better stop talking or *someone else* is going to hurt them." For the tribe described in the novel, using the third person when confronting another person allows for a high degree of face-saving, since threats are spoken indirectly.

For the test, you will need to be aware of several other aspects of sociolinguistics, including linguistic relativity, idiolects, isoglosses, sociolects, and dialects. These areas will probably constitute only one or two questions on the exam, but that might mean the difference between passing and failing the test. Therefore, you will learn about only the most important aspects of this area.

Linguistic Relativity.   *Linguistic relativity* asks the question, *Does one's language limit or broaden their experience of life?* The Whorf (1956) hypothesis would answer the question in the affirmative. Certain Inuit tribes in Alaska and Canada have several hundred words for snow. There is snow that is good for hunting, snow that is good for building, and snow that can kill you. I grew up in a part of Minnesota where there is just as much snow as in Alaska, but I can only come up with about five words for snow (besides snow): sleet, slush, powder, fluff, and *sparkly.* Whorf would argue that my experience with a snowy world is limited and that the Inuits have a much broader and therefore "better" appreciation of their word because of their extensive linguistic repertoire.

This example seems innocuous, but it isn't. Bernstein (1964) had a similar idea about linguistic relativity. He looked at elaborated and restricted codes among the social classes in England. Elaborated codes are the varieties of English spoken among the educated upper class members, and the restricted codes are the varieties of English spoken by the lower class members. He reasoned that speakers of the restricted code must have restricted thoughts, given their restricted and limited language, whereas speakers of the elaborated code have much broader and deeper thoughts due to their higher variety of language.

The counterargument to Whorf (1956) and Bernstein (1964) is descriptive linguistics (rather than relative linguistics). Here, any language variety can express any thought that the human mind can conjure up. Although one's vocabulary may be limited, it can grow and expand through experience and understanding. Therefore, all language varieties are equal; only our perceptions of language varieties vary (sometimes unfairly).

These considerations bring us to other sociolinguistic considerations about the language of individual speakers (idiolects), social groups (sociolects), and regional varieties of English (isoglosses and dialects). Let's now look at each of these areas.

Idiolects.   *Idiolects* characterize the language that we, as individual speakers, use when speaking. All of us have our own verbal tics (saying "uh-huh" or repeating phrases) and our own way of expressing ourselves. For example, I had a friend who said, "on the thing" all the time as filler speech. "On that thing, I'm going to get on that thing just as soon as I'm done getting on this thing." That phrase belonged to him, and I've never heard anyone else use it in quite the same way. It is also an example of an idiolect.

Sociolects.   *Sociolects* characterize the language used by subcultures, ethnic enclaves, social classes, and speech communities. Teens use language in interesting ways that can be described as a sociolect. Peer groups exert a great influence on many children's speech patterns, and "teen talk" has its own terminology that separates it from the adult world. The most recent additions include *phat, bling-bling,* and *shnizle. Can* is also becoming an adjective, as in *That's so can!* Teen sociolects can be further reduced into different social groups. The language that athletes use may not be the same as what one hears in other social groups. Consider the following terms:

- Spange (spare change), squat (temporary home) used by homeless teens.
- Sketchy (unstable), coping (skate park accessory) used by the "skater" crowd.
- Freds/Wilmas and Barneys/Bettys (unattractive and attractive people) used by the "popular" kids.

Note too that sociolects are highly volatile and that phrases can be "in" one day and "out" another. "Valley Talk" that was popular in the 1980s is seldom heard nowadays, unless one is speaking "nostalgically." Phrases like *Gag me with spoon* seem to have gone the way of *far out, wowie zowie,* and *twenty-three skidoo* before it. "Teen talk" has an ever-changing quality about it that seems to change the moment that "too many outsiders" catch on to it.

Sociolects vary greatly and mark individuals based on the language that they use. Ethnic enclaves can develop their own sociolects, too. Studies of African American communities note that the auxiliary *be* has acquired a new tense for some speakers of this sociolect (Goldstein, 1987). *I be scared sometimes* is used systematically to express temporality, and the feature is particular to speakers of this variety of English (not necessarily African Americans).

Social classes also speak sociolects. The most famous study of this phenomenon was done by Labov (1972). He looked at the way that different social classes use English in social settings and the attendant class effect. Informal speech involves phonological reductions (as you now know). Sometimes, when we say *running* casually, we say *runnin'.* That reduction happens because casual speech is usually rapid speech, and we must reduce the language to speak quickly. Labov looked at another reduction: dropping the sound *r* at the ends of syllables in the way that a phrase like *fourth floor* would be spoken as *foath floah* (a common reduction in New York English). He found that upper class speakers would say *foath floah* in casual speech but not in formal speech; *however,* members of the lower class would say *foath floah* **both** in casual speech and in formal speech. This indicated that the most formal speech of the lower classes is the casual speech of the upper classes. Although one variety might not be better than the other, some people may look upon us with derision based solely upon the sociolect that we speak.

Jargon is another variable of one's sociolect. The terminology that medical professionals use is different from what auto repair technicians use (see Table 3.40):

TABLE 3.40   Jargon

MEDICAL PROFESSIONALS	AUTO MECHANICS
■ Scalpel	■ Cross point
■ Stethoscope	■ Allen key
■ Sphygmomanometer	■ Impact wrench

Workplace terminology is important, because it reveals who is an insider and who is an outsider. For example, hearing your doctor say, "Hand me the pointy thing," during your next operation might not inspire much hope for your survival. Language and our perception of another person's competence seem to go hand in hand.

Isoglosses and Dialects.   *Isoglosses* and *dialects* reflect sociolect. An isogloss is a variation of English that differs between cities or closely connected areas (state borders); dialects are regional variations, like the difference between Midwestern and Eastern English and Northern and Southern English. There are identifiable differences in phonology, morphology, syntax, and semantics.

In Minnesota, there is an isogloss that exists in the phonology of natives of Minneapolis and the natives of St. Paul. It can be heard in the short vowels of certain words (see Table 3.41).

TABLE 3.41   Isogloss

MINNEAPOLIS		ST. PAUL
■ Irish	/irish/	■ /ireesh/
■ plaza	/plaza/	■ /PLA-za/

These differences really do have an impact on perception, and the isogloss marks one as being from one city or the other. What accounts for the differences is a lack of contact among members of each city, because each group is separated by a river. Because travel and movement is quite common, this phonological difference may disappear one day.

Isoglosses can also mark a person as being from one state or another. This is true for certain words that are particular to Minnesota but may not be heard in the adjoining state of Wisconsin. The variation is not so much phonological but semantic, as the words for certain nouns are different (see Table 3.42).

Again, these differences do mark one as having been reared in one state or the other. The differences can be quite humorous, too: Imagine someone calling a tuna casserole a "tuna casserole" as opposed to its proper name—*hot dish.* How absurd.

TABLE 3.42

NOUN	MINNESOTA	WISCONSIN
water fountain	drinking fountain	bubbler
soft drink	pop	soda
tuna casserole	hot dish	tuna casserole
rubber band	rubber binder	rubber band

Dialect differences are much broader than isoglosses. They often involve differences in syntax and semantics, but the differences are most apparent in phonology. Consider the examples in Table 3.43 of Midwestern, Southern, and Eastern word pronunciations:

TABLE 3.43

	MIDWEST	SOUTH	EAST
car	car	cawer	cah
bar	bar	bawer	bah

Southern speech tends to lengthen vowels. The phrase *My dog died* might sound like *Mah dawg diahed* because of this phenomenon. Similarly, some speakers in the eastern states tend to drop the /r/ from spoken words, giving their speech patterns a very distinctive and identifiable sound quality.

Dialect differences can also appear in syntax and semantics. Some Southern English speakers use "might" as a "double auxiliary":

- I might could come tomorrow.
- I might could do it.

In the Midwest, one hears *you guys* in casual speech quite frequently, and in Texas *y'all* (perhaps singular) and *all y'all* (perhaps plural) is the common casual form. These differences also mark one as being from one part of the United States or another.

Summary of Sociolinguistics. To summarize this discussion of idiolects, sociolects, isoglosses, and dialects—all of these elements mark one as being from one area, state, or region of the country. These elements can flatten out and nearly disappear from an individual's or groups' speech through language contact. Through transit, migration, and mass media, languages can shift and change and become more homogenous as one has contact with different language groups. "Teen talk" often changes when one enters the workplace and must adapt and conform to different expectations. Language is fluid and changing. Very briefly, there is change *toward* or *away from* a variety of English (accommodation theory), generation change, and historic change.

ACCOMMODATION TOWARD. Language variations can decrease and even homogenize through contact or through conscious effort. When a speaker wants to be part of a group, he or she can learn to alter his or her language to be part of a group. Members of the working class, for example, often experience their language changing when moving from their home to college; upon returning home, their families and friends may even comment on how different they "sound." This phenomenon may be the result of the speakers' conscious or unconscious attempt to sound like their new speech community.

ACCOMMODATION AWAY.   Adolescents often exemplify accommodation away from one social group in favor of another. For example, they may develop their own "language" with its own accepted style, jargon, and meaning. In the first place, this linguistic change marks a change in their identify from their family. Second, it then associates them with a particular peer group, since different peer groups may adopt different styles, jargons, and so forth. Thus, accommodation away from one group helps one to assimilate into another group, and this is accomplished linguistically.

GENERATION CHANGE.   In immigrant communities, there are often generational changes that result in a phenomenon called *hypercorrection*. When immigrants arrive to the United States, they bring their native phonologies with them. When they learn English, they often have an accent because their first language lacks features found in English. In sections of New Jersey, many immigrant groups lacked the sound /er/ in their first language, resulting in their pronouncing *girl* as /goil/. Their children, who learned English as a first language, noticed something was wrong with this pronunciation and dropped /goil/ from their vocabulary using the common form /gerl/ instead. But the second generation did something very interesting: they *hypercorrect* their parents' misuse of the /oi/ sound. This resulted in the second generation pronouncing **anything** with /oi/ in it as /er/ (see Table 3.44).

TABLE 3.44

GENERATION ONE		GENERATION TWO	
girl	/goil/	girl	/gerl/
		oil	/erl/
third	/thoid/	toilet	/terlet/

Generation language change does not have to be due to the hypercorrection of an error. Notice how the auxiliary *shall* has all but disappeared from our language. If you listen carefully to the speech of the elderly, you may hear them using *shall* far more frequently than younger people do. In a generation, *shall* just might disappear altogether from English, in the same way that *thou* (the formal you) most certainly has. It seems that the most formal aspects of the language tend to be lost from the language, and the casual speech of yesterday becomes the formal speech of tomorrow.

HISTORICAL CHANGE.   English, as we speak it today, did not begin like this. It has had three major periods: Old, Middle, and Modern. The transition from Old English to Middle English is marked by the Norman Conquest of 1066 (O'Grady, Dobrovolsky, & Aronoff, 1993). During this period, the Great Vowel Shift occurred, where many long vowel sounds became short, and short vowels became long. This shift affected not only the way that words sounded, but also their syntactic forms. The original word for *mouse* and its plural form lend an example.

Before the vowel shift, the singular for mouse was *mussi* and the plural form was *mussen.* After the vowel shift, the singular form became *mouse,* while the plural form went from *mussen* to *mice.* The same thing happened with *goose* and *geese.* Other shifts occurred and affected the way that we spell words today.

TABLE 3.45   **Historical Change**

	OLD ENGLISH	MIDDLE ENGLISH	MODERN ENGLISH
NAME	*/nama/*	*/name/*	*/nAm/*

As shown in Table 3.45, the old English pronunciation of *name* was a two-syllable word, /nama/. After the shift, it was still a two syllable word, but with a different vowel in the second syllable: /name/. In the modern English period, it became the word that we say today: /nAm/ with the long vowel. The problem with this word occurred when we first began writing English. In the late 1500s, Mulcaster and Coote decided to regularize English spelling and published a book on spelling rules. They decided that long vowels in certain words would be marked by adding a *silent e* to the end of words: *Name* and *like* are examples, because they could be spelled in a variety of ways (nayme, naim, etc.) before the *silent e* rule. This rule was applied across many words with odd-sounding vowels, resulting in the exceptions that we have today: *love, have,* and *done.*

Content Area Two: First- and Second-Language Acquisition

With the aforementioned areas of phonology, morphology, syntax, semantics, and pragmatics behind us, you now need to learn about first and second language acquisition.

Since you may be asked questions on first and second language acquisition, you will learn about the major areas of them next in terms of phonology, morphology, syntax, semantics, and pragmatics. There are a few terms that are common to both first and second-language acquisition and others that belong to second language acquisition only. Let's look at the commonalities first.

Terms and Concepts Related to First- and Second-Language Acquisition.

The Critical Period.   One important universal is the notion of the **critical period** for acquiring a first language (Lenneberg, 1967). Some researchers of first- and second-language acquisition hypothesize that children who learn their first languages after (maybe) 3 years of age will miss an important window of opportunity. Animal studies of songbirds suggest this idea: When young birds are kept from learning songs until after a particular age, they are then unable to acquire them. Since we cannot ethically isolate a child from learning his or her language until age 10 to see if the same idea is true, we can only assume that there might be a critical period for learning a first language.

Occasionally, examples from horrible life circumstances do arise. Two famous cases exist (Curtis, 1977). The first is from France, where a child was discovered living in the wilderness who presumably had no interaction with language from the time he was lost until the time he was found. Since he learned French after age 5, the quality of his language acquisition was rather poor. In the United States, a preadolescent child named Genie (a pseudonym) was discovered living in absolute isolation in a room of a house. Her family never interacted with her verbally (hardly emotionally, either) and she had no spoken language. The quality of her language, especially her phonology and syntax, was very poor. In fact, she sounded as if she were a hearing-impaired person when speaking English, even though her hearing was not damaged. Both of these cases show that there may be a critical window for learning a first language, in spite of the fact that we may never know if either child experienced brain damage that subsequently affected their language development.

The critical period may also affect second-language acquisition (Asher & Garcia, 1969). The onset of puberty may account for the difficulty nonnative speakers have in losing their accents. Because the brain lateralizes (assigns specific areas of the brain to perform particular functions), it may not store the second language in quite the same way. In addition, the phonology for one's first language may be fixed; and that will also play a role in how one sounds when speaking the new language.

Developmental Stages.   Some aspects of first and second language acquisition are subject to nearly identical developmental stages (Pfaff, 1987). For example, learning *wh- questions,* like *Where is Chris going?,* happens in a particular order by both children learning English as a first language and adolescents and adults learning English as a second language. These shared stages are thought to indicate that there is a psycholinguistic aspect to language acquisition (e.g., it is **not** a matter of simply memorizing the correct forms).

Developmental Orders.   Like developmental stages, certain aspects of first- and second-language acquisition occur in an order. Consider how the morpheme /s/ is acquired: The plurals (*cars*) occur before the possessives (*Chris's*), and the third singular -s (*runs*) is acquired last. Again, this fact lends credence to the shared psycholinguistic aspects of first and second language acquisition (Larsen-Freeman, 1976).

Hypothesis Testing.   First- and second-language learners test out their current level of language acquisition against reality (Bley-Vroman, 1986). For example, when a child says *goed* to form the past tense of *go,* she does so with the belief she is correct. Only later does the child change this assumption through exposure to the correct form. Second-language learners do the same thing—for example, when English learners say *wented* to form the past tense.

Terms and Concepts Related to Second-Language Acquisition.

Silent Period.   The silent period is an interval that occurs before English language learners start producing language (Hakuta, 1974; Huang and Hatch, 1978). During this time, the learner may only produce memorized chunks of language—or no language at all—for months as they adjust to a new language and new environment. The notion is that learners do not start producing language until they feel comfortable enough to do so (Krashen, 1983).

Transfer Phenomenon.   Adolescent and adult language learners bring their first language with them when learning the second language. This fact can both hinder and help second-language acquisition (Odlin, 1989). Transfer can occur when the English language learner "defaults" to his knowledge of the first language and applies phonology, syntax, semantics, and so forth, to the task of speaking and understanding the second language (Newmark,

1966). If the first language interferes with the learning or producing the second language, then it is called **negative transfer.** An example of negative transfer is when a learner whose first language is Spanish says *house white* instead of *white house,* mainly because he uses Spanish syntax to produce the English form. **Positive transfer** occurs when the first language helps the second language. Cognates are found across many languages. Many of the names of the months in Spanish are the same in English: *Febrero/February, Marzo/March, Abril/April, Junio/June, Julio/July, Agusto/August, Septiembre/September, Octubre/October, Noviembre/November, Diciembre/December.* These similarities may make learning the names of the months easier in the second language, because they are similar to what is found in the first.

Interlanguage. As coined by Larry Selinker (1972), interlanguage is the distance between the first language and the second language. Errors reveal how far the learner is moving from the first language and into the second language. Generally speaking transfer errors (resulting from negative transfer) show less progress in the second language, whereas errors resulting from developmental stages and orders (errors that occur when children learn English as a first language) show more progress (Taylor, 1975). The reason is that transfer errors suggest that the learner is relying heavily on the first language, but developmental errors demonstrate that the learner is moving into the second language more fully.

Fossilization. This refers to second-language learners who get stuck at a particular level in English and cannot seem to progress beyond a particular level. Fossilization is most obvious in one's accent and seems tied to the onset of puberty. In families with children who immigrated after the age of 15 and with younger children who were subsequently born in the United States, the older children may have very profound accents while the younger children speak with no accent at all. Fossilization and the age of immigration appear to play a role in how one will ultimately sound in the second language.

First-Language Acquisition. Developmental stages and orders dominate first-language acquisition at virtually all of the linguistic levels. What you need to understand about first-language acquisition is captured in Table 3.46 (Ingram, 1989; Owens, 1984).

TABLE 3.46   First Language Acquisition

PHONOLOGY	MORPHOLOGY	SYNTAX	SEMANTICS	PRAGMATICS
Sounds are acquired in an order.	Inflections are acquired in an order.	Grammar is subject to stages.	Meaning is acquired in an order.	Family Language. Peer Language. Social Language.

Let's look at each area in greater detail.

Phonology. In the first place, please note that all babies babble the same from birth, regardless of where they are born. For example, newly born children in the United States, China, or Russia all babble the same sounds over and over again, the most common sounds being /b/, /p/, /s/, and /k/. This suggests that these sounds are **universal** to all human beings, since all "normally developing" children start out with the same set of phonemes right from birth.

Newborns, regardless of their place of birth or ethnicity, can distinguish between pairs and strings of phonemes (Elmas, 1975). **Diachronic listening studies** show that children can tell the difference between **voiced** and **unvoiced consonant** sounds like /p/ and /b/ when they hear them. These studies are conducted by having a given newborn listen to a string of **phonemes** like the **unvoiced stop** /p/ over and over again while their heartbeats are measured. Then, the **voiced stop** /b/ is introduced and the heart rate is measured. Many studies show that the child's heart rate increases when the voiced phoneme is introduced, and this physical response suggests that the child can demonstrate an understanding of the appreciable (yet subtle) difference between each type of phoneme.

Universal babbling and diachronic listening studies suggest that children are predisposed to learn languages, since they babble from birth (though indistinguishably) and can even tell the difference between pairs of sounds. Humans, it seems, are "hard wired" to acquire the ability to speak, given these innate abilities of producing and distinguishing sounds. Consider also that race and ethnicity play no role in how well one acquires a language—it is done right from birth. Around 6 months of age, the sounds one hears in a child's babbling change, probably because the environment is providing the child with **input** to be acquired. For example, if we compare the babbling of children in the United States with Chinese and Japanese babies, differences begin to emerge (see Table 3.47):

TABLE 3.47   Cross-Cultural Babbling

BORN IN THE UNITED STATES	BORN IN CHINA	BORN IN JAPAN
■ Babbling voiced and unvoiced stops.	■ Babbling voiced and unvoiced stops *and tones*.	■ Babbling voiced and unvoiced stops *and syllables*.

These differences are important, because children begin to babble differently after this age. Because Chinese is a **tonal language** and Japanese is a very **syllabic language** (meaning that these language use tones and syllables to distinguish words and meaning when speaking), children begin to note and acquire these differences even before they begin to use language to communicate. Obviously, the differences between the languages continue to grow remarkably from this point forward.

In English, the following phonemes tend to be acquired before others (Lock, 1983).

- **Six months:** Voice and unvoiced stops (p, b, t, d, k, g)
- **Two years:** Voiced and unvoiced fricatives (f, v, s, z)
- **Four years:** Voiced and unvoiced infrequent fricatives (**th**in, **th**an, **sh**ip, a**z**ure).

NOTE: The terms *acquired* and *learned* will be used interchangeably here. In first-language acquisition, both terms indicate that children can produce them **when they want to produce** them (e.g., when saying words). It takes time for children to be able to produce and control these sounds. On their way to producing these sounds, children do quite a bit of **consonant reducing** and **deleting** (see Table 3.48).

In the beginning, children may think that they are producing the correct form; later, they may become aware that they are unable to articulate the sound correctly and may display frustration at this inability.

TABLE 3.48

TARGET	CHILD	
stop	top	(initial sound deletion)
try	ty	(medial deletion)
sleep	sweep	(initial blend reduction)

Morphology.   Inflectional affixes are acquired in a particular order that is common to all children learning English as a first language (Brown, 1973). As mentioned earlier, children tend to learn the plural -*s* before the possessive -*s*. Third person singular -*s* (*runs, hits, jumps*) tends to be last. This is probably due to the fact that plurals and possessives are concrete and third singular is abstract. It is easy to understand plural and possessive forms, but third singular -s is more for decoration; therefore, this third singular form is learned later.

Learning how to form the past tense morphologically occurs in stages as shown in Table 3.49. First, the child learns the form -*ed* to make the past tense, and then **overgeneralizes** this inflectional ending to any verb to make the past tense.

TABLE 3.49   Stages of Language Acquisition

STAGE ONE *OVERGENERALIZATION*	STAGE TWO *HYPERCORRECTION*	STAGE THREE *UPTAKE/SELF-CORRECTION*
Parent: What did you do yesterday?	Parent: What did you do for your birthday?	Parent: What did you do for your birthday?
Child: I **goed** to the store.	Child: I **wented** to the zoo.	Child: I **wented** to the zoo.
Parent: You **went** to the store?	Parent: You **went** to the zoo?	Parent: You **went** to the zoo?
Child: Yes. I **goed** to the store got a toy.	Child: Yes. I **wented** to the zoo and saw lions!	Child: Yes. I **went** to the zoo.

The Table 3.49 shows how a child might move from one stage of hypothesis testing to another on the way to learning how to correctly form the past tense for irregular verbs in English (*go/went, run/ran, sit/sat*). Please note that the forms the child uses in stages one through three (*goed* and *wented*) are seldom heard in their environment since the child's caregivers (parents and teachers) probably use the correct forms of the verb when speaking to the child. Yet the child uses these incorrect forms *anyway,* because they make the most sense to him or her. Overgeneralized forms (*goed*) and hypercorrected forms (*wented*) are common here.

Syntax.   Developmental stages affect the acquisition of English syntax. The most common stages are discussed below (Chomsky, 1969; Cairnes, 1996):

HOLOPHRASES.   Holophrases occur around 12 to 18 months. These are one-word utterances that the child uses to mean a variety of phrases. For example, the word *me* can mean a variety of things: *I'm hungry. I'm tired. I need to be changed. I'm really hot in this jumpsuit—could you please take it off?* Often, the child's caregiver is able to understand what the child wants based on the single word either by intonation or through trial and error.

TWO-WORD STAGE.   Two-Word Stage occurs shortly after the one word (holophrastic) state when children put two words together. *Chris car, kitty here,* and *no wash* are probably things that I said at this stage and so did you. The important idea to note is that grammar is emerging at this stage, though it is very reduced and stripped down.

TELEGRAPHIC STAGE.   Telegraphic Stage occurs when the child strings words together with a discernable grammar. *Daddy go, Milk all gone,* and *I now tired* are examples of the telegraphic stage. In each case, there is a subject and a verb form in the utterance. The utterances are becoming structurally correct, even though they lack "unessential" elements of determiners, prepositions, and so forth.

COMPOUND SUBJECTS AND ADVERBAL MODIFIERS.   Compound subjects and adverbial modifiers are in place and in production about kindergarten. For example, *Mike and Chris ran and jumped far* is a viable sentence at this stage, and prepositional phrases as modifiers may be in place by the end of kindergarten. This is because spatial concepts for words like *in, on, near,* and *far* must be established first before attaching a spoken or written label to them.

As children improve in their language, they go through other stages. Question and negation forms are examples that emerge around age two as shown in Table 3.50 (Klima & Bellugi, 1966):

TABLE 3.50   Acquisition Orders

DO + QUESTION	WH + QUESTION	NEGATION
You like?	Where go?	No run.
You do like it?	Where you go?	I no running.
Do you like it?	Where you did go?	I'm not running.
	Where did you go?	

The orders for learning the *do, wh- question,* and *negation* forms are quite universal for children learning English as a first language. The orders seem inescapable (linguists do not bother studying these forms any more, because they are so common). These orders suggest that there is a psycholinguistic aspect to learning English as a first language. In the first place, children are not hearing "you like" or "where go" or "no run" in the environment, *yet they produce these forms.* Some kind of linguistic structuring must be taking place in the child's mind for these odd forms to be produced on the way to learning how to correctly form the syntax of each of these statements.

Semantic Acquisition.   The meaning of certain words and phrases are acquired in an order. In the beginning, children overextend and underextend the meanings of words. For example, a "woof-woof" may be any animal with four legs and a tail (dogs, cats, beavers, lions, etc.), but "kitty" may only refer to the *child's cat* and to no other cat-like animal.

Subordinate clauses and *passive voice sentences* are among the last things to be acquired. These elements can be acquired as late as fourth grade, if not beyond. The problem is understanding the meaning that these sentences convey. A sentence like:

> If I had run for just twenty-five minutes longer, then I would have
> won the race; and I would not have to be here writing this book.

is a pretty complicated sentence to understand (for anyone), and it makes sense that the form is acquired late.

Passive constructions and complex sentences are also acquired quite late (Turner & Rommetveit, 1967).

A. Cookie Monster ate the cookie.
B. The cookie was eaten by Cookie Monster.
C. I will have been standing here for five hours when the clock strikes three.

Because position dominates in understanding what sentences mean, sentence A is easy to understand. The agent (subject) carries out the action on the goal (object). However, sentence B is tricky; and a child might act out the sentence with a puppet by having the *cookie* eat *Cookie Monster* instead of the other way around. Children might believe that the first position of the sentence always contains the agent, so they act upon that belief. Again, position is what children might rely upon for meaning; and this accounts for why passive sentences are acquired later. The last sentence is highly complex and requires knowledge of time and contingencies to be fully understood. Cognitively speaking, some children may not be ready to understand such a sentence without experience and knowledge of time.

Pragmatic Acquisition.   Acquiring a sociolect also occurs in an order. The child typically learns the "family language" first, meaning that he or she acquires the variety of English that the parents speak, along with the caregiver's idiolect and the regional isogloss and dialect. At school, peer groups exert a greater influence, especially during adolescence, and aspects of the child's language may move away from what his or her parents and teachers speak. Later, when the child grows up and moves into the workplace, the language of that environment will tend to dominate as he or she tries to accommodate into that world.

Second-Language Acquisition.   Adolescent and adult second language acquisition share similar developmental orders and stages present in first-language acquisition, but there is the additional characteristic of positive and negative transfer. This is because second-language learners bring a complete (or nearly complete) linguistic system to the second language learning experience. You will see how these factors play a role in learning a second language at each linguistic level.

Phonology.   Recall that transfer is specifically related to second-language acquisition. For second-language learners, more negative transfer issues emerge when second-language learners encounter English (Gass & Selinker, 1983) because the first language has sounds that are different from what one finds in the first language. Subsequently, the English sounds that English language learners produce are negatively affected. For example, the Spanish phoneme /s/ is often heard as /es/. This affects the way that English words are pronounced:

- Smoke   /esmok/
- Cereal   /eserial/

If the first language lacks similar phonological processes, the first language may still interfere with the pronunciation of English words. The phoneme /th/ at the ends of English words is often heard as a /t/:

- English: with
- Spanish Influence: /wit/

Final consonants are often voiced at the ends of words that native speakers of English devoice:

- English: /werkt/
- Spanish Influence: /werk-ed/

In short, negative transfer issues are most apparent at the phonological level, perhaps because of the critical period cited earlier (where the brain has already specialized phonology before the introduction of the second language).

Morphology.   There is a similar developmental order to learning English morphemes that you saw in first-language learning. The plurals tend to be learned before the possessives, and third person singular comes in last. These stages tend to be moved through quickly, because adults can grasp the abstractions more quickly than children can. Overgeneralizations of *-ed* are common, too, and *goed* and *wented* are common developmental errors at this level as a result of hypothesis testing.

Syntax.   Both transfer and developmental errors are common when learning English syntax. As cited earlier, Spanish speakers who place the adjective after the noun are relying on their first-language syntax to produce English. Developmental orders for questions (*do* and *wh-*) are common here. A similar pattern is present for negation, though the form *no sing* is ambiguous for many romance languages, since they form negation with *no* + verb (one cannot readily say if this interlanguage error is the result of transfer or development). Conditional sentences and passive voice sentences are acquired later, just as you saw with first language acquisition.

Semantics.   Transfer may also occur when the learner thinks there is enough similarity between words in the first and second languages (Kellerman & Sharwood-Smith, 1986). This strategy will work for true cognates in each language but not for false cognates. English language learners can sometimes draw upon their first language to get at the meanings of words, because our language has borrowed words from German, French, and Spanish. By proxy, German, French, and Spanish borrowed many words and roots from Greek and Latin, so there has been much filtering into the language that accounts for so many true cognates found in English and other languages (see Table 3.51).

Morphemes, too, are similar in many languages. Greek and Latin morphemes are found in both English and Spanish, which can be affected by positive transfer as shown in Table 3.52.

TABLE 3.51

ENGLISH	GERMAN	SPANISH	FRENCH	GREEK (DIMOTIKI)
School	Schule	Escuela	Ecola	Scholeio
Number	Nummer	Numero	Nombre	Numero
Cat	Katze	Gato	Chat	Gato

TABLE 3.52

	ENGLISH	SPANISH		ENGLISH	SPANISH
in-	inept	inépto	-able	insupportable	insuportable
im-	impossible	impossible	pre-	precede	predecir

Negative transfer can hinder semantic development, though, particularly where false cognates are concerned. False cognates are words that look very similar to words in English, yet have very different meanings (see Table 3.53):

TABLE 3.53

ENGLISH WORD	SPANISH WORD
embarrassed (ashamed)	embarasada (pregnant)
molest (criminal act)	molestar (annoy)

Idiomatic expressions are also challenging and can be subject to developmental errors. While at a college party, an exchange student wished to express how the group was "really partying" hard and how much fun he was having. He climbed on to a table and announced: "*We ALREADY party now!*" Such expressions might be hard for second-language learners to grasp at first, so be sure to look for errors in idiomatic expressions in the data on the test.

Pragmatics. Pragmatics is also a part of second-language acquisition (Bates & MacWhinney, 1981). You have learned about different registers of social speech in different genres of language use. For example, two friends who are playing poker (the genre) will probably use an informal speaking style (register) during the game. Their requests will be informal, direct, and maybe even jovial (if they are winning). This type of language use may not be appropriate during a funeral, though.

Language learners need to learn about these different genres and the registers within them. Making requests, for example, must be taught directly, but so must the appropriate level of formality required. Consider the following:

- Lemme see that article.
- Give me the article.
- Excuse me, could you please hand me the article?
- Pardon me, but would you be willing to allow me to view that article for just a moment?

Each of the sentences above means the same thing: It makes a request. But *how* each utterance achieves that goal is different. Language learners need to be taught not only how to make requests, but also how to accomplish the request appropriately. Because second-language learners may have a difficult time with the pragmatic aspects of the language, they will also have a tough time accessing the concepts in the language.

Theories of Second-Language Acquisition.   You may be asked questions about the major theories of second language acquisition. They fall into three general categories: behavioral, natural, and sociolinguistic.

Behavioral Theories.   Behaviorist B. F. Skinner (1957) proposed that languages are learned just like any other behavior: through rewards and reinforcement. As children grow, the environment provides them with input, and they learn the language through rewards and reinforcements that their caregivers provide to them. Hearing the words *cat, dog, run,* and so forth, over and over again provides the child with the stimulus needed for acquiring the words. As the child repeats what he or she hears correctly and is praised or rewarded for doing so, long strings of stimulus and response chains are formed. Thus, human language is something that is modeled and reinforced for the child from birth and beyond.

Natural Order.   Stephen Krashen is the major theorist of the natural order of learning a second language (Gass & Selinker, 1994). Because English has developmental orders in it, Krashen theorizes that language can be acquired in the same natural way. He also hypothesized that learning and acquisition are not the same thing. When one develops a vocabulary in a second language, he or she does so through acquisition, thus obtaining the language without consciously trying to do so, much like children do when growing up. Language learning, on the other hand, is very effortful and unnatural (but necessary): It entails learning formal grammar, standard forms of the language, and the like. One view is not better than the other. Instead, each area serves a different purpose: Acquisition is for obtaining the language naturally, and learning is for developing the capacity to correct one's grammar when writing or speaking. Other important principles to know in this area are discussed below.

THE MONITOR MODEL (LARSEN-FREEMEN & LONG, 1991).   The monitor is what we use *learned* language for. When we study grammar rules and do grammar exercises, we are *learning* (not acquiring) language. The monitor is what we use to fix our errors when *producing* the language. Think of the monitor as a quality control specialist whose task is to ensure that the utterance is grammatically and socially acceptable. This job can be done well only if the learned information is correct and can be applied to the utterance.

THE INPUT HYPOTHESIS.   Krashen (1985) believes that learners must have comprehensible input to acquire language. That is, input that is at and just a bit beyond their current level of competence in the language. This is captured in the $i + 1$ model. Think of it this way: If you have a learner who can comprehend the plural forms, then your goal is to move him from the plurals to the possessives (and later, third person singular -s). Acquiring language occurs naturally through exposure and experience (**not** direct instruction), through input that has been modified by the speaker to be understood by the learner just above the learner's current stage of development. The silent period occurs because the learner is building up competence through comprehensible input.

THE AFFECTIVE FILTER HYPOTHESIS (KRASHEN, 1981).   The affective filter can be characterized as the degree of resistance one has toward learning the language. Generally, if the student is full of anxiety or anger toward the speaker of a given language, then learning is probably going to be made more difficult. Teachers, too, can raise students' affective filters. If the teacher displays negative attitudes toward a learner's primary language and native culture, then the student may feel shame and anger and acquisition may not take place. A high affective filter will impede one's receiving comprehensible input, the necessary ingredient for acquisition.

FIRST LANGUAGE LITERACY.   Krashen (1983) also posits that children need to be literate in the first language to make the process of acquiring the second language easier. He theorizes that first-language skills will transfer to the second language positively. For example, the concept of reading letter patterns and direction of sentences and the meaning of stories will make sense in English if those ideas are grasped first in the native language. The same is true for narrative text schema and other elements of literature (plot, setting, character, etc.). The theory can be summarized as follows (Krashen, 1983):

> One acquires a second language through input that teachers make comprehensible.
> In addition, one's affective filter must be low enough to allow the input to enter.

According to Krashen (1983), comprehensible input is the only variable that can be measured by researchers.

Sociolinguistic Theories: BICS and CALP.   Some researchers, James Cummins (1979) in particular, make a distinction between Basic Interpersonal Communication Skills (BICS) and Cognitive Academic Language Proficiency (CALP). BICS amounts to social language, and the idea is that learners will acquire interpersonal language rather quickly—the language for playing and working with others on the playground and in the classroom. CALP, on the other hand, is the language of academics. Understanding metaphor and entropy, for example, is more cognitively demanding *in this view* than making a request for a date on Friday night. Teachers need to be aware of this distinction and try to ensure that both BICS and CALP develop equally. If not, then the learner may be very socially proficient but remain academically challenged. One must be careful to instruct both social and academic language to English language learners so that both aspects develop equally. (See Communicative Approach for BICA and CALLA for CALP in the next section.)

ESL Methods.   ESL instruction has the ultimate aim of mainstreaming English language learners into the "regular" classroom. This means that absolute beginners who are learning English must be taught quickly enough to move them into an academically demanding classroom where they must learn not only the English language but also academic concepts like metaphor, mathematical functions, and scientific methods. The following are general ESL methods that appear on the test.

Audiolingual Method and Grammar Translation.   Pattern drills and memorized dialogues typify the audiolingual method, where the constructed features of language are reduced to memorized chunks of information and practiced through repetition. If you imagine a work-sheet with sentences (perhaps out of context) for students to read and repeat along with a tape recording, you have grasped the idea of this approach:

- I **want** to learn English.
- I **want** the anesthesiologist to stay in the room during the appendectomy.
- I **want** a library book.

These approaches are very behavioral, given the emphasis on memorization and stimulus–response. The rest of the approaches take a more "naturalistic" approach to the acquisition of English.

Language Experience Approach.   LEA activities will be described in detail in Content Area Six. For now, understand that teaching English language learners to associate spoken and written language can be accomplished through LEA activities. Here, the teacher and the student discuss an experience and the experience is written down (usually one sentence in length). If the learner cannot write yet, then the teacher writes the sentence down. In either case, whatever the learner says is what is written in print (errors and all):

I goed to the store this yesterday.

The principle behind LEA is this: *What was discussed is written, and what is written is read.* Later, the errors can be corrected, but error correction is not the focus of early LEA. Instead, the goal is to help the learner make the link between spoken and written language. The same is true for conceptual knowledge. For example, if the teacher is instructing the theme of friendship and loss, it may be necessary first to try to relate to the student's own notions of this experience. The student can be asked to think about what it was like to leave friends from the home country when emigrating to the United States. This way, the student can relate a real experience to the text and not have to struggle with both the language and the content simultaneously.

Total Physical Response.   TPR is a method of instructing basic ESL (Asher, 1969, 1982). You model concrete actions and present concrete objects to language learners to help them make the connection between spoken language and the things they describe. Imagine that you have a group of absolute beginners and that you want to teach them basic commands like stand up, sit down, turn left, and turn right. Using TPR, you model each of these commands from the learner by saying the command and demonstrating the action. Then, you work with the learners to guide them in both saying and acting out the command. Finally, you say the command and have the learner demonstrate the action.

TPR is useful for teaching more complicated commands and nouns (see Table 3.54).

TABLE 3.54   TPR Examples

COMMAND	NOUN
Touch your	Nose
Show me your	Hair
Where is your	Arm

Here, the teacher models and guides the learner in learning these commands and requests, along with the concrete nouns.

Other TPR activities use labels around the classroom. Every concrete object in the room is labeled with a readable index card (e.g., *clock, chalkboard, light switch, desk,* etc.). These labels become part of TPR activities that are carried out daily as part of the morning routine.

REALIA.   Realia means using concrete objects, materials, and observable experience to teach abstract concepts. Think of how you would teach words like sweet and sour without realia. The task is much easier if you bring in a lump of sugar and a slice of lemon. That's using realia! Only using words to describe abstractions is ineffective for many learners, but especially for ELLs whose skills in the target language may be limited.

Communicative Approaches.   These activities include having students learn applicable language on a continuum from the easiest to the more difficult tasks. The continuum begins with the most **concrete** use of language (using present tense in immediate social situations) to more **abstract** uses of language (using past or future tense, expressing wants and desires in more abstract social situations). Consider the following examples and their linguistic demands on the speakers.

- Discussing what they do in the morning.
- Discussing their favorite activities.
- Discussing what they did for their last birthday.
- Discussing what they would and would not like to do on summer vacation.

The first activity is the most concrete. It asks the students to talk about what they do in the morning (e.g., wake up, eat breakfast, dress for school, etc.). The rest of the utterances are more abstract and involve more complicated utterances. The last item, for example, requires expressing choices using lots of modals, which is beyond the concrete linguistic demands of simply discussing what one does in the morning. Other types of communicative activities include having students answer questions about what they like to do and to then develop a list of their own questions to be posed to their classmates. As students work together to find and write down answers to their questions, they can work on both oral and written language development simultaneously.

If you have taken any foreign language classes during your college career, then you are probably already familiar with the communicative approach. First, you learn vocabulary in a given social situation, like being *at the bank* or *in the classroom.* You probably saw lots of pictures and vocabulary with an English translation. Then, you practiced a dialogue of some sort in the target language before learning a simple grammar point. The rest of the lesson then had you applying both the contextualized vocabulary and the grammar point in a variety of reading, writing, speaking, and listening activities. An example of the communicative approach for English language learners is shown in Table 3.55 on page 102.

The point is to teach vocabulary and grammar within a defined social context so that it is immediately applicable and usable by the learner. This approach is much different from the audiolingual method where the vocabulary can be decontextualized and the grammar points quite obscure.

TABLE 3.55   Communicate Sequences

GENRE	VOCABULARY	DIALOGUE	GRAMMAR POINT	COMMUNICATION
At the bank	Would like loan money collateral	Hello. I would like a loan. Why would you like a loan?	Future will + verb would + verb	Listening Speaking Writing

Natural Approach.   Krashen and Terrell (1983) synthesized approaches like LEA, TPR, realia, and communicative approaches into a singular method called the *Natural Approach.* It is based on the *Natural Order Hypothesis* described in the ESL theories section. Briefly, the natural approach relies on comprehensible input, exposure to rich vocabulary in context, listening and reading over speech production, and an anxiety-free learning environment to keep the affective filter low. The goal is to move students from no skills in English to an intermediate stage over a period of time (greater than one year). Learners also move from basic communication skills to more academic skills before transitioning into sheltered content classroom (described next) or into mainstream classrooms.

The natural approach divides learners into four groups: preproduction, early production, speech emergence, and intermediate fluency. Preproduction learners are not producing any language yet (or only chunks), so they are taught using high level of TPR, realia, and modeling. They are not expected to produce language at this point, but rather to receive and "build up" their comprehension through comprehensible input. Early production learners have some speech that is emerging on its own (they are now ready to produce language) and instruction begins to ramp up to include wh- questions and so forth. At the speech emergence state, learners perform more linguistically demanding activities, such as predicting, comparing, and describing. Finally, when they are intermediately fluent, they learn to handle academic tasks in English and prepare to move into a sheltered or mainstream classroom.

The natural approach model is shown in Table 3.56.

TABLE 3.56   The Natural Approach

PREPRODUCTION	EARLY PRODUCTION	SPEECH EMERGENCE	INTERMEDIATE FLUENCY
TPR modeling	TPR with responses	Predicting	Essay writing
Yes/no questions	Role playing	Comparing	Analyzing charts and graphs
Pictures	Wh- questions	Describing	More complex problem
Realia	Labels and realia	How and why questions	solving and evaluating
Simplified language	Simple response expectation	LEA	Prewriting activities
		Listing, charting, graphing	Literary analysis

As the learners' communicative abilities increase, the teacher talk decreases. In addition, the scaffolds move from TPR to more academically oriented tasks (e.g., writing essays, analyzing charts, etc.). Checking listening skills also varies from the preproduction stage to the intermediate production stage. For example, in the preproduction stage, one could have students demonstrate comprehension by carrying out concrete tasks. For example, asking students to place an "x" inside, to the left of, on top of, and beneath a box drawn on a piece of paper will tell you whether the student understands basic commands and prepositions.

Similarly, one can read a story and have students select pictures that best reflect what was just described orally. Again, in all of these tasks it is important to target only the skill in question and not others. For example, it would be inappropriate to have students write notes or summarize the requests in writing during the listening comprehension task. That is because one would be assessing two competing skills at once, which would be unfair to the student and would cloud your knowledge of the students' listening skills. Plus, such an assessment might be beyond the students' current level of language.

Means of checking speaking skills will also vary across the language levels. In the preproduction stage, little beyond memorized greetings might be expected. Later, informal conversations might be the focus. In all cases, the task must match the purpose. Having the student complete a dialogue about a conversation, for example, does not match the purpose of seeing if the students can carry on a conversation. Only a truly informal conversation between the teacher and the student can accomplish that.

Cognitive Academic Language Learning Approach (CALLA).   CALLA activities teach students academic content as they learn English. This approach is also known as sheltered English instruction. Academic content, like metaphors in literature, the Pythagorean theorem in mathematics, and expressionism in art, is modified and taught to English language learners, through specially designed academic instructional designs. As you can see, the focus is on learning the content of a subject (math, science, social studies, language arts, etc.), rather than on simple English language communication skills (see BICS and CALP earlier in this section).

The following are CALLA activities that address academic content and English language development (Chamot & O'Malley, 1986).

PREVIEW/REVIEW.   This method preteaches (previews) vocabulary and academic concepts in a lesson before actually undertaking instruction (Lesslow-Hurley, 1990). This way, the student will not be lost in the language she is struggling to acquire while also trying to understand an academic concept like *entropy* in a science class. In addition, realia and pictures may also be used to introduce the topic in advance. For example, before listening to a brief lecture on plant and animal cell similarities and differences, students will be shown pictures of both types of cells, along with the labels that describe each part. The pictures will provide concrete support (a scaffold) to students before they learn unfamiliar information in the lecture. The lesson ends with a review of the vocabulary and academic concepts to ensure that the students have learned both areas through the lesson.

Visual cues and realia-based demonstrations are very helpful. They are **advanced organizers** and provide concrete referents that summarize and support the information that one is going to explain verbally. Here, students' minds will be prompted to think about what the lecture is going to be about. In addition, they will also have a support system upon which they can rely that is **not** based on the language, of which they may only have a thin grasp. They will have a visual support to guide them through the lesson.

Study Skills.   Teaching study skills is also important. When asking ELLs to carry out a task in a science classroom, it may be beneficial to have the students write the steps down first so that they can have a scaffold to carry with them into the task. Without the list, the students may find it difficult to remember all of the spoken words that they have just heard in a language that they have not yet mastered. Keep in mind that note taking is a part of study skills. This is not an appropriate way to measure listening skills in general, because it adds an additional skill of writing to the task thereby clouding what the student can and cannot do when listening to directions.

CALLA Assessment.   Finding ways to assess ELL students' knowledge of content is important. This type of assessment is different from traditional assessment, in that the teacher must find a way to reveal what the student understands about a subject without testing her language skills at the same time. These assessments may include many demonstrations or other nonlanguage based means of assessing what the child understands. This extends to the first language as well. If the child supplies words correctly from the first language into the second language to describe the content, then it shows that the child is actively engaging the material. What the student must learn is how to express the same idea in English, though that would be done through separate instruction and assessments. CALLA assessments ensure that the student will not be unfairly assessed on both language and academic skills simultaneously. The student has the opportunity to show what he really knows about a subject without being limited by his English learner status. A sample CALLA lesson that utilizes these principles appears in Table 3.57.

TABLE 3.57   CALLA Science Lesson

CALLA SCIENCE: TEACHING A SHELTERED ENGLISH LESSON ON OCEAN LIFE

Preview: Introduce the academic content using lots of visuals and charts that are not language dependent. For example, when teaching the difference between mammals, crustaceans, and cephalopods, use pictures, objects, and other hands-on materials to convey the differences among these different elements of sea life.

Teach Vocabulary: Teach the vocabulary to associate with the objects and the concepts using speech, print, and modeling. Have the students use labels to identify different pictures or have them draw the items in their journals before attempting to read the content.

Guided Practice: Provide students with a scaffold for the reading. The scaffold should offer more support to the text as they read and look for information. The scaffold can be a visual outline of the paragraph or a cloze activity (fill-in-the-blank) where the students supply the correct label in the text using the vocabulary that they have learned.

Review: Close the activity by reviewing the outline or the cloze activity and reteach the vocabulary that has been introduced. *Assess the students in the same way that the lesson was delivered:* having the students label pictures, complete cloze activities, or draw and label items in their journals.

In summary, CALLA activities focus on academic content, along with providing English language learners with multiple opportunities to both learn and to demonstrate their understanding of the academic content in ways that are not necessarily language dependent.

Constraints on Second-Language Acquisition. The final area that we will consider pertains to constraints on language learning. How well one learns English as a second language is dependent upon a variety of factors. Assuming that the environment provides all the input that a learner needs, along with plentiful opportunities to learn, the following factors appear to play a role in how well one will acquire the language.

Age. *Age* does appear to have a great impact on how well one learns a second language. In general, adolescents and adults learn the basics of the language faster. This is because adolescents and adults have access to deeper analytic functions than children do. But children learn the language better in the long run, because adolescents and adults fossilize more quickly. Fossilization means that they get stuck at a particular level in the language and have an accent that they cannot lose or must speak only in the simple present, past, and future tenses because more complicated tenses remain too elusive. Fossilization may occur because of brain lateralization, where certain brain functions are assigned to particular sides of the brain (language acquisition being one of the functions). In short, children may acquire the language more slowly, but they tend to learn the target language more completely than adults do. In short, before puberty, less fossilization; after puberty, more fossilization.

Motivation. Motivation itself is an important ingredient in learning a second language, though it is unclear what kind is best. There are two types of motivation to consider. The first is intrinsic and internal, and the second is extrinsic and instrumental. The distinction is simple. Intrinsic/internal motivation is motivation because of a deep desire or want to participate with other speakers of the target language because of appreciation, and so forth. Extrinsic/instrumental motivation, on the other hand, is more utilitarian: One wants to learn the language to get something (e.g., better grades, jobs, etc.).

Learning Style. Learning style, too, is important but not a great determiner. Students who are easily frustrated and cannot handle ambiguity may spend a great deal of their time feeling angry while learning the second language, whereas students who can tolerate degrees of uncertainty may learn more comfortably. However, learning style is not an absolute indicator of how well or poorly one may ultimately learn the target language.

CONCLUSION

In this chapter, you have learned about English linguistics (phonology, morphology, syntax, semantics, and pragmatics), sociolinguistics, and first- and second-language acquisition. The next chapter presents another major area of the exam: literacy. Much of what you have already learned from the section on linguistics has already prepared you for this chapter, so you are now in a good position to learn what the test-makers view as the process of learning to read.

CHAPTER FOUR

LITERACY INSTRUCTION

This chapter covers literacy and how to view the process of learning to read (Content Area Three), assessment principles (Content Area Four), and literacy instruction (Content Area Five). After finishing these content areas, you will have completed all of the major ideas contained within domain one. Please note that teaching English language learners to read English texts follows the same model presented in this chapter, with the addition of all of the areas covered in the previous chapter under ESL methods.

CONTENT AREA THREE: LITERACY

The easiest way to view Content Area Three is to make a distinction between learning to read and reading to learn (O'Mally, 1998). Just imagine that during the learning to read phase is where you teach a child all of the foundational skills so that later he can read to learn independently, *just as you are doing right now in preparation for the test.* Table 4.1 shows a model associated with this content area, and it is important for you not only to learn it but also to commit it to memory. We will go into this model in greater detail throughout the remainder of this chapter, so do not worry if you are unfamiliar with some of the terms and concepts.

To begin, "learning to read" is to occur in grades kindergarten through third grade. Look at the table and notice that **concepts about print** and **phonemic awareness** are taught early in kindergarten. From late kindergarten through grade three, children start learning beginning, intermediate, and advanced phonics. **Regular** and **irregular sight words** are also instructed during the reading-to-learn stage though in separate activities. Heavy emphasis is on skills instruction, particularly in the areas of learning to decode print and the foundations that precede that ability. By the end of grade three, children are expected to be **fluent decoders of text,** so that they can begin to focus on higher level vocabulary and reading comprehension. Comprehension instruction does take place, though it is mainly through listening comprehension that continues in discrete activities (30 to 60 minutes per day) until second grade.

"Reading to learn" occurs in grades four and above. Here, students learn how to gain knowledge independently from a variety of narrative and informational and scientific texts. To do so, they will need **vocabulary instruction** that starts with syllabication and moves on to etymology. In addition, students will also need **comprehension instruction,** so that they can understand a text literally, inferentially, and critically (evaluative comprehension).

TABLE 4.1　Literacy

KINDERGARTEN	FIRST	SECOND	THIRD	FOURTH	FIFTH +
CONCEPTS ABOUT PRINT PHONEMIC AWARENESS					
	Decoding Instruction		Fluent Decoding		
	VOCABULARY				
	Regular Sight Words	Irregular Sight Words	Syllabication	Structural Analysis	Etymology
LISTENING COMPREHENSION		READING COMPREHENSION			
		Literal		Inferential	Evaluative

This means that they will need instruction in strategies that will allow them to work with text independently and to demonstrate that they have understood what they have read, regardless of whether the text is a short story or an article on gene therapy.

Let's begin with the foundations of kindergarten through third grade literacy: concepts about print, phonemic awareness, and decoding instruction.

Concepts about Print

Concepts about print (CAP) includes all of the functions of a book that one must learn in order to make it work. Since humans are not born as readers, we must learn about all of the principal parts of a book before it can be used as a tool for learning. This is a top-down process, where the largest concepts are taught first (Gray-Schlegal & King, 1998):

- Book Concepts: title, picture, author's name, etc.
- Sentence Concepts: where to start, direction, return sweeps.
- Word Concepts: word boundaries, first and last letters, word reading.
- Letter Names: names of upper- and lowercase letters out of sequence.

Memorize the order above. The highest level of CAP is letter naming, where the child sees an upper- or lowercase letter and says its name. This ability is extremely important, because the child will later attach a variety of sounds to the letters that she says by name. Consider the letter *s*. First, the child will learn the name of the letter, /es/. Later, she will learn to attach other sounds to it when she sees it in print, as in cat/s/, dog/z/, and wash/ez/. Letter–sound associations cannot happen until the child can see a letter and say its name. Please recognize that letter–sound associations take place in separate activities and after **phonemic awareness** (the subject of our next area of discussion) is in place.

CAP instruction involves big book readings, and all elements of CAP can be modeled this way (Park, 1982). As the teacher reads to a group of students, she points to each word as she reads aloud. This is a very common practice for making the association between spoken and written language, since we were not born simply knowing this relationship. Using a pointer or having the child read with his finger to track print are common techniques to teach children directionality, though it must be discontinued later on as it may interfere with fluency.

Reading aloud to students is important, because it exposes them to book language and helps to provide them with a rich oral vocabulary. In addition, it also begins to teach them about story grammar or schema: the elements and organizational framework of a story. Though they cannot read on their own yet, the students will begin to acquire ideas about plot, setting, character, and so forth, at this point, which will greatly assist them when they begin to read and try to comprehend these elements independently. Assessments can also follow oral reading, where students' literal comprehension of a story that has been read aloud to them can be assessed. Students can be asked to order story panels or to draw pictures of the events in the story, and the teacher can see what the children have and have not understood.

Language experience activities can also be used for CAP instruction. For emergent readers, language experience approaches are common to help them develop reading readiness. It targets requisites for reading, like language and conceptual development. These approaches have children experience something, like going to a zoo or to a grocery store, and then creating a story about it. This activity helps them to develop oral language expression and to develop the foundations for reading, like **concepts about print,** where one links spoken and written language together (e.g., directionality, word concepts, word boundaries, distinguishing words from letters, etc.). Early in development, the child might not understand that written words represent what we say in speech, so this concept will have to be taught explicitly (Taylor, 1992).

Language experience approaches can also be part of early reading assessment. By having children discuss an experience and write it down, you can see their current level of concepts about print (directionality, word boundaries, letter sounds), spelling development, and letter formations. During early LEAs, student utterances are written down word for word, errors and all. If the child says, *I goed to the store today,* then that is what is written. Why? Because the goal is to illustrate that what can be spoken can also be captured in print.

After the sentence has been written down, the child can "read" the sentence with the teacher and point to each word as it is read:

I   goed to   the   zoo   today.
            ↑ ↑

Corrections can be made, as in the example above. Here, the child has *syllabicated* today into /to/ and /day/. The teacher can indicate that the word is to be read as whole by pointing at the word and running the finger beneath the word while saying it. Then, the student can practice the skill. This way, the student will understand how to read a multisyllabic word correctly.

Later LEAs can target corrections to fix *goed/went* confusions. The utterance is written on note cards and amended as you see below:

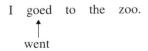

Morning message activities are also a form of language experience. Here, the teacher writes a "message" on the board each morning and has the students "read" the sentence with the teacher:

Today is Friday, March 11, 2005.

Students can take turns reading each word aloud with a pointer with the other students, or the teacher can simply model the reading for the students before having them choral read the text. Such an activity will teach the students many aspects of CAP, including capital letters at the start of sentences (*Today*) and for proper nouns (Friday, March) and correct placement of commas and periods. Furthermore, students learn about directionality, word boundaries, and letter names. In sum, morning message activities incorporate all aspects of CAP and are appropriate choices if you are asked to identify a proper activity for fostering CAP development with young children.

Note too that you may be asked questions about using multisensory techniques to teach letter formation often involving environmental print. Examples of environmental print include familiar logos seen often in the child's world. This is good for teaching letter recognition, along with copying the alphabet through multisensory techniques and metalinguistics. Copying the alphabet, for example, targets the motor skills necessary for legible handwriting and may also help children to memorize the letter patterns. Accompanying multisensory techniques, such as writing in the air, in sand, or tracing sandpaper letters while saying them aloud, are effective for helping to distinguish easily confused letters like *p/b, d/q*—letters that are orthographically similar. Finally, metalinguistics also play a role in teaching children how to form letters. Telling the difference between making a *b* and making a *d,* for example, might occur by having the child associate language with the formation: stick and circle for the letter *b* and circle and stick for *d* might help them make the distinction when printing the letters on paper.

In summary, children with caregivers who read to them at home will be at a distinct advantage because they come to school with many concepts in place. Families should be encouraged to read with their children for this reason. Having students take books home to read with their families is an excellent way to foster family literacy. In addition, second-language learners from literate households may have the same advantage. Regardless of the language, many aspects of CAP will transfer and students will learn the schema of narrative text, because these concepts are common to all linguistic groups. Developing a list of books to be found at the local library is another way to foster family involvement in literacy. This will also ensure that the messages that one receives from school are consistent with what one hears in the home.

Phonemic Awareness

The next area of kindergarten through third grade instruction focuses on phonemic awareness, where no print is used during instruction because the goal is to teach children to have a very important awareness of sounds.

Phonemic awareness is the understanding that words are made up of individual sounds (Yopp & Yopp, 2000), and it is considered to be the earliest predictor of a child's ability to read (Adams, 1990). Studies of children with reading difficulties indicate that they have very poor phonemic awareness; so the rationale is that if phonemic awareness is addressed early on, then reading difficulties may be avoided later on.

Phonemic awareness is a foundational skill that prepares a child to associate individual sounds to individual letters through direct instruction in first grade. This cannot happen unless children learn to distinguish sounds within words, and that is not easy. When we speak, individual sounds in words, and even whole words in sentences run together, making it hard to distinguish one sound from another. Early on, children must be taught to distinguish one sound from another until they can actually break a spoken word into its individual, constituent sounds in an activity called segmenting (Ball & Blachman, 1991).

The order of assessment and instruction for phonemic awareness is as follows:

- Matching sounds.
- Substituting sounds.
- Blending sounds into words.
- Segmenting sounds from spoken words.

The whole point of phonemic awareness is to teach children to segment spoken words into individual sounds like this:

Spoken Word: cat   /k/ /a/ /t/

Segmenting is the endpoint of instruction and, along with letter naming from CAP, it is the entry point into decoding instruction.

Phoneme counting is an important activity to understand for segmenting. Having the child listen to a word, say it slowly with the teacher, and then count the sounds in it is a very typical activity. Do be careful when reading test data. If you are asked to count phonemes on the test, do not be fooled when looking at letters. Remember that phonemic awareness deals with sounds, not letters, and that some letters are not heard in words (see Table 4.2).

TABLE 4.2

book	/b/ /u/ /k/	three sounds
cake	/c/ /A/ /k/	three sounds
rain	/r/ /A/ /n/	three sounds

Elkonin boxes are a way to make sounds heard in words concrete so that they can both be counted and identified. Since trying to segment a spoken word like /kar/ (*car*) into its constituent sounds can be hard (it seems to have only two sounds, /k/ and /r/), teachers use Elkonin sound boxes for instruction. Using a picture of a car, sound boxes drawn beneath it, and markers for the children to move into the boxes, teachers can instruct segmenting like this (see Figure 4.1).

In the activity above, the student looks at the picture and says the word /kar/. With the teacher's help, the child moves the markers up into the boxes while saying each *sound* (not letter) in order to make the sound segments concrete. Doing so helps the child to "see" the sounds in the word and to understand that spoken words are made up of individual phonemes. Later, those sounds will be attached to the letters that they can identify from CAP.

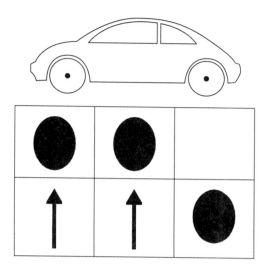

FIGURE 4.1   Sound Box

Assessment of phonemic awareness can take place formally, where the teacher reads or shows pictures to the child and asks him to identify initial sounds or to segment the spoken words into individual sounds. Results can be compared with other students in the class and needs can be targeted through small group or individual instruction. Assessment can also be informal, where the teacher simply asks a child to identify the sounds heard at the beginning, end, and middle of the child's name or in a simple, three-phoneme word like /mat/.

Games are frequently devised to teach children to become aware of sounds. The easiest starting point is with the child's own name or the names of other children. Children can be prompted to guess the names of their classmates after the teacher prompts them with a sound, or they can identify the initial sounds heard in their own or others' names when they are spoken (e.g., what do we hear at the start of Chris's name?). Such an activity will promote the notion that words are made up of individual sounds, even though we really only hear strings of sounds at once in spoken speech. Reading rhyming books or patterned books aloud to children can cue their awareness to sounds in the English language, too.

Be sure that you do not confuse phonemic awareness for phonics instruction. Phonemic awareness deals with sounds only and readies a child to associate individual sounds to letters; however, the activities do not use print when they are pure phonemic awareness activities (Williams, 1980). Phonics activities may import a sound from phonemic awareness, but they always include print.

As a final note on both concepts about print and phonemic awareness, please note that they are taught separately but consecutively:

- 9:00 A.M.   Concepts about Print Instruction
- 10:00 A.M.   Phonemic Awareness Instruction

Remember that the highest level of CAP (letter naming) and the highest level of phonemic awareness (segmenting) must be in place to begin decoding instruction, so it makes sense to ensure that they develop in tandem.

Decoding Instruction

Decoding instruction begins when the letter naming and segmenting are in place. Children in first, second, and third grades move through the process of learning to decode text. Look at Table 4.3 and familiarize yourself with the patterns. Pay particular attention to the distinction between phonics and regular and irregular sight word instruction since they are separate areas of instruction.

TABLE 4.3   Learning to Read

Kindergarten	First Grade	Second Grade	Third Grade
	Beginning Phonics		
		Intermediate Phonics	
			Advanced Phonics
Regular Sight Words		Irregular Sight Words	

Phonics instruction is distinct from sight word instruction. Consider the following sentence:

The cat sat on the mat.

This sentence contains two types of words. The sight words are underlined and the decodable words are not. Sight words are words that cannot be decoded easily. *The,* for example, ought to be pronounced /tuh-he/ or /th-eh/, but it isn't. So, sight words must be recognized and this ability must be taught.

Decodable words are those that the child can decode by looking at the letters and then seeing and saying the patterns: *c –at, s –at, m –at.* In order for a child to be able to read the sentence above, he or she will need to be able to recognize and automatically say the sight words, while also looking at the decodable words and "cracking" their codes.

Sight Words

Sight words are words that cannot be decoded easily, because the combinations of letters do not correspond to regular phonics rules. There are two categories of sight words: regular and irregular. Regular sight words are taught very early. They are words like *a, an, the, saw, was, here, there, on, by,* and so forth; they are called "regular" because they are both frequent and quite short. Irregular sight words are different. The words *though, threw, through, throughout,* and *thought* are examples. The pronunciation patterns are not stable across the words, even though they look very similar. They are hard to syllabicate, too, so normal decoding strategies may not apply to them. Emergent and developing readers must learn to recognize them automatically based on repetition or memorable features that distinguish one sight word from another sight word.

Look at Table 4.4 and note the span of instruction across the early grades.

Although the words are certainly not precise by grade level, you should note that the sight words that children are expected to recognize grow more and more complex as the time

TABLE 4.4   Sight Word Instruction

LEARNING TO READ			
Kindergarten	*First Grade*	*Second Grade*	*Third Grade*
Regular Sight Words a, an, the, was, saw, here, there, to, on		*Irregular Sight Words* though, through, thorough, throughout	

in school increases. Highly irregular sight words like *aforementioned* and *heretofore* would be among those introduced in later grades, given their complexity and infrequency in print.

One activity that will help students to learn sight words is to teach by feature and to underline each of the sight words as it appears in text to draw attention to it (Hennings, 2002). Visual discrimination is most effective, because students' attention is focused on these irregular words. Having students try to pronounce words like *though* and *throughout* is ineffective because the words do not follow regular phonetic patterns. Thus, another sense (like sight) must be used to teach these words, so that children can automatically recognize them in text.

Assessing sight words can take place using a list of words out of context and then in context. For example, sight words like *when, then, the, an,* and *who* can be assessed orally in a column and then in the context of a sentence. This allows the teacher to isolate the words that she wants to know if the child can recognize and to see if the child can identify the words out of context and within context.

Word walls are another common method. As children encounter sight words in print, they can be written or tacked to the word wall. The words can then be used in separate sight word activities (writing them down, sorting them by feature, etc.) or as cues when reading them in context.

Before moving into phonics instruction in greater detail, let's move from sight words that must be recognized automatically to decodable words that can be sounded out and decoded with some regularity.

Decodable Words

Decodable words are those words that the child can decode based on their letter combinations. Consider the words *cat, sat,* and *mat.* These words fit logical patterns, and if students can recognize the letter, the sound, and the common patter *–at,* they can say the word. Children can be taught to recognize *–at* and then learn to manipulate lettered index cards with *c, s,* and *m* to form the words *cat, sat,* and *mat* in decoding activities.

The way that sight word and decoding instruction mesh is as follows. First, recall the sample sentence that contains both sight and decodable words in it:

The cat sat on the mat.

As you now understand, children will need to know both sight words and decodable words to decode the text. You can imagine instruction to read the sentence to look like this:

- 9:00 A.M.   Sight Word Instruction (the, on)
- 10:00 A.M.   Decodable Word Instruction (*mat, cat, sat*)
- 11:00 A.M.   Practice (*The cat sat on the mat.*)

TABLE 4.5   Decoding Instruction

LEARNING TO READ			
Kindergarten	*First Grade*	*Second Grade*	*Third Grade*
Letter Names Sound Segments	*Beginning Phonics* Letter Sounds Onsets/Rimes		
		Intermediate Phonics Blends/Digraphs Vowel Patterns Phonics Rules	
			Advanced Phonics Syllables Fluent Decoding
	Regular Sight Words	Irregular Sight Words	

Decoding instruction needs more discussion. You need to understand beginning, intermediate, and advanced phonics instruction for the test. Look at Table 4.5 and note the progression of instruction. Though some of the terms might be unfamiliar to you, just try to get a sense of the progression for now.

Look at kindergarten first and recall that students are supposed to leave kindergarten knowing their letter names and their sound segments. That is because they will then associate the letters and sounds together in first grade during beginning phonics instruction. This is important because many letters in the English alphabet do not follow the alphabetic principle. The alphabetic principle is that one letter represents one sound. That works for words like *ape* and *ace,* since the letter *a* says its name in each word. But now think of words like *apple, ant,* and *aunt.* As you can see, there are many variant sounds (allophones) associated with just the letter *a.* Thus, learning to read English is challenging because it is a phonetically irregular language.

Table 4.5 also shows that instruction moves from letter–sound correspondence to onset/rime instruction during beginning phonics instruction to more complex elements of print during intermediate and advanced instruction (blends, digraphs, rules, and polysyllabic words). This is because the goal is to have children who can fluently decode print by the end of third grade, so that instruction can then focus exclusively on comprehension. Note that sight word instruction parallels decoding instruction and also increases in complexity.

Beginning Phonics Instruction.   Let's now look more closely at decoding instruction, so that you will be prepared to answer questions about it on the test.

As you know, decoding instruction begins with letter–sound correspondence and then moves on to decoding simple onsets and rimes in simple consonant–vowel–consonant (CVC) words (e.g., *cat, sat, hat,* and *mat*). Learning to decode words like these focuses on consonants first, because they are easiest to recognize especially in initial position. Early decoding activities teach children to decode words by word family using simple onsets and rimes. Onsets are the first consonant or consonants in a syllable, and the rime is the vowel you hear in the word plus any consonants that follow it. Consider the common onsets and rimes in Table 4.6:

TABLE 4.6

ONSETS	RIMES
C	-at
M	-an
T	-ake

Look at all of the simple, monosyllabic (one) syllable words we can make from these onsets and rimes: *cat, can, cake, mat, man, make, tan, cake, make, take.* Beginning phonics instruction focuses on these decodable words using these easy-to-generalize patterns. Along with sight words, the decodable words can be used in simple decodable sentences that the children can begin to decode independently.

Intermediate Phonics Instruction. Phonics instruction increases in complexity, moving far beyond decoding simple onsets and rimes. During this phase, more complicated letter patterns and positions are used for instruction. Initial positions of letters are easy to recognize, but final and medial positions (in that order) are more challenging. Furthermore, letter combinations become more complicated. There are two types of letter combinations to know for the test. These are blends and digraphs. Blends are two or more consonants together and each consonant can be heard. Digraphs bring two or more letters together to make only one sound. To help keep blends and digraphs straight, just remember that the "bl" in blend is a blend (you can hear the *b* and *l*), and the "ph" in digraph is a digraph (you hear only one sound, not *puh-huh*).

See Table 4.7 for examples of each type of combination:

TABLE 4.7

CONSONANT DIGRAPHS	CONSONANT BLENDS
this	ship
with	blue
stop	bend

The examples in Table 4.7 contain consonant digraphs and blends. The digraphs are *th* and *sh*. Note the position of each digraph. The test maker wants you understand that digraph position presents its own challenges to children learning to decode digraphs: In the initial position, they are easier to recognize (**th**is, **sh**ip); but in the final position, they are more difficult (wi**th**). If you are asked questions on sequencing instruction, try to keep the "position" principle in mind.

Consonant blends in the example include *bl, st,* and *nd.* Again position plays a role in sequencing instruction because of the position principle. Activities to teach either digraphs or blends are the same as what you saw earlier with simple onsets and rimes. Index cards with the digraph or blend written on them can be paired with common onset to form words. This type of activity is appropriate for virtually all areas of phonics instruction.

There is another type of digraph and blend that you need to know for the test. These are called vowel digraphs and blends. The terms are the same here: Vowel digraphs contain vowels that come together to make one sound; vowel blends, on the other hand, bring vowels together to form two or more sounds (see Table 4.8).

TABLE 4.8

VOWEL DIGRAPHS	VOWEL BLENDS
paint	coil
meet	sow
boat	boy
tow	royal

As the table shows, vowel digraphs bring *ai, ee,* and *oa* together to make long vowel sounds (the vowel letter names for *a, e,* and *o*). Vowel digraphs are difficult, because there are many variations in how the patterns are decoded. Consider *ow* for example. As a digraph, it makes *tow, row,* and *bow;* however, it also makes variants like *cow* and *sow,* which are vowel blends (discussed next). The letter combinations, *oa* and *ee* are relatively stable since their pronunciations do not vary wildly, but the rest of the digraphs have many short and long vowel associations attached to them. This makes vowel digraphs a challenging area of decoding instruction.

Now let's look at vowel blends. Vowel blends bring two vowels or letters together to make two or more distinct sounds. Say the words *coil, cow,* and *boy* to yourself. You should have noticed that you said more than just one vowel sound when saying these words. That is because vowel blends are also **vowel diphthongs.** A diphthong contains two vowels that make up two distinct sounds. So, *coil, toy, ouch,* and *bow* (as in "take a bow") all have diphthongs in them. In fact, *coil* /koyul/ and *royal* /royul/ are **triphthongs,** since they have three separate vowel sounds in them.

Phonics Rules.   Phonics instruction grows even more complex as it turns to phonics rules. Phonics rules are also called phonics generalizations, and they are dependable patterns that can be extended across many kinds of words. These rules are easily recognized from common sense (phonics is *not* rocket science).

The easiest rules to remember for the test are ones that you already know from experience.

- Consonant-Vowel-Consonant (CVC) and Consonant-Vowel-Consonant-Consonant (CVCC) Patterns: The medial vowel is usually short, as in *cat, sat, bet, set, mitt, sit, lot, hot, but, rut,* and *tack, sack, with.*
- CVCe (silent e) Patterns: The silent e makes the medial vowel long or it says its name: *name, mite, cove, mute.* There are exceptions: love and have.
- Two Sounds of C: When *c* is followed by *e, i,* or *y,* it sounds like /s/: *cereal, city,* and *cytoplasm.* It is hard like /k/ elsewhere: *cat* and *cot.*
- Two Sounds of G: When *g* is followed by *y* or silent *e,* it sounds soft like /j/: *gym* and **garage.** It is hard like /g/ elsewhere: *get, got,* **ga*rage.*

- VV patterns usually make the first vowel long and it says it name as in *main, each, moan,* but there are many exceptions. The combination *oo,* for example, makes *book, look, took,* but also *spool* and *fool.* Also, *ou* makes the */oo/* in *through* and the */O/* in *though.* The most stable patterns to remember are *oa* and *ee,* since their long vowel associations (/O/ and /E/ respectively) remain constant (Bear, Invernizzi, Templeton, & Johnston, 2000).
- R-Control: Some words are hard to read or spell because the *r* is overpowering or says its name. Examples: *car, tar, bar, far, bird, curb.*

The Word Sort. Before discussing advanced phonics instruction, let's close with the most common activity used to instruct all of the aforementioned areas: the word sort. Here, children sort word cards into two or more piles based on their sound. For example, when learning to read and write words based on the hard and soft *c* phonics rules, the children will sort the words *city, cereal,* and *cytoplasm* into one pile and *cat, cot,* and *cut* into another pile. This activity helps the children recognize patterns that help us when reading and writing both familiar and unfamiliar words according to these generalizable patterns (see Figure 4.2).

FIGURE 4.2

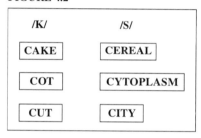

Such an activity will work for short onsets/rimes, vowel digraphs and blends, and all of the phonics rules. Sight words, too, can be instructed in this way, even though they are not decodable. Sight word sorts have the children learning to automatically recognize sight words based on features that they can recall within the words (see Figure 4.3):

FIGURE 4.3

The point is to teach children to automatically recognize words in isolation before having them return to text, so that they can say them immediately when they see them in context.

Advanced Phonics Instruction. The ultimate aim of decoding instruction is fluency. By third grade, all children are expected to be able to fluently decode print. Remedial instruction in problematic areas of print takes place until print is no longer an issue for them. This is because of a singular idea that we will revisit again: *Fluency enables comprehension.* If children cannot decode text fluently, then they spend their time making and correcting errors. Since their attention focused on struggling through the text, the idea is that they will not have enough attention left over to comprehend what they have decoded. Plus, decoding errors can simply interfere with comprehension. Decoding *car* for *cat* throughout a passage on kittens will leave the reader with a vastly different impression from what the author had in mind. Thus, fluency is critical for comprehension; and that is why kindergarten through third grade instruction is so preoccupied with teaching children to rely on print.

Polysyllabic Words

So, the last area that children need to be able to handle are multisyllabic words. After learning how to manage simple and complex onsets and rimes, phonics rules, and regular sight and irregular sight words, polysyllabic words become the focus. Let's look at how this type of instruction is handled.

Decoding polysyllabic words (words with more than one syllable) probably emerges later in development. To be fluent decoders, children must be able to handle these kinds of words. Polysyllabic words are challenging, because many of them are made up of open and closed syllables. An open syllable is one without a consonant in the rime; a closed syllable has a consonant in the rime. Let's look at the difference. Put your hand under your chin and say the following words:

- Mama
- Dada
- Haha

Each time your chin dropped, you marked a syllable. Syllables are built around the vowels that we can hear in words. Each of the example words has two syllables: *ma / ma, da / da*, and *ha / ha*. Each of these syllables is open, because there is no consonant in the rime. Now say these words (hand under chin) for a contrast:

- Batman
- Catman
- Antman

These polysyllabic words have two closed syllables in them, because there are consonants in the rime positions of the syllables: *bat / man, cat / man, ant / man*. Decoding polysyllabic words with open and closed constituents is important, because upper elementary texts are filled with them. Consider the four types of polysyllabic words (Vacca & Vacca, 1989):

- Compound words, like *Batman, toolbox,* and *weathermen.*
- Complex words with prefixes and suffixes, like *unrecognizable* and *antidisestablishmentarianism.*
- Decodable words, like *calculus* and *elephant.*
- Irregular words, like *Wednesday* and *February.*

Being able to decode polysyllabic words and complicated sight words (*throughout, however, therefore*) fluently are the requisites for moving from the learning-to-read stage into the reading-to-learn stage.

Some types of polysyllabic words are the result of adding certain inflectional affixes. Consider what happens when adding *–ed* and *–ing* to some words (see Table 4.9):

TABLE 4.9

-ED		-ING	
run	runned	run	running
pin	pinned	pin	pinning
step	stepped	step	stepping

Doubling these consonants occurs in English to preserve the short vowel sounds in each of these words, *run, pin, step,* when adding *–ed* and *–ing.* It is possible that you may see decoding data that has a child decoding words with inflectional affixes like this: */run/ /ed/,* */pin/ /ed/,* or */step/ /ping/.* Obviously, these would have to be corrected. The appropriate type of activity would involve word cards and would be performed like a word sort:

Here, each card would be read separately before being united and read as one word.

running

The teacher would then return to the text and ask the child to read words with these types of inflectional endings within the context of print.

Fluency

Fluent decoding of complex, polysyllabic text separates learning to read and reading to learn. Fluency is the ultimate aim of instruction and refers to smooth and accurate decoding of text. Once children can decode text fluently and accurately, then they are ready to focus on comprehending vocabulary and the text itself (Adams, 1990).

Fluency is defined as reading a text at a good rate of speed and with correct intonation. Reading accurately but too slowly, for example, may mean that the child is focusing too much on the print and not enough on the meaning of the passage. Both areas could be separate targets of instruction if deficiencies are present in either aspect. After students become fluent, they will be able to devote the majority of their attention to textual meaning and comprehension.

Three types of activities are appropriate for fluency. The first is for increasing speed. Repeated reading of familiar texts at the child's independent reading level is always appropriate, whether it is followed by a discussion, done in pairs, of performed with a tape recorder (Samuels, 1997). The second activity is for eliminating flat and monotone reading behaviors. Choral and echo reading activities where the teacher models how to read a passage that has been copied and highlighted to emphasize a rising and falling voice are appropriate (McCauley & McCauley, 1992). The last activity is for repeating behaviors, where the child repeats words, phrases, or whole sentences. This behavior is usually due to lack of confidence (trying to confirm what one has read), or it may be a simple directionality problem. In either case, a scaffold like running the finger beneath the text can help or the edge of a note card can be used to guide the child. *It is important to wean the child off using either the finger or the note card eventually, as these crutches can interfere with fluency later on.* Note also that that the texts used for repeated readings are always familiar and are at the child's independent reading level (to be discussed in Content Area Four: Assessment).

Spelling Development

One area of instruction that spans kindergarten and beyond is spelling instruction. This section will describe spelling instruction for primary and upper elementary students that you need to know for the test. The terminology associated with spelling instruction will be presented first, before examples of analysis and instructional methods are described for you.

The terms, *prephonetic, phonetic, transitional,* and *conventional,* are used to in many of the test registration bulletins to characterize the stage in which a student's spelling can be categorized. An important idea is that children move through each of these stages on their way to becoming proficient spellers. The following are characteristics for each stage that you should know for the test (adapted from Bear & Barone, 1989; Bear & Templeton, 1998; Invernizzi, Abouzeid, & Bloodgood, 1997):

The **prephonetic stage** describes the spelling that one sees in the writing of children who have little to no knowledge of spelling. Here, children will often scribble when asked to spell words, because they have not yet learned to associate the sounds that they hear with letters. Later, the scribbling may include discernable lines or symbols that look like regular print. This reflects a child's emerging awareness of the symbolic nature of language. Invented spelling is common at this stage, where children write random symbols or draw pictures of words they are asked to spell. Invented spelling is important, because this will tell you how a child's spelling falls along a continuum of spelling development (from prephonetic to conventional).

The **phonetic stage** begins when the child begins to write letters to represent the dominant sounds she hears in words. Phonetic spellings show development in associating sounds to letters. This stage depends greatly on how much prior knowledge and instruction the child has had in *encoding orthographic letter patterns.* Sounds pretty serious, huh? All that means is that the child can form the appropriate letters based on the sounds she hears and can write common letter combinations.

The **transitional stage** represents a level where the child encodes all of the dominant sounds heard in the word and *attempts* to include the complexities found in words. Spelling a word like "bread" as *brade* is an example of this stage of development, since the child is attempting to encode a complicated vowel digraph (**ea**) by adding a silent *e* to the end of the word. This stage reflects very late development and is a goal of spelling instruction.

The **conventional stage** in spelling is the stage where children correctly spell the majority of words they write. This does not mean that they spell every word correctly, though. Common misspellings at this stage include words like, "*independance*" and "*confidant.*" In the upper-elementary grades, children at this stage of development will use spelling to increase vocabulary, particularly *content-area vocabularies,* as they learn to spell words that use prefixes, suffixes, and roots. A full discussion of this area of spelling instruction will take place when vocabulary instruction is covered later in this chapter.

Let's look at these concepts in context. Table 4.10 illustrates spellings that typify each stage of development (all data are hypothetical):

TABLE 4.10 Spelling Stages

Pre-phonetic	Phonetic	Transitional	Conventional
	t r	Tre	tree

Each of the spelling data for the word *tree* reflects the spelling stages that you need to know for the test. The prephonetic example for *tree* shows that the child moves from pre-phonetic scribbling to phonetic encoding (writing) the most dominant sounds heard in the word—the consonant blend *tr*. In the transitional stage, the child has successfully encoded all of the dominant sounds heard in the word. The child would need instruction in encoding long vowel patterns to move into the conventional stage.

Activities like words sorts (that end by having the child write the words down in lists) or spelling activities, such as writing words in the *–at* family, are common. Elkonin **word boxes** are also typical; *though word boxes are <u>never</u> used during phonemic aware-ness, only sound boxes are.* Word boxes help children hear sounds in words where the vowels or other sounds are hard to discern (as in r-control words) by first marking the sounds and then adding the letters.

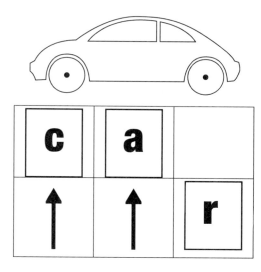

FIGURE 4.4   Word Box

In Figure 4.4, children have the opportunity to identify the sounds first, make sound letter associations next, and then spell the words using tiles. This way, they can learn to spell words that are inherently difficult because of the particular features within them. This type of activity is also appropriate for students who are reluctant to spell words because they are afraid that they might misspell them. Word boxes help to elicit a response from the child, because the child can write what she thinks she hears in the word by pronouncing the word to herself and then writing it down. The word boxes can then be used to compare what the child said with what she had written down and to provide her with a strategy that she can use when spelling unfamiliar words and to reduce her anxiety about spelling.

For questions at upper elementary levels, keep in mind that the spelling of one word can reveal how to spell a very similar word. Consider the following:

- Nature: Natural
- Critic: Criticism
- Special: Specialist

Teaching words in this manner will help students develop an awareness of how words and their spellings relate to one another. In upper elementary classrooms, children can be taught to spell words based on Greek and Latin roots as shown in Figure 4.5.

FIGURE 4.5

This can take place in the content areas, too. For example, children can be taught to spell scientific terms like *thermal, microscope, thermometer, meter, centimeter,* and *sphygmomanometer* within the context of content area vocabulary instruction.

Vocabulary

Extensive oral vocabulary fosters comprehension. Once a child can decode a word correctly, he will comprehend it because what he has decoded will register meaning in his mind. Consider the written word *cat.* If the word is in the child's oral vocabulary and he understands its meaning, then it is likely to register when the word is decoded the for the first time. Vocabulary in upper elementary classrooms is beyond this level and vocabulary from the sciences can be very elusive. Decoding a word like *entropy* for the first time might not help one comprehend it. Adding its definition as the *second law of thermodynamics* might not help much either, because the word is conceptual in nature and highly specialized. Highly complex words like *antidisestablishmentarianism* present their own challenges, because they are polysyllabic and contain many derivational affixes. Thus, vocabulary in upper elementary classrooms requires a variety of strategies. However, without these strategies comprehending what one reads might not be possible.

To understand the challenges that children face when learning upper elementary vocabulary, you need to know about the five types of words that they may encounter in text (Armbruster & Nagy, 1992; Dunn & Graves, 1987):

- *Words that they know when reading and use when speaking.* These vocabulary words are the most accessible words to children, because the meanings "register" when they read them. For example, when they encounter the word *cat* for the first time and decode it, it is likely that they will understand the word if it is already part of their spoken vocabulary. The only real challenge here is to decode the word correctly.
- *Words they know connotatively or denotatively.* Often, there are differences between a word's **connotative** and **denotative** meaning. Connotation is a word's implied meaning, and denotation is a word's "dictionary definition." Many words that we use in English acquire connotative meanings through use and change, thus acquiring meaning outside of their dictionary definition. The word *cool* is a good example. The denotative meaning of *cool* is something "cold to the touch" or "below room temperature." If we hear students say, "Ms. Johnson is a really cool teacher," they are using the word connotatively to mean that the teacher is "hip" or "nice" or "aware." Obviously, if a student is aware of only one type of meaning for a particular word, then she will take away an entirely different meaning of the above sentence. Understanding "Mrs. Johnson is below room temperature" would be a strict denotative understanding of the word "cool."
- *Words that they know when reading but rarely use when speaking.* The most obvious examples of such words are those like *heretofore* and *aforementioned.* They represent words that we know in reading, but probably rarely use in casual conversation. As children read more and more varieties of text, they will develop a reading vocabulary that includes words like these and the collection may exceed their spoken vocabularies. Homographs, too, can present challenges. Knowing whether to say *mínute* or *minúte* depends on context: *Give me a minute* or *that sample is minute* may not be readily discernable to students when first encountered in print.
- *Words that they have seen before in only certain spoken or written contexts.* The target vocabulary of developmental activities are the words that the student knows only in certain contexts and words that are completely unfamiliar to her. Homophones fit this category and are words that sound the same but are spelled differently (for example, *their, there,* and *they're*). The child might have been saying the word *they're* for years, but not recognize it immediately when reading it for the first time. Confusion in writing may also occur with homophones like *site, cite,* and *sight,* when the child does not have a firm grasp on the spelling and usage of each word.
- *Words that they have never seen before or have never used when speaking.* Highly specialized vocabulary words from the content areas, like *entropy,* name concepts that they child might not have any clue about. So, even if words like these are decoded correctly, they will not conjure a familiar idea and register meaning. Structurally complex words fall into this category. For example, the difference between *denationalization* and *internationalization* might not be immediately recognizable unless the child has particular skills to "get at" the meaning of each word.

Please note that the variety of upper elementary words that you will focus on here are ones that are beyond the simple word recognition level. Teaching *word recognition* is different from instructing *word meaning.* In the former, one asks the students to see and say a word; whereas in the latter, one asks the students not only to see and say the word, but also to understand it. Early on, word *recognition* can be taught by reading the words aloud to the children while they look at the words and then write them down. This is also thought to determine their level of vocabulary development, because if they cannot decode the word fluently, then they will not be able to comprehend it while reading.

Early word *meaning* instruction can be taught by simply previewing the passage, pulling difficult vocabulary out, and preteaching the terms to the students before they either read it alone or with the teacher. In addition, reading aloud to children is another early word meaning activity. Here, you reduce the decoding demands on the student by reading to them and discussing any unfamiliar words with them as you go along. Actively questioning and discussing the words with them will help to engage their attention and, hopefully, lead to their understanding of the words in context. Please recognize that this is **not** an effective way to teach **decoding:** When teaching decoding, have the students decode text. When teaching early comprehension, take attention off of decoding and focus it on understanding and context.

These considerations lead us to consider how to instruct higher-level vocabulary words, particularly during the reading-to-learn process for children in grades four and above. Table 4.11 presents these considerations.

TABLE 4.11   Reading-to-Learn (Vocabulary)

VOCABULARY DEVELOPMENT			
Third	*Fourth*	*Fifth*	*Sixth–Eighth*
Syllabication	*Structural Analysis*	*Roots*	*Etymology*
■ Polysyllabic words ■ Open/closed syllables	■ Inflections ■ Derivations	■ Greek and Latin roots	■ Word origins ■ Word history

By the end of third grade, children are expected to be able to successfully decode text, particularly polysyllabic words. We discussed activities associated with decoding text when we presented polysyllabic words during the learning-to-read process. The important idea to keep in mind is that children need to leave the third grade with the ability to syllabicate, because **syllabication** will allow students in upper elementary grades to apply structural analysis to highly complex words.

You learned about **structural analysis** in Chapter 3, when we discussed both *morphology* and *semantics*. Here is how it applies to vocabulary instruction. Consider these two polysyllabic words: *chimpanzee* and *denationalization*. In the case of the former, syllabicating the word might trigger an image in the child's mind if the word is in the child's spoken repertoire; in the latter example, an image might not come to mind, because the word is not part of the child's spoken vocabulary. Thus, a different set of activities will be required for each word as shown in Table 4.12.

In the case of *chimpanzee*, getting at the meaning of the word is a matter of syllabicating the word and saying it correctly. There is nothing to analyze structurally within the word, because it has no prefixes, suffixes, or root words. *Denationalization*, on the other hand, requires a number of skills that the child must learn in order to comprehend what the word means. To structurally analyze the word, the child needs to be able not only to syllabicate but also to identify base words, roots, prefixes, and suffixes. Skills in these areas can be applied to vocabulary strategies that the child can use when reading.

TABLE 4.12

CHIMPANZEE	DENATIONALIZATION
1. Recognize the letters.	1. Recognize the letters.
2. Syllabicate the word.	2. Syllabicate the word.
3. Say the whole word.	3. Find the base or root word (*nation*).
	4. Identify suffixes and their meaning (*-al, -ize, -ation*).
	5. Identify the prefix and its meaning (*de-*).
	6. Reassemble and say the word.
	7. Check context.

Root word instruction and instruction in **etymology** can also help to develop a child's vocabulary. In the former, having children learn a root word like *tele* and then apply it to a list of words like *telephone, telegraph,* and *telex* will provide them with a tool to access complex vocabulary words. In addition, students can create root word webs and connect them together to see how words relate to one another (see Figure 4.6).

FIGURE 4.6

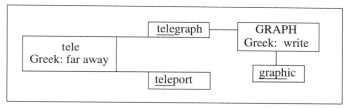

Etymology can also help with teaching word meaning. Activities for etymological studies can be applied to the names of the months or the days of the week as shown in Table 4.13:

TABLE 4.13

December	Tenth Month
November	Ninth Month
October	Eighth Month
Wednesday	Odin's Day

Such an activity can lead to discussions of why the calendar only had ten months in it at one time, who Odin was and why a day of the week was named after him, along with how the spellings of many words give clues to their origins and meanings. Note that looking up words in a dictionary, although an important skill, takes place in a particular context, mainly during etymology research. These skills must be taught and applied explicitly though please recognize that this activity is not used for either word recognition or word meaning, because it is too cumbersome and time consuming. The dictionary is also appropriate when one needs to understand how to pronounce an unfamiliar word that does not follow regular phonics generalizations. For example, *archaeopserinx* and *rhamphorincus* have many letter combinations that are not common in English; therefore, a dictionary will be helpful when determining how to say these words correctly.

At this point, you must be wondering: Where is context? In the test maker's view, context is a wholly unreliable predictor of a word's meaning, so it is deemphasized in this model in favor of relying on the print and the structure of a word to get at its meaning. For some words, though, context is the only way to know what word is correct, appropriate, or how it is pronounced in a sentence. This is particularly true for homophones and homographs:

- Homographs: The sample is **minute.** Give me a **minute.**
- Homophones: I need to go _____. (there, their, or they're?)

The only way to know where to place the stress on the word *minute* depends entirely on context. Similarly, the only way to know which *there* to use is also based on context. Thus, context does play a role in the exam, but it is relegated to this level and should not be your first choice when answering questions on vocabulary.

One important activity to know for the exam that combines print, grammar, and meaning together into one activity is called the *cloze* activity. Cloze activities are nothing more than fill-in-the-blank activities that require children to rely on visual information, syntactic (grammar) information, and semantic (meaning) information to complete the activities. Cloze procedures are also common ways to test comprehension, because they ask students to construct meaning from what they read in order to fill in the blanks with words that make the most sense in the passage (Barnitz, 1998).

Sometimes, cloze activities are used to assess a student's ability to use visual, syntactic, and semantic information to supply correct words within sentences. Consider the examples in Table 4.14:

TABLE 4.14   Grammar and Comprehension Cloze Activities

EXAMPLE ONE	EXAMPLE TWO
Give me ____ apple.	Literary _____ are common. They are _____ that compare unlike things. For example, _____ use *like* or *as,*
I bought ____ car.	but _____ use neither one.
a, an	*analogies, symbols, similes, metaphors*

Example one targets a grammar point. Here, it is assessing a student's knowledge of when to use *a* or *an,* and that depends on visual information and their knowledge of English syntax: If the noun that follows the article begins with a vowel, use *an;* if the noun begins with a consonant, use *a.* In the second example, relying on semantic clues (called, "cues") is required to identify the appropriate word for each blank. This cloze activity assesses a student's knowledge of literary terminology and the vocabulary words related to literary analogies (to be covered in Chapter 5). In both cases, cloze activities can assess and teach vocabulary, though their purposes vary depending on the focus of the instruction.

A note on assessment: Assessment of word recognition and of meaning should use the words both in isolation and in context. This will ensure that the child has the opportunity to demonstrate word recognition skills in both contexts and the teacher will have a better picture of what the child can and cannot do. During oral assessments of vocabulary and reading, the teacher's role is to record the behaviors and to assess the student's ability.

No interventions are permitted, such as supplying words or helping the student successfully decode the text or print, for either word recognition or meaning assessment.

Comprehension

Recall that fluency is the gateway to comprehension in this model and that by grade three, children are expected to be able to decode print fluently. This skill will enable them to have the opportunity to comprehend what they read. The test makers divide comprehension into two categories: *listening comprehension* and *reading comprehension*. Reading comprehension itself is further divided into literal, inferential, and evaluative comprehension. Review the model in Table 4.15 to get a sense of how these areas relate to one another across grade levels.

TABLE 4.15 Comprehension Instruction

KINDERGARTEN	FIRST	SECOND	THIRD	FOURTH	FIFTH +
Listening Comprehension		*Reading Comprehension*			
			Literal	Inferential	Evaluative

Comprehension, particularly listening comprehension, is taught early in grades K–3, but **not** during decoding instruction. Since focusing on comprehension during decoding instruction would take attention away from print, it is not part of decoding instruction. Thus, listening comprehension **is** taught to children during the learning-to-read process, though it is done in activities separate from what the teacher undertakes to instruct print. The day might look like this:

- 9:00 A.M.   Decoding Instruction
- 9:30 A.M.   Oral Reading and Listening Comprehension

For example, after decoding instruction, children might be read to for a period of time and would then be asked to retell the story. Oral retellings are a common means of assessing comprehension. The teacher can direct a question to the children about the plot, sequence, or characters in the story. To ensure the effectiveness of this assessment, the teacher would have to preview and list the most important characteristics that the students must include, along with notes about how much prompting the teacher had to provide to elicit such responses.

Another activity can ask children to draw the stories based on what they have heard, since having a goal beyond the reading is also important to keep them engaged during the reading. After hearing the story, the children can draw a picture of the main character and his or her adventure. After drawing the picture, the children can then narrate their stories to the teacher to foster early literacy development. Not only will such an activity keep them engaged, it will also give children with other learning styles the opportunity to use those abilities to express themselves. In summary, all of these activities will prepare children for *reading-to-learn.*

Since comprehension is the primary focus of the *reading-to-learn process* in upper elementary grades, let's look carefully at literal, inferential, and evaluative comprehension (see Table 4.16).

TABLE 4.16 Reading to Learn (Comprehension)

COMPREHENSION DEVELOPMENT		
Late Second–Third	*Fourth–Fifth*	*Sixth–Eighth*
Literal	*Inferential*	*Evaluative*
Factual questions	How and why questions	Fact, opinion, propaganda

The sequence of instruction in this model moves from the easiest to more complicated tasks. Literal comprehension is seen as being easier than inferential comprehension, and evaluative comprehension is viewed as the highest level of all. In addition, one area depends on another area: Without literal comprehension there will be no inferential comprehension; without inferential comprehension, there will be no evaluative comprehension.

Literal Comprehension. Literal comprehension is the most basic level of comprehension. Children learn to answer basic factual questions, like simple *wh-* questions: *who, what, where,* and *when.* Sequences and details are also very important for literal comprehension. Having students list events in the order in which they took place in a story is one way that teachers instruct and assess a student's literal comprehension. Students are not asked to make inferences nor to evaluate the events at this point, but merely to list the events and the details in order to ensure that they have understood the factual elements presented in the text.

Inferential Comprehension. Inferential comprehension is a higher level of comprehension. Here, the teacher asks students to make inferences about what they have understood literally. In this stage, students learn to answer more challenging questions about **how** and **why** things happen in a story. The teacher can ask them to generate alternative endings to the stories they have read or have heard that are consistent with what the main character would probably do. The teacher can then determine whether the students' literal understandings were sufficient to make the correct inferential assumptions about the character. In summary, if children do not have literal comprehension, they will not be able to make correct inferences about how and why things happened; and this will be reflected in their retellings and answers to inferential questions.

Evaluative Comprehension. Evaluative or critical comprehension is the highest level of all. Instruction in this advanced area takes place after students are proficient in comprehending what they read or hear both literally and inferentially. Critical thinking involves identifying reason and logic in a text to determine whether the author's point is valid, reliable, and worth considering or whether a work represents fact, opinion, or propaganda. Evaluative comprehension of a literary work would also consider how well each part of the work functions as a whole. This moves beyond merely analyzing character, plot, setting, and the like into asking students to think about whether the novel holds together through each chapter of the text and whether the main and subplot lines are believable and effective when viewed comprehensively.

Nonfiction stories from news articles can also be evaluated for instances of bias and propaganda. Copies of news articles and editorials can be circulated, and the students can categorize them into fact and opinion piles and then justify their decisions. Such an activity will help the students recognize when text contains only facts and when it also incorporates opinions in the passage. Another type of activity asks students to outline the major points found in an article or a speech and then asks them to propose alternative arguments to each point that they have identified. Students can research alternative ideas for the purpose of comparing what they have found with what the author has proposed. Comparing and contrasting ideas moves beyond mere literal and inferential comprehension into evaluating ideas. In this way, students learn to be critical readers who can identify facts, opinions, and propaganda in the articles they read.

The types of text being read is the final area to consider in the reading-to-learn stage. Chapter 5 is devoted to the language arts and will explore these areas in greater detail, so we will only introduce you to the major concepts here.

The test makers divide texts into two separate categories: narrative and expository. Narrative texts are short stories, novels, and other works of fiction, while expository texts are informational pieces that include reading in the content areas (science, math, social studies, math word problems, etc.). Text type is important because the organizational patterns of each category is different. Narrative text, for example, has plot, setting, characters, and action, whereas expository texts often have only lists of details, comparisons and contrasts, and are otherwise hard to understand because they use language in highly specialized ways (e.g., word problems requiring proportions).

Schemata

Because students may need explicit instruction in the organizational patterns of text in order to comprehend what they decode fluently, let's learn about each type of text now.

Schemata is the organizational format of text. Children acquire narrative text schema from direct experiences such as having stories read to them and even from watching cartoons on television. They learn to anticipate characters, plots, and setting, however rudimentary, through these experiences. As a result, narrative text comprehension tends to precede expository text comprehension. Expository text is different. Its organizational pattern, especially in mathematics, may be very abstract. A child who reads a text about different types of butterflies might get lost in the details, because she goes into the reading expecting a story but finds neither characters and nor action to speak of. She finds the text difficult to comprehend, because she lacks the mental framework necessary to follow the organizational schemata of the text. Thus, this will have to be taught explicitly.

Table 4.17 on page 130 presents the two basic organizational patterns to know for the test.

Briefly, narrative schemata includes story sequence, grammar, and something else that you will learn about in Chapter Five called *Freitag's Pyramid*. Stories are a part of the life of classrooms from kindergarten through the eighth grade, though in the early grades (where either the foundations of decoding or decoding itself is the focus) narrative schemata are developed mainly through listening and other oral language activities. Expository schemata, on the other hand, are more elusive, because they are not as accessible as narrative schemata. This is because expository schemata involve abstract thinking, understanding cause and effect patterns, and evaluating proposed solutions to described problems.

TABLE 4.17   Story Schemata

KINDERGARTEN–EIGHTH GRADE	FOURTH–EIGHTH GRADE
Narrative Schemata	*Expository Schemata*
■ Story sequence	■ Details
■ Story grammar (plot, character, setting)	■ Sequence
■ Freitag's Pyramid (background, plot, rising action, climax, resolution)	■ Cause/effect
	■ Comparison/contrast
	■ Problems/solutions

Activities for teaching children to comprehend each type of text differ, yet they all share a common pattern for prereading, during reading, and post reading. Let's look at the basic structure of all schemata activities as they relate to narrative and expository text reading (see Table 4.18). Note: The descriptions here will be brief for both narrative and expository text activities, because they will be discussed in detail in Chapters Five and Six.

TABLE 4.18   Structuring Reading Instruction

PREREADING	DURING READING	POST READING
■ Prior knowledge	■ Think aloud	■ Literary response
■ Advanced organizing	■ Graphic organizers	■ Research process

Prereading, during-, and post-reading activities are very important in teaching children to comprehend narrative text. They learn to access their prior knowledge before they read a story, to stay engaged in the reading as they read the text, to develop story maps while they read, and to elaborate and extend their knowledge after they have read something. As students become more and more capable readers, they are asked to focus more and more on story elements, like figurative language, character types, and themes, along with engaging in more challenging tasks such as comparing stories cross-culturally and thematically. In short, teaching children to access narrative text schemata is critical to the reading-to-learn process.

Expository text comprehension is also highly dependent upon schematic patterns. Students need to learn how to read a variety of texts that are organized around lists of details, sequences, cause–effect patterns, and problems–solutions. Prereading, during-, and post-reading activities are very important here, as well. Students need to learn how to access prior knowledge and to apply it to the text as they read. Furthermore, they need to learn how to make expository text schemata concrete through various types of visual aids, including Venn diagrams, concept maps, and basic outlines. Finally, students need to learn to elaborate and extend the knowledge that they cull from an expository text though other experiences like the writing and research process (to be discussed in Chapter Six).

Now that you have some idea of the learning-to-read and reading-to-learn process, our next major area of focus is on how reading is assessed in this model of literacy instruction. You will see the major assessment models presented next.

CONTENT AREA FOUR: ASSESSMENT

There are two types of assessment to know for the exam. These are individual and group (standardized or norm-referenced) tests. Individual assessment tells you what an individual student can do at one point in time (IRIs) or over time (portfolio evaluation). Group assessment tells you about one moment in time and allows for between group comparisons (individual student and her class, a class with another class, or a school district with another school district). Let's begin with the informal reading inventory.

Informal Reading Inventories (IRIs)

Informal reading inventories include graded word lists and graded reading passages. If you have a fourth-grade student, you start with a wordlist at about a second-grade level. You keep moving up the word lists, until you find the grade level that frustrates the child (where he misses more than 20 percent of the words on a list).

The next step is to have the student read the graded passages. If the frustration level for a fourth grader was at a fourth-grade level, you drop back a grade and start assessing at the third-grade level. You have the child read the passages and note any deletions, substitutions (reading *cat* for *can,* for example), and mispronunciations. After the child reads a passage, you perform the following calculation (Clay, 1993b):

$$\frac{\text{\# of words read} - \text{errors}}{\text{\# of words}}$$

You count any words that were deleted, substituted, or mispronounced as errors. For 100 words read with 11 errors, our calculation would look like this:

$$\frac{100 - 11}{100}$$

This yields a percentage of 89 percent. The percentages correspond to the following reading levels (Clay, 1993b):

- Independent: 100%–95%
- Instructional: 94%–90%
- Frustration: 89% and below

The passages usually correspond to books in a series. Green books might be at a level one; yellow books might be at a level two; and red books might be at a level three. If the child's independent level is at the green level, then those books are sent home to be read with the family or are to be read freely in class during sustained silent reading. If the yellow books are at an instructional level, then those texts are used for individual and small group instruction based on the child's need. Finally, frustration level books are withheld until further IRIs indicate that the child is ready to move on to that level. In short, today's instructional-level books become tomorrow's independent-level books; today's frustration-level books become tomorrow's instructional-level books.

An advantage that informal reading inventories have over other types of assessment is that they are tailored to individual students and therefore reveal individual needs.

Interpreting results means considering how the present data reflect progress or regress against other recently administered assessments. IRIs assess students through graded word lists and graded passages and comprehension questions that move from literal to inferential to evaluative.

If the child reads aloud, then the focus is on decoding. If the child reads silently, then the focus is on comprehension. Why? Because of attention. In the former, the child will focus on performance, and there might not be enough memory left over to focus on understanding. Therefore, it is important for you to know what you're assessing: If it's decoding, have the student read aloud; but if she is to also comprehend what she has read, then have her read the passage once or twice silently before asking the questions. Passages that one selects for the miscue analysis should be able to stand by themselves and not depend upon other units for meaning. Just imagine trying to bake a cake with only half of the ingredients listed. The same is true here: If the passage does not have its own contextual integrity, then it will be difficult for the child to answer any comprehension questions based on this passage alone.

Miscue Analyses

After the child has read aloud, perform a miscue analysis. This tells you what *cueing system* the child relies upon when reading. You have already learned something about the cueing systems when you learned about cloze activities. Recall that there are three cueing systems to know for the test. The **semantic cueing system** is based on **meaning,** where we look at a multiple-meaning word like *ring* and determine whether it means *to ring a bell* or refers to piece of jewelry. The **syntactic cueing system** helps us figure out the grammatical category of a word in a sentence. The **visual cueing system** (called *graphophonemic,* meaning letter–sound correspondence) helps us read words based on the sounds they represent.

After a child reads aloud, the teacher analyzes each substitution to see what cueing system was at work while the child was reading. In Table 4.19, the child's substitution appears above the line; how the text actually read appears below the line. Meaning, Syntax, and Visual correspond to *M, S,* and *V* in the table. The Xs in the boxes below M, S, and V tell you what system was at work at the point of error.

TABLE 4.19   Miscue Examples

EXAMPLE ONE			EXAMPLE TWO			EXAMPLE THREE		
$\frac{cat}{car}$			$\frac{man}{boy}$			$\frac{cheeseburger}{girl}$		
M	S	V	M	S	V	M	S	V
	X	X	X	X			X	

In Example One, the child substituted *cat* for *car.* Since there is no semantic relationship between each word, the M column is blank. Because there is a syntactic (grammatical) relationship between *cat* and *car* (they are both nouns), the S column is checked. And because the words look similar, the V column is checked.

In Example Two, the child substituted *man* for *boy*. Since there is a semantic relationship between each word, the M column is checked. There is also a syntactic relationship between each of the words (both are nouns), so the S column is checked. However, the V column is left blank, because neither *man* nor *boy* are visually similar.

In Example Three, the child substituted the word *cheeseburger* for *girl*. Neither the M column nor the V columns are checked, because there is no semantic or visual relationship between these words. The only relationship that exists between each word is grammatical (they are both nouns), so the S column is checked.

Each of these analyses boil down to one thing: *The child does not rely on print enough when reading.* Even when the V column is checked in Example One, the child is ignoring the final consonant in the rime. Additional work is needed in that area of decoding. In Examples Two and Three, the child is obviously relying on information beyond the print when decoding text, because the V column was not checked. Thus, print decoding problems abound in the data, and this would be the focus of instruction in all three cases.

Be cautious when looking at any miscue or informal reading inventory data. If the miscue is a simple dialect difference and not a semantic, syntactic, or visual miscue, then it is not considered an error. Exchanging a short vowel for diphthong is a common regional variation. Substituting /peyen/ for *pen* is not a critical error, unless it interferes with comprehension. Therefore, as long as the dialect difference does not detract from a student's reading comprehension, it is not to be targeted as a need for remedial instruction.

Self-corrections can also be analyzed. When a child reads a word incorrectly and then self-corrects it, one can analyze why they did so. The same M, S, and V columns are used; you ask yourself if the child corrected the error based on meaning, syntax, or visual information.

Portfolio Assessments

In contrast to the narrow informal reading assessments, portfolios take a very long view of a child's literacy development: They are collections of artifacts that reflect a child's ability to read, write, listen, and speak. The items are taken from as many sources as possible, so that the portfolio shows a complete and authentic picture of a student's abilities (Courtney & Abodeeb, 1999). The artifacts can include everything from early drafts of writing to audio recordings of the child reading aloud from her favorite book. This way, a teacher can have a complete and "contextualized" view of who the child is, what she can do, and what her needs are. Two portfolio sections that are important for you to know about for the test will be described next. They document reading and writing (Mitchell, Abernathy, and Gowans, 1998).

Reading Sections.   Portfolios can include all of the child's running records, including informal reading inventories, miscue analyses, and wordlists, so that you and the child can see the progress the child has made over the year. These documents will also illustrate areas of continuing need that you and the child still must address. Reading lists are also important. They show the numbers of books and their genres, magazines, and other types of literature that the student is reading in and outside of class. This helps both the student and the teacher see progress in the kind and quality of books that the child selects for reading (or avoids). In short, this section should reflect a total picture of the child's reading ability from the beginning of the year to the present moment.

Writing Section.   The writing section collects all of the pieces of writing that the child creates, errors and all. These artifacts can be drafts of poems, complete poems, informal notes, letters to characters from stories, and so forth. They also document all of the work that goes into a paper that the child has written for research projects. This means that all of the prewriting, the inspirations for writing, including pictures, graphics, and early notes are part of this section. Drafts and revisions of drafts are also made part of this section, along with comments from the teacher and peers regarding the strengths and needs of the writing. All of these items are important, because they help the teacher and the child to see all of the work that went into writing a research paper. Instead of only looking at the final product and assigning a grade to it, portfolios allow one to have a comprehensive view of a child's development. If you have ever felt that a final number on a test or a letter grade was an inadequate means of assessing the real amount of work that went into something that you've done, then you can appreciate the purpose of the portfolio's long view of student development.

Conferences.   Conferences with the child about the portfolio are essential. During these conferences, the teacher and the student discuss the progress the child has made, along with areas of continuing need. For example, the reading section might show that the child reads many simple narratives but few expository pieces from journals. The teacher and the student together can set goals to improve this area of the portfolio. Similarly, the writing section will tell both the teacher and the student where the child's strengths and needs lie. For example, the writing might reflect strong organization and a high level of interest, but not style. The teacher and the student can discuss this need and make plans for how the student can improve this area of the writing. Subsequent conferences would look at progress in this area, as well as new ones, as they arise.

Other Portfolio Sections.   Speaking and writing can also be included in portfolios. Audio and video recordings of public speaking are artifacts that one could collect, along with assessment records of listening comprehension. In Chapter Five you will learn about reading response journals and learning logs, which can be included as part of the portfolio, too. Here are other items that might be included in the portfolio:

- *Interest Surveys.* Early in the year, it is important to uncover each student's preference for working alone or with others on projects, preferred types of reading materials; and other topics of interest for future study. This knowledge will help the teacher design the learning environment to include specific experiences preferred by the children. In addition, knowing the students' preferences and interests will enable the teacher to include appropriate reading materials for each student.
- *Observation Checklists.* Teachers can also use their own observation checklists to gauge student learning. The teacher can note how students behave during SSR or how they answer questions about what they have read. These checklists can indicate how well the student relates the main idea about what he has read, including facts and details from the story; events that took place and their order; and words from the story that describe, rhyme, or mean something different in a variety of contexts. Observational checklists can also be used to indicate any reading problems that can then be targets for small-group or individual instruction.

■ *Observation Records.* Keeping anecdotal records is also a form of subjective assessment. Noting whether the child is engaged or disengaged during Sustained Silent Reading, for example, will indicate that the child may be in need of some kind in reading instruction. The child may not be engaged because she can't find anything interesting to read or because she is not comprehending the book she has selected because it is too hard.

Portfolio Evaluation

Two types of evaluations take place around portfolios. There is student self-assessment and teacher assessment. Student self-assessment has the child reflect on specific areas of the portfolio to identify strengths and needs in the work. Students select items for their portfolios based on the learning and growth represented in work done over a period of time. The student's reflections might address whether he is meeting or has met any stated goals, whether he recognizes his own strengths and needs, and whether any new goals need to be set or revised. Setting goals and making plans to meet those goals can help the child to develop a sense of inner control and self-direction (Serafini, 2000/2001). This is a highly personal approach that differs drastically from standardized testing, which only shows a child's progress at one moment in time.

Students can have a hand in developing the criteria by which their portfolios will be assessed. For example, the students and the teacher can work together to develop a list of qualities that should be reflected in the portfolio. They can also establish what shows various levels of progress toward meeting or exceeding the established criteria. It is also important to review the assessment rubric with the students after it has been generated. Doing so will ensure that the students understand how they will be assessed and time can be given to answer students' questions and to clear up any misunderstandings. Table 4.20 provides a brief example of criterion-referenced assessments, which are discussed in the next section.

TABLE 4.20

POINTS	CRITERIA
3 Points	Has met the criteria for punctuating declarative sentences.
2 Points	Has nearly met the criteria for punctuating declarative sentences.
1 Point	Has not met the criteria for punctuating declarative sentences.

Criterion-Referenced Tests

Criterion-referenced tests are the last type of group assessment that you need to know for the test. The terms associated with these tests include *benchmark* and *rubric* (Ediger, 1999). Like the other assessments described in this section, you will have to know how criterion-referenced tests work, what they tell you about a student's performance, and what is done with the results.

In the first place, criterion-referenced tests look at both product and process. For example, these assessments consider what the child is doing when she writes her answers, along with whether the answer she has written is correct. For example, a criterion-referenced spelling test would look at whether the spellings were correct as well as at *how* the child actually spelled the words:

- Desember
- Febuary
- Janury

The product side of the assessment would be handled through the benchmark score for the test, and the process side would be viewed through preselected rubric criteria. Here is how it works:

If a perfect score on spelling the months of the year is the exit criterion for third-grade children, teachers will want to know who is performing at or below this expectation and what to do to help them. Using a rubric can help. Rubrics typically rate students in terms of early, developing, or advanced stages of proficiency. If you assess the children in spelling the months of the year, you can begin to develop a view of which children are early, developing, and advanced based on their score and the *spelling processes* they use. The first item is obvious; the second one needs some explaining.

To achieve a twelve out of twelve on the spelling test, students must not only spell the words correctly but also must capitalize each of the words. The spellings of *January, February,* and *December,* for example, have some odd features about them. *January* has an odd vowel pattern (e.g., *ua*), *February* has a silent *–r,* and *December* ought to have the letter *s* in it, not *c*. Based on this information, spelling development criteria could be set for who is early, developing, and advanced.

- **Early**   *Does not capitalize the months of the year or does so infrequently. Spells the words by dominant sounds only (e.g., dsmbr).*
- **Developing**   *Capitalizes most of the months of the year correctly. Developing spelling patterns (e.g., desember).*
- **Advanced**   *Capitalizes all of the months of the year correctly. Frequently spells the months of the year correctly, with very few exceptions (e.g., Febuary).*

You can assess the children throughout the year with this rubric to see how they are doing and to determine what they need. For example, if you have two children who consistently get a six on the spelling test, you can figure out why that is so. For the first child, it might be only because she does not capitalize the months of the year. Fixing that will bring them nearer to reaching the benchmark. For another child, capitalization might not be the issue; instead, it is with writing *er* at the end of some words and with writing all of the sounds not heard in the words (e.g., *February*). Criterion-referenced assessments are useful for identifying strengths and needs in children and for helping them to reach particular benchmarks in their development. These assessments take both product and process into account.

Norm-Referenced Tests

Norm-referenced tests locate a student's score on the normal curve against the performance of other students in the same normative group (of the same age, grade level, and demographic group). Scores tell teachers how well a child is performing in relation to similar students who have taken the same test. When a teacher reviews norm-referenced scores for

English, he can compare his children's level of English comprehension with the performance of their peers on the same exam.

They are also considered to be less subjective, because of their objective assessment of a group of students under the same conditions. This allows one to compare the performance of a given student against the scores of other students in the class, district, state, and nation.

The terms that you need to know for norm-referenced reporting include raw scores, percentile ranks, and grade-equivalent scores, and scaled scores.

- The *raw score* on a spelling test is simply the number correct out of the number of items given. A child who spells the names of six months correctly has a score of six out of twelve. In short, the raw score is simply the unaltered number correct.
- *Percentile rankings* are different from raw scores. They make comparing the individual to the group, and a group of individuals to other groups of students, much easier. The scale can go form one to ninety-nine, and you locate the student's raw score on this scale to figure out how much "better" one student did in relation to other students. A student who spelled all of the items correctly would be said to have scored "in the ninety-ninth" percentile, meaning that she did better than 99 percent of the people who took the test. A student who scored zero did worse than 99 percent percent of the people who took the test. Finally, a score in the fiftieth percentile means that the student did "half-as-well" (or "half-as-bad," depending on your perspective) as other students.
- *Grade-equivalent scores* describe a student's academic performance, telling us the grade and achievement levels from one *academic year* to the next. For example, a fourth-grade student's score of 5.9 tells us that the fourth grader performs *like* a fifth grader who is in the ninth month of the academic year (May), though we cannot say that the child is "ready" to do fifth-grade work. Remember that grade equivalent scores are based on the September to May calendar and that September is the first month and May is the last month in this system. Note also that grade-equivalent scores will only tell you about the individual's performance in relation to other individuals; it is not appropriate for group descriptions.
- *Scaled Scores* are raw scores converted into a standard format so that results can be compared.

All of this should seem quite simple to understand. When you encounter questions about what norm-referenced tests do and do not do, keep this spelling example in mind. Furthermore, if you are asked about how you would report results to parents or other caregivers, keep in mind that they are not experts. Pick answers that make thinks very concrete for parents to understand, yet retain the correct ideas. For example:

> Your child scored in the ninety-ninth percentile, yielding an above-average, grade-level equivalent score of ten out of twelve items. You should be proud.

would need to be amended to

> Chris got all twelve items right on his spelling test. This means that he scored better than 99 percent of other students who took the test. Since most fourth graders only get ten items correct on the test, his perfect score means that he is doing better than most children his age. You should be proud.

This way, the information is made accessible for parents who probably are not experts in the language of standardized assessments.

Other terms to know are reliability, validity, and conditions. *Reliability* means that a test will provide the same result each time it is given. Giving a spelling test by having the students spell the words aloud before their peers isn't reliable, because it will produce different effects for each student. *Content validity* means that you have a test that measures what it says it will measure. Having students spell December by asking them to spell "the name of the twelfth month of the year" is not valid, because this tests memory and spelling together. Finally, conditions must be the same among all tests if one is going to compare scores. If one group of literature students uses their notes for a quiz, but another group cannot, then you may not compare the scores of each group. The scores will not mean the same thing, even if the tests are reliable and valid.

CONTENT AREA FIVE:
INSTRUCTIONAL CONSIDERATIONS

Something that makes answering questions about literacy instruction difficult is not knowing what the test makers are really asking. Consider our opening question again:

> A fifth-grade teacher wishes to implement the process approach to writing in her classroom. Which of the following statements best represents the action that the teacher should take first?
>
> A. Consider the grammar points that the students know already and the ones that they will need to learn through the activity.
>
> B. Plan to have the students brainstorm topics that they might like to write about before attempting the first draft.
>
> C. Prepare the students to work together to develop a rubric so that they can participate in how the writing project will be scored.
>
> D. Demonstrate each step of the writing process for the students first and then work with them to carry out the steps together.

True, you have to understand the writing process to answer the question, but you also have to understand the principles behind instructional activities, like preplanning, to really get it. To understand why D is the correct answer, you need to know how to preplan and to implement activities in the classroom. In the question above, you are asked to implement an activity in the classroom for the first time. Because the writing process involves many steps (see Content Area Ten), you must first model the whole process for students. If not, then any content that you try to teach them will be lost in the confusion of trying to figure out how the activity functions and what the expectations are. So, for any questions on implementation, be sure to look carefully at answers that have modeling as an option. To make this process easier for you, ten key principles are discussed here. These principles will help you to answer questions like the example above (where all the options look good).

1. Understand how to plan activities. There are three things to consider when planning activities. What will I have the students do before, during, and after the activity?

Before: One method that is effective for helping students to comprehend what they read takes place before they even approach the text. Having students generate questions before and as they read, for example, will keep them actively engaged in the task of understanding (Langer, 1981). Without questions to guide them through the story or information, they may lose interest or otherwise become disengaged during the process of reading the story. Posing and answering question, then, keeps active reading alive.

Pretesting is also a good starting point in the planning process because pretesting tells one how much students know about a topic before it is introduced (Ogle, 1986). This helps guide the teacher in planning based on what the children know and do not know about a topic. For example, in a unit on dinosaurs, the teacher can introduce a topic and then have the children work in pairs to list what they already know about them. If the children already know enough about the types of dinosaurs that existed, then the teacher can scale her instruction up based on this information. If anticipatory questions will be used, then writing answers to the questions that the teacher expects to hear from the students is also a good place to begin.

During: The test makers believe that learning occurs best when students participate completely in the learning process, especially in gaining and constructing understanding. Student interest is most important in this model of learning. Having the students pose their own questions and then have the opportunity to answer these questions while they read will keep them actively engaged in the learning process (Carr & Ogle, 1987). The teacher's role is to ensure that the learning environment will allow for such endeavors. In sum, because the goal is to have students become independent learners, students must learn to pose and answer their own questions, along with identifying ways to identify resources to satisfy their intellectual curiosity.

After: Groups of students can work together to answer questions about who, what, where, why, and when after reading a story. Writing answers to these questions when applied to the story will teach students a strategy that they can generalize to other passages that they will read independently. These activities are enrichment activities, where the teacher helps students to elaborate and extend their knowledge using other forms of communication (speaking and writing) to do so (Bryan, 1998).

2. Know how to adapt materials for different learning styles. Teachers need to adapt a variety of instructional materials to meet the needs of their students and their diverse interests and learning styles (Armstrong, 2000). Academic learners, for example, may be able to rely on the textbook entirely to gain understanding (Chapman, 1993). Visual learners, however, might need more graphic organizers to ensure understanding, and auditory learners might need small group discussions and lectures on tape to help them comprehend the material (Lazear, 1999). Finally, kinesthetic learners may need hands-on activities and active demonstrations to remain engaged in their own learning, like highlighting details or creating graphic organizers (Lazear, 1998). Teachers must preplan their lessons based on who their students are and what their learning styles demand.

3. Recognize the difference between deductive (direct) and inductive instruction. Direct instruction compartmentalizes learning the section language into distinct and discreet parts (Carnine, Silbert, Kame'enui, & Tarver, 2004). For example, one

learns skills in the language one at a time. This is also called the "bottom-up" approach, where students are taught to decode words, identify sentence structures, and other "parts" of the language first. Note: It is safe to assume that this type of instruction is favored for teaching children to decode print.

Inductive approaches are different. Inductive approaches teach academic concepts indirectly (Gunning, 2004a). For example, in a deductive approach, the teacher simply presents the concept and then directly teaches it to the students. In inductive instruction, the teacher creates a situation where the students must arrive at the concept that the teacher instructs in the same way that detectives solve crimes. When teaching a grammar point, the teacher might write two examples on the board in the form of a cloze activity.

- I gave the student ___ apple.
- I bought myself ___ new car.

Here, the students are supposed to supply the correct article in the space. Once they do so, they might then be asked to generate the rule: *An* is used before words with starting with vowels; *a* is used before words beginning with consonants. The students can then present the rule, along with examples of their own based on the inductive examples. This type of instruction helps students see themselves as capable of solving problems on their own and actively engages them in more rigorous levels of thinking. Note: This type of instruction is not favored for decoding.

4. Use metacognition. Metacognition means "thinking about thinking" (Baumann, Jones, & Serfert-Kesson, 1993). When studying for your exam, for example, you, the reader, may have to stop sometimes and think about whether you've understood an explanation. If not, then you reread the passage and ask yourself if you think that you've understood it. If the concept is still unclear, then you may consult another source or ask a qualified person to help you. But you do not quit. That is because you have metacognitive processes that help you to answer your own questions and to motivate you to find solutions.

Metacognitive processes need to be modeled for students and can be as minimal as simply asking questions of oneself while reading, or can be as concrete as writing down questions based on the headings and subheadings in a text and then writing down answers to these questions while reading (Tadlock, 1978). For example, if one wants to have students self-monitor their own reading and ask themselves if what they're reading makes sense or who the main characters are, then the teacher must explicitly teach this skill through modeling, guided practice, and independent practice (Baumann et al., 1993).

5. Use multisensory techniques. Learning to recognize letters is often accompanied by multisensory techniques (Clay, 1993b). For example, children can be asked to trace felt or fuzzy letters to reinforce the shapes using another sense. This is especially true for letters that are hard to visually discriminate because they are orthographically similar. The idea to keep in mind is that if the concept being taught orally or visually doesn't stick, then try another sense rather than just repeating the ineffective approach over and over again. This type of technique can be expanded to upper elementary levels, where children are asked to highlight relevant details in a story. They are using kinesthetic and visual skills to make abstract concepts concrete.

6. Use ability grouping for skills and heterogeneous groups for strategies (Gunning, 2004b). In general, grouping students, whether heterogeneously or homogeneously, will require preplanning. The teacher must consider how to configure the groups, how to populate them, and then how to assign specific goals and tasks to each member of the group to ensure that all members make positive contributions to the effort.

   Homogeneous grouping will help readers who are not at the same level as their classmates have their specific needs met and may reduce feelings of inferiority that might otherwise arise if they are placed in situations where their needs are constantly exposed but not addressed (Gunning, 2004b): They may feel more comfortable expressing themselves in this type of environment and become more independent learners as a result. Homogenous grouping will also allow opportunities to meet the needs of advanced students who can receive developmentally appropriate materials that take their interests and abilities into account.

   Heterogeneous grouping is effective for cultivating a sense of appreciation and sensitivity in diverse classrooms (Gunning, 2004b). The same is true for groups of students with varying ability. The key is to structure the groups to play to each of the students individual strengths, so that each member can utilize his or her talent to the fullest and not be made to feel inferior. For example, activities can be structured for the group such that each student, regardless of whether he or she is an academic, visual, or kinesthetic learner, can use their talent to the fullest.

7. Understand individual instruction and minilessons (Tompkins, 2003). Individual tutoring may be very effective for remedial instruction. This is because needs can be identified and addressed very quickly, something that might not be possible in small or whole group instruction. Instruction can also be tailored to the student's individual strength. If the child is a visual learner, for example, activities can be developed to target this child's strength and make the process of learning easier for him or her. Feedback is corrective but supportive in this model, since the goal is to encourage the student to continue learning and applying whatever skill or strategy the teacher is modeling.

   Planning lessons for individual children begins by addressing the most immediate need of the child in reading, while also aiming the child toward the next level of development. For example, if a child is stuck at the level of blending in phonemic awareness, you address that need. In addition, you also try to aim the child toward the next level of development (segmenting). This way the child will continue to make progress on a continuum of development.

   After targeting any need, it is important to have the child practice the ability in context. Though instruction typically occurs separate from context, the goal is to have the child be able to apply the skill or strategy in a real situation. For example, if sorting words with the rime -*at,* the final step is to have the child try to read -*at* words in decodable text. So, after studying and practicing the skill apart from context, be sure to provide the student with the opportunity to practice in a real context. This will lead to independence.

8. Plan units and other field trips carefully. When planning units, define learning goals early on. For interdisciplinary units that unite one or more content areas, it is important to determine the learning objectives for each discipline and to define them

clearly (Burns, Roe, & Ross, 1999). The teacher must state in advance what skills the students are to acquire through the unit and how they will connect one area to another (Cooper, 2003). Obviously, one must understand the goals of a unit oneself before proceeding with the planning of the unit.

Consider a field trip to view art. As part of the preplanning, the teacher will consider how to activate the students' prior knowledge before leaving on the trip. In addition, he will also think about how to have the students remain engaged during the activity. To satisfy these goals, the teacher might begin with a discussion of concepts they have learned about art and list the concepts on the board. Then, the students will generate a list of questions that they will write in their learning logs and apply to the art that they view. When at the museum, the students can jot down notes about the characteristics they've learned about and how they apply to the real art that they are viewing. When they return to class, the students can work together to answer the questions in their learning logs, before having a whole-class debriefing on their original questions and the answers.

To assess the students' understanding further, the teacher can ask the students to develop their own art exhibition. They can create pictures based on the concepts that they've learned about and then display them in class. In this way, the students will be able to use all of the four skills for the learning experience, along with demonstrating their understanding of the elements of art that they have learned about.

9. Know how to select texts. One of the most important guidelines for selecting multicultural literature is to ensure that the culture is presented accurately and realistically (Jipson & Paley, 1991).

Equity is another important consideration (Traxel, 1983). Equity is different from equality. Equality means simply having enough books about girls and boys in the classroom. Equity means that one has analyzed each text to ensure that the representations are accurate, nonstereotypical, and help the children aspire to become whatever they want to become based on their interests and skills not on societal preconceptions. Selecting books that reflect unbiased views are also important, along with ensuring that the texts show both genders in a variety of nontraditional roles. This is because one wants students' aspirations to be based on their desires and abilities, rather than on someone else's stereotypical expectations for them.

In short, selecting a wide variety of genres, both fiction and nonfiction, are a must and they should also represent all reading levels (independent and instructional). Recent and award-winning books are always good candidates, especially to support the goals of the curriculum. Be sure to consider the grade level here. If the students are emergent readers, then pick books that will support phonemic awareness and letter recognition. Decodable texts with regular phonics patterns would be appropriate for developing readers. Finally, wide varieties of literature should be available for fluent readers. All of the texts should be of high interest.

10. Teach skill to strategy. This pattern always begins with assessing students' skill level (Carnine et al., 2004). Once they have the skill then they can learn to apply it. Think about syllabication. First, the skill must be developed, then it must be converted into a strategy that students can use when reading text with lots of polysyllabic words in them. This pattern is true for anything on the test. Reading techniques are no exception. The pattern is to develop prereading strategies, like finding out what they know

about a subject and what they want to know about a subject before reading, because this focuses student attention and gives them a skill that they can apply to other passages (Ogle, 1986). Furthermore, it will cue the students into what kinds of strategies to use when reading the passage to answer their questions (Carr & Ogle, 1987). Post-reading activities, like having them list what they have learned after reading the passage engages them in actively comparing what they thought they knew and what they wanted to know in relation to what they have read (Bryan, 1998).

This notion should also extend to teaching English language learners. Try to view answers along the lines of the four skills, *reading, writing, listening,* and *speaking,* and align the activities as shown in Table 4.21:

TABLE 4.21

READING	Concepts about Print Phonemic Awareness Decoding Instruction Comprehension Instruction CALLA Approaches
WRITING	Language Experience Approach
LISTENING	Total Physical Response
SPEAKING	Communicative Approaches

CONCLUSION

This chapter presented literacy instruction. You learned about learning-to-read instruction and reading-to-learn instruction. You also learned about different types of assessments that target individual children and groups of children. Finally, you reviewed ten principles that should help you answer questions about literacy instruction on the test. The next step in preparing for CSET Multiple Subjects exam is to learn about children's literature. The major elements of literature will be covered in the next chapter.

CHAPTER FIVE

LANGUAGE ARTS

DOMAIN TWO: LANGUAGE ARTS

Domain Two covers the genres (types) of children's literature available to elementary teachers (Content Area Six), the features of literature (Content Area Seven), and children's responses to literature (Content Area Eight). Most of the questions on the exam will ask you to apply your knowledge of literary forms, rather than simply ask you for the definition of a particular literary or poetic form. Therefore, it will be necessary for you to do outside reading to prepare for this portion of the exam if you do not feel that your knowledge of literary forms is adequate.

Content Area Six: Genres of Children's Literature

Rather than make grade-level assignments of texts, just divide the texts using the same distinctions discussed in Chapter Four. That distinction is between the *learning-to-read* literature and the *reading-to-learn* literature. Table 5.1 below categorizes these texts for you, and explanations of each variety follow.

Learning-to-Read Literature.   Learning-to-read materials are summarized by genre in Table 5.1 and focus on emergent and developing readers. Since the goal of using these materials is to teach *learning to read,* the structure of the books is more important than the subject matter. Emergent readers focus on the process of reading and the parts of that process; developing readers expand on the elements previously learned. Descriptions of the types of literature follow.

Emergent Readers.

WORDLESS BOOKS.   Two varieties of wordless books may be the targets of questions on the test. Vocabulary books present pictures of concrete nouns and verbs (actions) without words to stimulate oral vocabulary development without the burden of print. Many of them are organized by genre, and they can be used with initial English language instruction to develop an oral repertoire. Picture stories also include concrete nouns and verbs, but they tell a simple story in pictures. They might depict an activity like going to the zoo and may show what happened before, during, and after the activity. The goal is to teach basic story schema (event sequences) and oral language before introducing print.

ABC BOOKS.   Books that teach the alphabetic principle (one letter, one sound) teach children the alphabet through pictures and upper- and lowercase letter representations. The let-

TABLE 5.1   Genres of Children's Literature

LEARNING-TO-READ		
Emergent	Wordless ABC Letter-sound Picture books	
Developing	Pattern Decodable	
READING-TO-LEARN		
Tales	Traditional Folk Fairy Fables	Myths Epics Legends Allegories
Fiction	Realistic Historical	Fantasy Sci-fi
Non-narrative	Topical information Glossaries Tables of contents	Indices Expository text
Biography and Autobiography		
Poetry	Narrative Lyric	Limerick Haiku
Plays		

ters *A a* appear on a page, along with a picture that corresponds to the letter name *ape*. The texts can be used in concepts about print activities, where the teacher and student point to each letter and then associate the letter with a familiar picture. Many of these texts include fuzzy letters to provide children with tactile sensations during multisensory tracing activities to reinforce letter recognition.

LETTER-SOUND BOOKS.   These books present upper- and lowercase letters with pictures that represent other sounds associated with letters. For example, it is logical that *A is for Ape,* but there are other sounds associated with the letter, too: *ant, aunt,* and *apple.* Letter-sound books move beyond teaching simple letter names into more complicated sound–letter associations. Some of the texts can include sound–letter associations that are not as transparent. Short vowel sounds, for example, can be communicated through pictures that illustrate that *A* is also for *aunt* and *apple.* They can also be made part of kinesthetic activities, where children act out the pictures they see to associate sounds and letters with actions. The *Zoo Phonics* series is an example, where a gesture is taught along with a particular letter and its sound (*Aa = Ape*).

PICTURE BOOKS.   These books include richly detailed pictures and text, thus, offering early readers supported understanding through text and images. These books are ideal for reading aloud to the children, because the pictures are captivating and the text is imaginative. Books like *Where the Wild Things Are* and *Where the Sidewalk Ends* are examples. Note: These books are **not** favored for decoding instruction, because the test makers believe that pictures may take the children's attention away from the print, and thus delay the development of their knowledge of phonics.

Developing Readers.

PATTERN BOOKS.   Pattern books include pictures that support text that is presented with a predictable pattern:

> The boy got   **up.**
>   **down.**
>   **in.**
>   **on.**

The pattern changes with changes in the picture and the final word in the sentence. The texts are favorable for teaching concepts about print (book concepts, directionality, word matching, etc.), but they are not favorable for teaching early decoding. The test makers believe that the child will simply memorize and apply the pattern throughout the text, because the pattern and the pictures supply too many cues for the child to follow and attention is taken away from relying exclusively on print.

DECODABLE BOOKS.   These texts are favored on the exam for early decoding instruction. They include decodable elements as seen in the sentence below:

> The *cat sat* on the *mat.*

Typically, decoding instruction takes place with some isolated element of phonics, like identifying blends in the initial positions of words or digraphs in the final positions of words. In the example, it should be obvious to you that the rime *-at* is the focus of instruction. After teaching the isolated phonics element, decodable texts are used to reinforce the focus of isolated instruction within the context of reading. This way, the part can be taught in isolation and reinforced again in print within the context of "reading" decodable text. Needless to say, these texts are tightly controlled to ensure that the child must focus on the print in order to decode the text. The most severe decodable texts include no pictures, because the pictures may draw a child's attention away from the print. Computer-based texts are similar in that they are meant to reinforce elements of phonics that have been instructed in isolation.

Reading-to-Learn Literature.   Let's turn now to the reading-to-learn texts. Texts for teaching children reading-to-learn skills include both fiction and nonfiction. The stories include themes that will appeal to the child's age. They can, for example, include simple lessons on why obedience is a value to more complex presentations on facing divorce, family illness, or living with a family member who has a disability. Age appropriate themes are an important consideration, since you do not want to aim too low (and lose interest) or too high (and be "above their heads"). The literary elements of these texts will be discussed in content area eight. Each type of text has subgenres within it, and you should know their general characteristics for the test.

Tales.

TRADITIONAL LITERATURE. *Traditional literature* presents stories deeply rooted in the culture from which they are drawn. They can reflect the values, symbols, and worldviews important within a given culture. This makes traditional literature ideal for comparative analyses of such topics as animal symbols found in Native American literature, Greek fables, and Chinese folktales. Similarly, themes from Asian traditional stories can be analyzed for their collectivism and individualism with respect to the traditional literatures of Western cultures.

FOLKTALES. Folk tales are stories that began as a part of oral tradition and then because part of cultural narrative. The trickster figure embodied in Brer Rabbit, a figure from Southern literature, and his adventures exemplify a character who began as oral tradition and then became part of a cultural story where wits play a very important role in survival. Folktales provide a glimpse of a culture's worldview at a given time in history.

FAIRY TALES. Fairy tales are also cultural stories, though they include magical elements and depict struggles between good and evil. Think about Little Red Riding Hood, where the innocent Red travels to Grandma's house to perform a good deed and is stalked by the wolf. Hansel and Gretel is another example of a fairy tale. The original Grimm's versions of these stories are far more violent and, well, *grim,* than you might imagine (our versions are pretty sanitized). This is because the stories were meant to inspire obedience in the reader through fear and other "lessons."

FABLES. Fables use animals to teach moral lessons to children. *Aesop's Fables* are the most widely known. His writings from Ancient Greece include anthropomorphized animals who have human attributes and human experiences. These stories lend the reader some distance and objectivity when seeing how the animals make choices before reflecting on one's own experience. "The Tortoise and the Hare" is a memorable example of a fable, along with its theme of "slow and steady wins the race."

MYTHS, EPICS, AND LEGENDS. These stories are long narratives that celebrate the heroism of a culture and its extraordinary deeds. Myths often reveal a culture's religiosity and tell not only about life but also about the role that gods and goddesses played in human events according to their worldview. Epics, such as the *Iliad,* include historical elements and stories of actual battles recast within the framework of an epic. Legends may also tell magical stories of heroism, and they often include figures like kings, queens, and knights or other archetypal figures. They may also explain concepts like *chivalry* and demonstrate how one is to behave in the role of knight, king, or serf.

ALLEGORIES. Allegories are also cultural stories where the surface story actually tells another deeper story through symbolism. The *Wizard of Oz* by L. Frank Baum (2000) is an example. On the surface of the story, one learns about Dorothy, who encounters a Cowardly Lion, a Tin Man, and a Scarecrow on her journey down the yellow brick road that leads to the Wizard. Few readers may be aware that Baum was actually telling a political allegory of the William Jennings Bryan populist campaign (Parker, 1994). Dorothy symbolized the undecided voter, the tin man represented industrial workers; the scarecrow was the agricultural demographic, and the cowardly lion was Candidate Bryan (who needed courage to win).

Fiction.

REALISTIC FICTION.   This type of fiction offers readers plots and themes that mirror real life. The stories are believable and describe people engaging in activities and dealing with situations that one finds in everyday life: family conflict, growing up, managing friendships, or rites of passage. Rather than relying on fantasy, they portray situations that readers can place themselves in and explore how they might react if given similar choices. Such narratives like *A Separate Peace* (Knowles, 2003) tells the story of two friends, one who is gifted and one who is not, and an injury that befalls the talented friend that may have resulted from the other character's jealousy.

HISTORICAL FICTION.   Historical fiction conveys a sense of a history surrounding an event. One learns about an event and the times through setting descriptions, conflicts, and character choices. *The Chosen* by Chaim Potok (1995) is an example. The reader learns not only about the struggles and expectations of American Orthodox and Hasidic Jews in the creation of the State of Israel after World War II, but also about its effects on both communities as witnessed through a friendship. Through the story, the reader learns about the historical context through characters that the reader can relate to.

FANTASY AND SCIENCE FICTION STORIES.   Fantastic stories can also be about ghosts, horror, mysteries, and so forth, though science fiction is most recognizable. Science fiction stories are distinguishable from other types of fiction through the setting, which is often other worldly or set in the future, or because the story relies heavily on yet-unrealized technologies. The themes do not necessarily have to be outlandish, as they can be about love, friendship, or other realistic topics. Some can also be socially critical, like *The Hitchhiker's Guide to the Galaxy* (Adams, 1995), where a manic-depressive robot "puts up" with humans and other aliens on a variety of bitingly critical "adventures."

Non-Narratives.   These texts are topical and informational. They offer readers information about health, history (first flights, space explorations), historical figures, athletes, and so forth. Non-narratives can serve as an introduction to content area texts, because they often include tables of contents, glossaries, and indices. They also enable modeling of how to read expository text, which will also help in the transition from pure narratives to informational texts.

Biography and Autobiography.   *Biographies* are also an example. They tell readers about the life of an author or a historical figure (autobiographies are written by the author). The question that one always has about biographical writings is just how objective are they? Often, they present only the best or worst attributes about a person, and they can be very subjective and skewed. In children's literature, they tend to emphasize themes like hard work, perseverance, and staying in school. They are meant to inspire rather than titillate.

Poetry.   Poetry also appears on the exam, though your ability to interpret poetic forms is the primary focus. Poetry relies on its form and figurative language to convey meaning to the reader. The rhythm and rhyme of a poem can captivate a reader, and the language can stimulate our five senses (touch, taste, hearing, smell, and sight). For the test, it is more important for you to know how to interpret themes and moods based on the devices used in the poem than it is to tell the difference between a lyric poem and a haiku. Therefore, you will see here only a brief description of poetic forms found in elementary classrooms. We will spend more time on poetic devices in the next content area.

There are four types of poems to know for the exam. These include narrative poems, lyrics, limericks, and haiku.

NARRATIVE AND LYRIC POEMS.   Narrative poems tell a story and present us with a sequence of events. We will dissect one for you in Content Area Eight, when you learn about the features of literature. Narrative poems are distinct from lyric poems. Lyric poems contemplate a singular mood or feeling and capture it in verse. They can also ponder animals or other things. Here is one that uses *free verse:* unrhymed verses organized into a stanza or stanzas:

> **Congestion**
> Stuffed up
> Drip-Drip
> Sniffle-Snort
> Menthol Scarf
> Sleep.

LIMERICKS.   Limericks are humorous poems of five lines, where lines one, two, and five rhyme and have the same length, and lines three and four are shorter and have their own rhyme scheme. Here is a limerick appropriate to the task at hand.

> I once had to prep for a test.
> I felt that I'd never get rest.
> With the coffee I had,
> I'd thought I'd go mad,
> 'Til resolving to just do my best.

HAIKU.   A haiku is a brief poem that invites meditative insight. It functions like a flash of light that suddenly reveals something previously unseen, unfelt, unthought, or unimagined.

> Yes, the palm tree green
> something else that will always
> remain far from me.

This particular English haiku employs seventeen syllables, the conventional length of a haiku, arranged by some practitioners in three lines: five syllables, seven syllables, five syllables.

The traditional haiku contains a reference to nature, especially an image that reveals the season or time of year. Most importantly, a haiku involves a conflict, stated or implied, that is to be resolved by the reader. In this poem, the conflict is between the typical human response to nature's beauty—to befriend. At first a reader might not understand the poem because it says something positive but discusses something negative: distance and longing. After further meditation on the brief poem, an insight is possible—that human needs and wants are not always realized. A new respect for nature is the ultimate hope of this haiku.

Modern haiku may use fewer or more than seventeen syllables, and a reference to nature and season may be absent. But there is always a surprise in a haiku, a shock, a fresh awareness and new understanding.

Plays.   Since questions on plays will probably be few, we will spend very little time on them. What differentiates a play from the rest of the literature that we have discussed is that meaning is conveyed through character dialogue, action, and stage directions. We learn about the characters' state of mind by what they say and do on stage. Event-centered plays focus on the drama and action of the plot. Character-centered plays focus on one or two main characters and the challenges they face: One accompanies the main character on his or her journey through a number of events. Greek plays come in two varieties: comedies and tragedies. Comedies amuse the audience and can satirize human vices and foibles. Tragedies, on the other hand, are designed to arouse sympathy from the audience for the main character, who usually meets a tragic end due to some character flaw beyond his or her control.

Content Area Seven: Features of Literature

The majority of the questions that you will face on literature will ask you to apply concepts to passages to demonstrate your understanding of prose and poetic devices. You may be given only one line or entire passage or poem. You are less likely to face questions of mere definition, such as:

My love is like warm water is an example of which of the following poetic devices?

A. Metaphor

B. Simile

C. Assonance

D. Onomatopoeia

Instead, you will have to know the definition of the appropriate literary device and how it applies to a passage to reveal character motives, symbolism, mood, and the like. These types of questions can be challenging to prepare for because the test makers have an infinite selection of prose and poetry from which to choose. The best way to learn the material is to be armed with a few powerful examples of each literary device and know it well enough that you can apply it to the exam. If you have the time, spend a couple of Sundays with the *New York Times Book Review.* Their reviews dissect a variety of fictional, nonfictional, and poetic works every week.

Let's review the features of literature in prose and poetry. We will begin with the most common form of story schema, Freytag's Pyramid (Burroway, 1999), and the literary elements that often occur within it—foreshadowing, character types, narration, and theme. We will then look at other story elements that appear on the exam (metaphor, allusion, motifs, and flashbacks). Finally, we will end by looking at poetic devices cited most often in the registration bulletins.

Story Schemata.   Freytag's Pyramid captures the basic organizational pattern of elementary literature. It has five steps, including exposition, rising action, climax, falling action, and resolution (denouement). Table 5.2 shows how each step functions in works of literature.

TABLE 5.2 Story Schemata

EXPOSITION	RISING ACTION	CLIMAX	FALLING ACTION	RESOLUTION
Background information	Events building to a climax	Culminating event	Events after the climax	The final action that resolves the conflict
Narration Setting Foreshadowing Characters	Types of conflict	Realistic Fantastic Hyperbolic	Symbols and "truth" revealed	Theme revealed

In the movie *The Dead Poet's Society*, Robin William's character had his students tear something similar to Freytag's Pyramid out of their books, so that they could read and understand literature on their own. But since it may appear on the exam, let's explore each aspect in detail.

Exposition. *Exposition* provides us with background information, such as the type of narration that will occur in the story. First-person narration tells the story through the eyes of a central character. Third-person narration tells the story from the point of view of an observer/nonparticipating character. Omniscient narration is different, because the author provides a "God's eye view" of the story and uses narration that is above and removed from the text. One question that is always a good one to ask is whether the reader can trust the narrator. On the subject of *The Great Gatsby*, many Ph.D. dissertations could be written on whether one can trust the narrator's observations about Gatsby, because there is conflict about the subjectivity of his reporting.

The setting (where and when a story takes place) may also be established early. The story may take place in one room of a house, at a school, or at any other place that you might imagine. Science fiction stories usually have fantastic settings that employ descriptions not found in regular life. Descriptions of the setting might also provide us with elements of foreshadowing. In Poe's *Fall of the House of Usher*, the reader is treated to a lengthy description of the Usher home, complete with a gloomy exterior and a crack that runs down the length of the house, from the roof to the foundation. This description indicates that there is a flaw in the family that will probably lead to a tragic ending.

One of the most famous descriptions of setting that occurs during exposition is from Crane's *The Open Boat* (Crane, 1898), a story about four men (an oiler, a cook, a correspondent, and a captain) trapped in a small dinghy at sea:

> None of them knew the color of the sky. Their eyes glanced level and were fastened upon the waves that swept toward them. (p. 715)

Here, the reader learns of the chaos in which the characters are immersed because they cannot tell the difference between the ocean water and the sky above them.

Characters may also be established during exposition. There are two types of characters to know for the test. *Protagonists* are the main characters, and *antagonists* are the characters who provide opposition to the protagonists. Supporting characters help the protagonist on his or her journey or otherwise move the story along into subplots, provide comic relief, and so forth. We also learn about the protagonist's and antagonist's motivations and behaviors through their interactions with supporting characters in the story. One difference between literature for children and adolescents resides in how the characters change. Static characters, who are either good or evil, tend to populate children's literature, whereas characters found in adolescent literature may grow, change, and evolve.

Rising Action.   As the story moves out of exposition, the action rises. We learn about the type of conflict that the characters will face, whether it is realistic or fantastic. There are four types of conflict that you should be able to recognize for the test:

- The character in conflict with another character.
- The character against nature.
- The character against the "gods."
- The character against himself.

The dialogue and events may evolve around these types of conflicts and lead us to a culminating event. Students can be asked to predict and speculate on the nature of the conflict, and then read the climax to see if they were correct.

Climax.   The culminating event is the climax of the story, when the action reaches its highest level. Based on the four types of conflicts described earlier, the character finally has it out with his or her antagonist, has a showdown with nature or with the "gods," or at last has a defining emotional conflict. Please note that modern literature plays with this framework quite a bit. One frustrating aspect that you may remember from Literature 101 is the way that Faulkner tended to end his story at the point of climax, never offering the reader any resolution. That was probably not because he couldn't think of a way to end the story; instead, his preoccupation might have been with the interior motivations and psychological aspects of his characters, rather than their simple actions and "what they did."

Falling Action.   After the climax, "truths" about the characters are often revealed. Mysteries and detective stories are certainly famous for this, where the reader sees the fallout of the detective's having revealed who committed the crime. The reader also learns whether we have been treated to static or multidimensional characters as we see how they respond to the climax.

Resolution.   The *denouement* is the resolution of the story. This is where many authors reveal their point to us. We tend to get the theme (meaning or moral) of the story at the end, and we also learn if the story will end to our satisfaction. Themes can be as simple as *they lived happily ever after* or as complex as that found in *The Old Man and the Sea* (Hemingway, 1995), which we will discuss in the next section, Other Devices in Literature.

Other Devices in Literature.

Allusions.   Allusions are references to other famous stories within a given work. Bible stories often find their way into literature, as do children's stories. Many of the popular movies that we watch are little more than allusions to stories that we enjoyed as children. The movie *Pretty Woman* might be described as an allusion to *Cinderella,* where the Prince (Richard Gere) rescues a "fallen" Cinderella (Julia Roberts). Similarly, *Good Will Hunting* can also be characterized as a retelling of the frog–prince story, only here it is a psychologist (Robin Williams) who "kisses" the frog, Will (Matt Damon), and turns him into someone employable.

Flashbacks. *Flashbacks* give us background information and insights into character motivations. In *Slaughter House Five* by Vonnegut, the reader is treated to a character named Billy who can travel through time. He does so in his mind, as his past and present experiences move back and forth through his mind, until we finally learn of the central event in his past (the bombing of the civilian town of Dresden in World War II) that has left him distressed. Faulkner also uses flashbacks extensively in *The Sound and the Fury* (Faulkner, 1991) where the opening story is told from the point of view of a mute and mentally challenged character whose mind moves from the past to the present and back again as he encounters natural cues from his environment.

Analogy, Similes, Metaphors, and Symbols. Authors use a number of devices to describe elements in their stories. Similes are explicit comparisons of one thing with an unlike thing and use the words *like* or *as* in the comparison. Metaphors are often implied comparisons between two unlike things, though they can be direct statements or conveyed through symbol. Similes are pretty straightforward. You probably have said one at some point in your life:

> I'm as hungry as a horse.
> It's raining like cats and dogs.

You have probably also uttered a metaphor or two, as well:

> He has the attention span of a flea.

Extended metaphors are far more complex than similes because they rely on a collection of symbols to convey their meaning. *The Old Man and the Sea* (Hemingway, 1995) provides an example of an extended metaphor conveyed through symbol. For those of you who have not read the story in a while or missed it somehow or avoided it on purpose, here is a brief synopsis:

> An old man gets in a small boat and goes fishing on the ocean for what might be his last trip (he's pretty old, remember). He catches the fish of a lifetime and spends many pages bringing it in. It is so big that he has to keep it next to the boat. As he returns home, his prize fish is attacked and destroyed by sharks. All that is left of his wonderful fish is the skeleton. The old man sails one way and the skeleton floats to another part of the island. Later, the skeleton washes on shore and some tourists see it. They comment that a storm must have killed the fish.

Elements from the story can be considered as symbols of things outside of the story. At one level, there is the old man, his fish, the sharks that attack it, and the bones that are left. Beneath these elements are possible symbols that develop into an extended metaphor and symbol (see Figure 5.1).

FIGURE 5.1

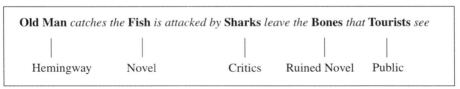

Beneath the symbols of the old man, the fish, sharks, bones, and tourists, we find a metaphor about life and what can happen when we pursue our goals and dreams. If we extend the metaphor further, we can even relate it to our own experience as shown in Figure 5.2:

FIGURE 5.2

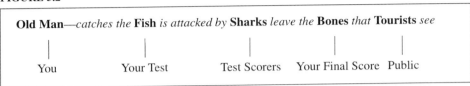

Old Man—*catches the* **Fish** *is attacked by* **Sharks** *leave the* **Bones** *that* **Tourists** *see*

You   Your Test   Test Scorers   Your Final Score Public

Before you get too depressed about this extended metaphor, keep in mind that Hemingway once said that *The Old Man and the Sea* was "just a fish story."

Themes.   Themes represent the main idea that the author explores in the work. Often, teachers select literature for their classrooms based on age-appropriate themes. This explains why you might find themes like obeying adults, being nice, and helping out in preadolescent literature, and why themes of conflict resolution, relationships, and coming of age are found in adolescent literature. In *The Old Man and the Sea,* one theme is that no one beyond the person who struggles to achieve a goal sees the difficulty inherent in the task or experiences the disappointment when it doesn't work out. Keep in mind that themes are also cultural. Other cultures that prefer more collectivist themes might argue that such a disappointment is to be expected if one wants to venture out on to the ocean of life completely alone.

Poetic Elements.   Like elements from literature, you need to prepare for questions that ask you to apply your understanding of poetic devices to lines or entire passages of poetry. To ensure that you understand what selected terms mean and so that you will know examples of each term to use in answering exam questions, we will explore several terms common to all of the exams. In addition, we will also dissect an example poem, and present mood, setting, imagery, and theme.

Assonance.   Assonance is a poetic device that repeats a syllabic sound in short intervals to make it memorable:

The black cat snapped back: attack!

This verse is an example of assonance in action.

Alliteration.   Alliteration is like assonance, but it repeats a consonant over and over again in verse. Here is a famous alliteration:

Peter Piper Picked a Peck of Pickled Peppers.

The repeated consonant sound /p/ gives the line its alliterative quality.

Onomatopoeia.   Onomatopoeia is a device that uses a word that closely resembles the sound it captures.

The ball *swished* through the net.
The car went *vrooom*! as it zoomed.

Personification.   Personification assigns human qualities to things and objects.

> The scorpion tattoos its way across the desert
> And stops periodically to unfurl its tail
> To declare victory over so much sand.

Figurative Language.   Simile and metaphor are common devices used in poetry and were discussed earlier in this chapter.

Poetic Elements Illustrated.   To give you some practice in reading and analyzing poetry, we will present a poem for you in *Tupparian* (i.e., bad) verse and describe it in terms of mood, setting, imagery, and theme.

THE DRS. ARE OUT

> 10,000 trumpets in my head they did blow!
> In search of a cure, hence did I go.
> Advice from the schooled is all I would need;
> Their help I would ask, their help I would heed.
>
> OPEN YOUR MIND the neon did read;
> I relished the thought of my newfound lead.
> As he sharpened his saw, he said, "by the way,
> For you a lobotomy—done free today."
>
> ACK! I screamed and ran'til I stood
> Under a sign that read Dr. Good.
> "Good is the name," he thrust his hand out.
> "A headache, indeed! Hated mother no doubt."
>
> I thought to myself, as he started to hop,
> If this next one can help, then dead I will drop.
>
> His name was quite simply Dr. Phil (O'Sophy),
> (A friend of the famous Ms. Oprah Winfree).
> "I have your answer," he shouted with glee,
> "A brand new Mercedes I'll buy just for me!"
>
> With new found disgust I walked slowly on.
> An aspirin I took. My headache? Soon gone.

Mood.   Poetic mood is much like our own personal moods. Humans can be happy, joyous, sad, depressed, dark, and so forth and so can poems. The language, structure, and descriptions in a poem convey these elements to us. Here, the mood of this poem is playful but a bit cynical. It opens with a narrator who is, despite his pain, hopeful and filled with expectation but ends with resignation and disillusionment.

Setting.   The setting is a journey down the road of self-discovery. The only description of the setting is hyperbolic (exaggerated). A neon sign that reads OPEN YOUR MIND is obviously absurd.

Parody, Satire, and Hyperbole.   Elements of parody and satire fill the poem. Parody describes writing that mocks a recognizable literary style, and satire makes fun of human foibles and fallibility. Dr. Seuss's style is parodied here. The sing-songy rhyme, ridiculously ironic characters, and social "message" are all contained in this world of lobotomizing psychiatrists, hopping psychoanalysts, and greedy pop psychologists. Satire occurs when a human weakness is held to ridicule. Here, it is the common desire of seeking help from others for problems that might be solved on one's own that is satirized.

Imagery.   Imagery is conveyed through figurative language. The poem opens with a metaphor where a headache is linked to 10,000 blowing trumpets without the use of the words *like* or *as* to accomplish the analogy (which would make it a simile). Onomatopoeia is also present. *Ack!* is a nonsense word that captures what a scream sounds like (for the narrator, anyway). The descriptions of the people in the poem are ironic. For example, Dr. Good isn't so good.

Theme.   The theme of the poem is revealed at the end, when the narrator discovers that the only cure for his "headache" is to learn to do for him- or herself. Another theme might include the fact that there is often a difference between reality and expectation, which sometimes can only be learned the hard way.

Content Area Eight: Interpreting Literature

This content area covers prereading, during-reading, and post-reading activities that teachers use in the classroom before children read, as they read, and after they have read. It is easiest to view these activities as they are shown in Table 5.3:

TABLE 5.3   Structuring Reading Activities

PREREADING	DURING READING	POST READING
Prior Knowledge	Strategies	Enrichment Activities

Let's look at each state of reading in detail.

Prereading Activities.   The purpose of all prereading activities is to set a purpose for reading a text and to activate prior knowledge (Langer, 1981). That's because students need to stay engaged during the reading (purpose) and to use their background knowledge to comprehend what they encounter (prior knowledge). Good prereading activities will set the purpose and activate background knowledge, so that students can confirm and deny assumptions they have about a topic, anticipate what is to come, and stay focused throughout the reading.

Making predictions is appropriate for any age. This process cues the students to begin thinking about what they are going to read and to see if what they predict can be confirmed or denied by the text. In short, engaging the reader's attention and cognition and previewing the text will improve comprehension and retention of information.

Generating questions to be answered will keep the students actively engaged in the learning process (Carr & Ogle, 1987). These questions will draw upon their newly revealed, prior knowledge. They will be able to test their prior knowledge against the lesson and to correct any misunderstandings that they might have about the subject.

The following are prereading activities for emergent and fluent readers that appear often in the registration bulletins.

Book Walks.   Book walks ready children for stories that they are going to hear in small or whole-class groups. The teacher shows the students the cover and asks them to report what they see and to offer statements about what they think the story will be about based on the cover and the title. This prompts students to listen to the story with the purpose of confirming or denying their initial impressions about the topic. Again, engaging attention and cognition in this way will improve the students' comprehension and retention of the information that they hear during the reading.

Introducing chapter books to upper-elementary students can also employ a book walk. For example, though students may be accustomed to reading short stories and short informational pieces, the first time they encounter a book with a table of contents, chapters, and an index may be startling. The teacher can model all of the parts to the students in a whole-group presentation to help them understand the purpose of the table of contents, the chapters, the glossary, and the index. Then, he or she can let the students look through the book in small groups to get a sense of how the book is assembled and to discuss its format.

Anticipation Guides.   Anticipation guides (Duffelmayer, 1994; Duffelmeyer & Baum, 1992) contain true and false statements that students evaluate prior to reading a passage. After they read the text, they revisit each of the question and reevaluate their original assumptions. For example, prior to reading a passage on sea life, students can answer true–false questions about the passage as shown in Table 5.4:

TABLE 5.4

1. Whales are fish.	True	False
2. Lobsters and cockroaches share a phylum.	True	False
3. Sharks never sleep.	True	False

After answering the questions, students read the passage and revisit their answers to see how many of their preconceptions were true and how many were false. As a prior knowledge activity, anticipation guides (like all prereading activities) set a purpose for the reading to keep the children engaged and also to cue their minds to be receptive to the reading. Finally, they reevaluate their original understandings making this a prereading, during-, and post-reading activity.

KWL Activities.   This acronym stands for *Know, Want to Know,* and *Learned* (Ogle, 1986). The *K* and *W* portions are the prereading activities, where students list everything they know about a topic and then generate questions representing what they want to know (see Table 5.5).

After they read the text, they complete the *Learned* column and revisit the *Know* column to ensure that what they thought they knew before they read the text was in fact correct. Any unanswered questions become topics of further investigation, and the teacher and students can work together to identify outside resources to answer those questions. This activity

TABLE 5.5   A Example of KWL

KNOW	WANT TO KNOW	LEARNED
Segmenting is the highest level of phonemic awareness.	What activity is used to develop segmenting?	Elkonin Boxes are frequently used for segmenting instruction.

ensures that the reading will be purposeful and that students will learn how to pose and to answer their own questions. They also learn how to correct their misconceptions and how to fill in gaps in their knowledge through reading.

SQ3R.   This acronym stands for *Survey, Question, Read, Recite,* and *Review.* Like KWL, this activity covers prereading, during-reading, and post-reading and is used mainly with expository (content area) text (Tadlock, 1978). *Study skills* are also taught using expository schema. Since many chapter books use titles, headings, and subheadings, teachers often use SQ3R to make the schema of expository text not only concrete but also a useful scaffold for teaching. SQ3R asks students to **survey** the titles first. During the *Survey* portion, students preview the text to see how the information is organized. They can learn to skim the selection to get the gist of the information and scan it for certain phrases to see what kinds of relationships will be drawn (see Table 5.6).

TABLE 5.6

because, since cause-effect	if, then contingency	before, after transition	first, second sequence

After surveying, they then turn each heading into **questions** that they write down in their note books. As the students **read** the text, they answer the questions generated from the headings. After reading, they **review** their questions and written answers to ensure that they have answered each question sufficiently. Finally, they read each question and **recite** their answers. They then compare what they remembered to what they had written. This is also an excellent prereading activity for expository texts, because it cues the students into what they will be reading about and prepares their minds for the information.

During-Reading Activities.   Literacy in the content areas is also important. For example, when solving word problems in math, the teacher could ask the students to write their solutions down in the form of statements or steps. This way, the teacher can see the students' thought processes at work, rather than just looking at the product the student arrived at after solving or attempting to solve the problem.

Note Taking.   This technique is applicable for expository text. The kinds of activities to select are ones that move beyond passively listing details or copying quotations. Instead, one wants to have students engage in an activity that requires both metacognitive strategies, self-monitoring, and learning how to pose and answer questions as they read. The activity can be as minimal as asking the students to note questions in the margins of copied passages they read or listing questions to be answered in their learning logs.

Students may have to learn that there is a difference between recording information and analyzing/evaluating it (Kesselman-Turkel and Peterson, 1982). T-journals are an example: One draws a large "T" on a piece of paper and writes the topic across the top of the page. In the first column, the teacher and students work together to pull ideas out of a text and list them. In the second column, the teacher and the students evaluate each of the ideas in the first column and write their responses (e.g., whether they think the point is fact or opinion or worse). Through this activity, students can learn the difference between extracting and evaluating information.

Outlining.   After taking notes, the information can be organized into an outline. The advantage of an outline is that it will help the student see how main ideas and supporting details relate to one another. Figure 5.3 shows an outline of the literacy section of Chapter Four of this text.

FIGURE 5.3

TOPIC: LITERACY INSTRUCTION

  I. Concepts about Print
        A. Book Concepts
            1. Cover
            2. Title
        B. Sentence Concepts
            1. Direction
            2. Return Sweep
        C. Word Concepts
        D. Letter Names
 II. Phonemic Awareness
        A. Matching Sounds
        B. Discriminating Sounds
        C. Blending Sounds
        D. Segmenting Sounds
III. Decoding Instruction
        A. Letter Sounds
        B. Onset/Rime
        C. Phonics Rules
        D. Syllables
 IV. Fluency

The topic is literacy and the main ideas are listed in items I through IV: CAP, phonemic awareness, decoding, and fluency. Supporting ideas are listed within the main ideas. For example, CAP is further subdivided into Items A through D: book concepts, sentence concepts, word concepts, and letter names. Any subordinate ideas that clarify the supporting ideas are listed numerically. Continuing with CAP, items A and B have two subordinate ideas. Each of the supporting ideas could have been supported by subordinate ideas throughout the outline.

Graphic Organizers.   Graphic organizers are effective tools for teaching students to diagram the schema of expository text to aid in their comprehension. Recognizing these organizational patterns will also help students with critical thinking, because it forces them to organize the details into recognizable categories and then judge the validity of the information. When studying a historical event, for example, students can be shown a time line with pictures supporting each event. This provides students with a guide upon which to rely as they read the story.

Graphic organizers are also helpful in reducing confusion that students may encounter when engaging with unfamiliar or complex expository text. A graphic organizer enables them to see relationships and to grasp the structure of the information before they attempt to embark upon abstract journeys of understanding. The concrete nature of the information displayed visually will also keep the students on task and engaged throughout the activity.

In the content areas, students can use graphic organizers to guide their identification of key concepts and their relationships (see Table 5.7).

TABLE 5.7   A Graphic Organizer for Biology

PLANT AND ANIMAL CELLS		
What plants have:	*What plant and animals cells share:*	*What animals lack:*
Cell Structures: Plants	Organelles:	Cell Structures: Animals
■ Cell wall	■ Mitochondria	■ No chlorophyll
■ Vacuoles	■ DNA	
■ Chlorophyll	■ Cell membranes	
Summary:		

Graphic organizers can also help students use dominant and subordinate categories of words that show the relationships among the concepts they name. Students can generate a list of everything that they know about a topic and then arrange the information to show how the terms relate to one another, as shown in Figure 5.4 (Stahl & Shiel, 1992):

FIGURE 5.4

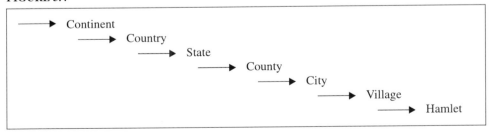

They can also add to their lists and make changes as their knowledge develops. Students can compare graphic organizers to identify any variations in the relationships they have identified. To extend vocabulary after reading, teachers can discuss words found in the story with the students. They can discuss synonyms and antonyms to words that they have learned about in the reading. Such an activity will enrich their reading vocabularies by first associating new words to words that they already understand. Later, when they encounter these new words in print and decode them correctly, they will have the oral definitions in mind and the terms will register.

Venn diagrams can help students understand expository texts that compare and contrast details about various subjects. Venn diagrams force students to categorize information by similarity and difference.

Guided Reading.   Guided reading teaches reading skills and strategies to individual or small groups of students (Manzo,1975). Here, one uses each stage of the reading process (prereading, during reading, and post reading) to assist students. For example, with the child or children, the teacher can conduct a prereading activity to draw upon the children's background knowledge and to prepare them for reading. Vocabulary can be pretaught or clarified. Questions to be posed and answered during reading can be generated. In addition, strategies to repair information breakdowns can be decided upon (let's syllabicate when we come to a big word and look for its meaningful parts). One common activity also has the students highlight important phrases or details within photocopied paragraphs to enhance their understanding and work on specific skills as they read.

Think Alouds.   Think alouds are also good metacognitive activities for students to use while reading (Babbs & Moe, 1983). Students can be taught to self-question their way through narrative text to learn how to monitor their own understanding independently. The teacher models how to pose *wh-* questions to the passage (Who is the main character? What are they doing?), sequencing questions (What happens first and next in this paragraph?), and inferential questions (Why is that character so sad?). Teaching students how to think through a passage metacognitively is an important strategy to know for the test.

Post-Reading Activities.   After students read a text, they can also elaborate on and extend their understanding of the material and the ideas that they have encountered (Bauman, Seifert-Kessel, & Jones, 1992). Post-reading activities are also known as *enrichment activities* to be used with students who have understood what they have read. Several of these activities are discussed here.

Literary Responses.   Responding to literature is meant to elaborate and extend understanding of both concepts and vocabulary. There are questions that one can ask before, during, or after one has read narrative text (Shanahan & Shanahan, 1997). Questions relating to characters, setting, plot, and evaluation are shown in Table 5.8.

Students can also use these questions as a guides to create visual representations of stories that have been read to them. This is another way to encourage children to develop their comprehension skills early. In this way, they can make the connection between the story that they have just heard and what it represents to them in their minds. The teacher can also have the children describe their pictures in order to gauge how well they have understood the story.

For writing, an effective way to have children respond to literature is to ask them to write letters to characters or from characters in stories. They can use details from the text to create realistic letters that a character might have written. This elaborates and extends

TABLE 5.8

CHARACTERS

- Who are the characters in the story? How are they described?
- Which characters are the antagonists? How do you know that?
- Which characters are the protagonists? How do you know?
- What is the setting of the story like? Is it realistic or fantastic? Why?

SETTING AND PLOT

- What is the plot of the story? Is it realistic or unrealistic?
- Who causes the problem in the story?
- What other problems do the characters face?
- How are the problems solved?

EVALUATION

- Would you have solved the problems like this? Why or why not?
- What did you like/not like about the characters? Why?
- Is this a story you would read again or recommend to someone? Why?

the children's understanding because they have to use their newly gained knowledge in a different form of expression.

Another enrichment activity has students elaborate their knowledge through literature discussions. Literature discussions are a good post-reading activity because people always take away a variety of interpretations from whatever they read. This activity capitalizes on that fact and allows students to share their points of view with the group, without fearing that their interpretation is simply wrong or not worth considering.

Activities for literary responses also address the four skills of reading, writing, listening, and speaking. Reader's theater is an example.

READER'S THEATER.   The purpose of oral language activities is to use another skill to support reading. Mainly, students use discussions to elaborate and to extend their understanding by sharing ideas with one another. The same idea is true when students have the opportunity to dramatize their understandings through activities like reader's theater.

Having students role play how the main character made good decisions can help children learn about their own values, assumptions, and beliefs. Role playing can also help children learn about different points of view. After reading about a historical period of time, for example, children can assume different roles. Some students can be characters from the period, while others can be interviewers. The students can take turns interviewing one another and learn not only about the events of that time period but also about the different points of view of the characters in the story.

Students can learn to connect personally with works of literature. When pretending to be characters in the stories, students not only learn about story elements but also how to think and maybe to empathize with the characters. They can also write alternative endings to the stories and then perform them. To accomplish either of these ends, students must use the four skills of reading, writing, listening, and speaking. In short, having students propose and develop their own versions of stories can also reinforce their understanding of literature.

Question–Answer Relationships.   Many content area textbooks include comprehension questions at the end of the section. The comprehension questions typically move from literal to inferential to evaluative. Students need to learn strategies to answer these types of questions. These techniques usually involve skimming the passage first to get the gist, reading the questions at the end, and then reading the passage to answer the questions. When answering the questions, the student can consider where they will find their answers. There are four types of questions associated with QAR (McIntosh & Draper, 1995):

- Right There   (literal).
- Think and Search   (literal).
- Think It Through   (inferential).
- On My Own   (evaluative).

Students read the question and then decide if they will find the answer right in the text or if they will have to answer it using details from the text and their own impressions. Such an activity helps them to use metacognition to self-monitor their understanding as they activity read the text and extend their understanding by answering these types of questions and satisfying their demands (Mesmer & Hutchins, 2002).

Motivating Children to Read.   Goal setting and rewards are important considerations in motivating children to read. Setting goals means discussing the plan with the child and working together to reach tangible goals, like reading a certain number of pages per night, bringing magazine articles from home to be read in class, and so forth. Rewards can be as simple as a token like a star or as public as posting their work on the board to highlight their individual accomplishments, though you are better off considering community-based methods of motivation here. Book clubs are an example of community-based activities. Students get to discuss books that they enjoy with one another as well as engaging in the self-selection of literature based on what they want to read.

Motivation is also required if a child is stuck in one particular genre. Anecdotal records may indicate that a student only chooses books from a specific genre, series, topic, or author thereby limiting his exposure to new formats, vocabularies, and concepts. Certainly, goal setting is an option here, though another approach might be worth considering.

Fostering Appreciation of Reading.   Enjoyment of reading is extremely important because students who avoid reading at all costs do not improve their reading skills. One way to help unmotivated or struggling readers, beyond identifying their needs in decoding, fluency, or comprehension, is to ensure that they have high-interest materials available to them that is at or near their independent-reading level. The interest value of the material might draw them into the process of learning to read, and having it at their independent-reading level will allow them to succeed.

Fostering appreciation of literature occurs by reducing external demands on students. For example, taking time to read aloud to students from a novel without asking them to write papers on the topic or having any other expectation for them beyond listening and enjoying the story may help foster their appreciation of reading. Here, they can simply enjoy hearing the story for the sheer pleasure of it.

Sustained Silent Reading (SSR) is another option (Krashen, 1993, Trelease, 1995). Here, students select high interest texts independently and read them for 20 minutes per day without interruption or papers due at the end. Being allowed to discuss stories afterward with other classmates can also help them to develop student interest and enjoyment of literature. Another by-product of sustained silent reading and reading for pleasure itself is that one's vocabulary will also increase. Since they will see words used in different ways in a variety of contexts, they will elaborate and extend their personal lexicon and have a greater source on which to draw when reading new texts.

CONCLUSION

This chapter covered a variety of literature designed to foster the learning-to-read and reading-to-learn processes. You also learned about a number of literary elements, including Freitag's Pyramid and other common terms (metaphor, theme, etc.). The final area that you need to consider for the exam concerns written and oral language development. Let's now turn to the final chapter to learn about these two elements.

■ ■ ■ ■ ■ ■

CHAPTER SIX

WRITTEN AND ORAL COMMUNICATIONS

DOMAIN THREE: WRITTEN AND ORAL COMMUNICATIONS

This chapter presents the final domain about written and oral communications (Domain Three). The content areas of this last domain include writing applications (Content Area Nine), the writing process (Content Area Ten), the research process (Content Area Eleven), the editing process (Content Area Twelve), and verbal and nonverbal communications (Content Area Thirteen). As in the previous domain, you will be asked to apply the information in these content areas to texts or dialogues, so you need to prepare to transfer the information that you learn to those circumstances. Let's look at writing first.

Content Area Nine: Writing Applications

This content area concerns applications of writing, including the form, function, and content of different pieces. These pieces include narratives, expository essays, persuasive essays, and research reports. Table 6.1 presents them at a glance.

TABLE 6.1   Applications for Writing

NARRATIVES	EXPOSITORY ESSAYS	PERSUASIVE ESSAYS	RESEARCH REPORTS
Freitag's Pyramid	*Informational Patterns*	*Persuasive Patterns*	*Research Designs*
Plot outlines	Schema	Objective data	Focus question
Setting descriptions	Facts	Authority Statements	Analysis method
Character	Objectivity	Testimonials	Data collection
Descriptions	Main ideas	Emotion and logic	Data analysis
Sequences	Supporting ideas	Call for action	Findings
Chronology			Recommendations

Narrative Writing.   The important function of narrative writing is to tell an interesting story and, in the words of Mr. Kopesky, my eighth-grade English teacher, "to delight and entertain." Narratives contain rich descriptions of setting and character and plots that are fully developed, consistent, and resolved.

You will find narrative writing easy to remember if you recall Freitag's Pyramid. The steps include: **exposition, rising action, climax, falling action,** and **resolution** (denouement). Try to remember what takes place during the writing of each stage of this model. For example, during *exposition,* the students will be doing character sketches and plot outlines to ensure that they will have richly developed characters, setting descriptions, and an interesting and engaging plot. During *rising action,* the students can sketch the chronology of events to ensure that there are no sudden or illogical shifts in the story. The *climax* can also be written in a way that is consistent with all of the characters, their actions, and the plot, so that the effect is powerful and believable. Finally, during *falling action* and the *resolution,* students can write themes that express the main points of their stories. If you remember these steps and what can take place within them, you will be in a better position to analyze the narrative writings in the data sets that you will see on the exam.

Expository Writing.   Unlike writing narratives, expository pieces are designed to inform or to persuade.

Informative Writing.   Expository writing that is meant to inform can take a number of different formats and serve a variety of purposes (see Table 6.2):

TABLE 6.2   Expository Writing Designed to Inform

DEFINITION	CAUSE/ EFFECT	COMPARE/ CONTRASTS	PROBLEM/ SOLUTION	NARRATIVE ANALYSIS
Describes a theme or process	Explains how and why something happens	Explains similarities and differences	States a problem and describes solutions	Analyzes characters or literary elements

The function of any one of these expository formats is to provide a balanced and factual account of the information without arguing for or against a particular position. Learning to separate fact from opinion is important here, because students must learn how to substantiate their claims with objective facts and to use unbiased sources.

Persuasive Writing.   Persuasive writing uses a formula of gaining attention in the opening sentence or paragraph, organizing objective data, authoritative quotes, and emotional testimonials to make a case, and then calling for action at the end (changing one's position, voting a particular way, etc.). The function of these essays is to move someone to act or to cause change. Undoubtedly, you are familiar with persuasive arguments, though you may not be able to name the form. As an example, consider this request for a donation:

> [Emotion] 1,000,000 children die of starvation every year. [Fact] 1,000,000 children could be saved with $1.00 worth of food. [Logic] For less than the price of a fast-food cheeseburger, you could save the life of a child. [Call to Action] Won't you please donate 100 cents toward a child's life?

The content of persuasive pieces includes logical and subjective arguments and reasoned and emotional appeals to move someone to take the position of the author or to do what has been asked. In the example above, emotional arguments are offered (child starvation) along with logical arguments (feeding them is inexpensive). The persuasive piece ends with a call to action (donate 100 cents toward a child's life). The format is standard, and it may appear on the exam as a paragraph followed by questions that ask you to identify the correct element in a multiple-choice question. Please note that persuasive items need not be this dramatic. Having students write letters to school board members or to the media on a particular issue like the dress code are examples of how persuasive writing is used in classrooms.

Research Reports.   Research writing has the format of posing a question, explaining a method to answer it, presenting data and data analysis, offering findings, and making recommendations. Students can create in-class opinion surveys on a variety of topics, administer them, and collect and analyze the data. They can then write up their findings and present them to the class both in writing and in speeches. Because the research process represents a separate content area, you will learn about this process in greater detail later in this section.

Summary and Precis Writing.   Summary or precis writing is another type of expository essay, where one locates the main and supporting ideas in a piece and summarizes them quickly and faithfully in one's own words. A student simply lists the major topics in their sequence without attention to the minor details in a work. Since summaries tend to be brief, our discussion of them will also be short and end here.

Content Area Ten: The Writing Process

The next content area is about the writing process, which is applicable to narrative, expository, and persuasive writing. Research writing uses a similar approach, but there are some additional steps to consider; thus, we will give research writing its own topic (Content Area Eleven).

The general process for writing that appears over and over again on these tests has five steps: brainstorming, drafting, editing, revising, and publishing. You must know not only what purpose each step serves, but also what occurs within each step. Table 6.3 below captures these important details (Hoffman, 1998):

TABLE 6.3   The Writing Process Illustrated

BRAINSTORMING	DRAFTING	EDITING	REVISING	PUBLISHING
Quick Write	Outline	Organize	Transitions	Conference
Web	Rough draft	Clarify	Grammar	Layout
Sketch	Focus	Expand	Mechanics	Print
Discuss		Contract	Word Choice	Present
			Spelling	

Each step in this approach to writing is modeled for the students first so that they know what is expected. The process can also be made part of the daily routine so that it becomes something natural for the students to carry out independently and in small groups. Students can participate in establishing the criteria to be used to evaluate the final product.

Brainstorming.   *Brainstorming* is the prewriting phase. Students generate ideas based on how the purpose has been set for the writing. For example, they might be responding to literature to analyze a character's actions, or they might be working on a narrative piece that places a main character in a new setting with a new challenge. The following activities are common during brainstorming. The *Catcher in the Rye* (Salinger, 1991) will be the vehicle through which we will illustrate these elements.

Quickwrite.   Students write for a sustained period of time and either list or write continuously in stream-of-conscious style to generate as many ideas as they can before trying to identify a topic or to create an outline for their first draft from what they have written. No attention is paid to grammar in this form of writing.

> Holden Caufield is conflicted confused dropout antihero…

Webs.   Students can also make webs and maps to sketch out their ideas. As shown in Figure 6.1, a central topic is placed in the center of the page and related details and ideas can be connected to it. For example, a main character's name can be written in the center and all of his or her attributes can be listed (both good and bad) so that a complete sketch is created.

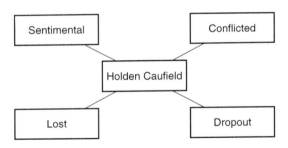

FIGURE 6.1

Students can be paired or grouped heterogeneously to discuss their ideas without fear of criticism, since all ideas are on the table at this point in the process.

Drafting.   The next step in the process is to develop the draft. Students can organize outlines and try to list dominant and subordinate ideas before writing the draft. Paragraph frames that scaffold writing a paragraph can also be used. They look like this:

1. Topic: Holden Caufield is lost in nostalgia and sentiment.
2. Details: He drops out of school because he is disillusioned by the choices in life and longs to keep life still and unchanging as what one finds in a museum.
3. Conclusion: It is a story of a character's inner conflict with the external world and a longing for stability.

Students can share and discuss their outlines and drafts and receive feedback about what to expand or to contract to make the piece more effective and interesting.

Editing.   Editing occurs when the draft is read silently or aloud to help shape the piece into an appropriate format. Sequences are verified and ideas are strengthened with details and quotations. The idea is to ensure that all of the details and events have been completed and organized effectively. Extraneous ideas are also eliminated during this phase of the writing process.

Revising.   Revision occurs at the paragraph, sentence, and word level, where transitions, grammar, mechanics, word choice, and spelling are reviewed. Checklists for these items are common, and grammar points are often taught separately before they are applied to the writing. We will review the principles of revising writing in Content Area Twelve. For now, just accept that revisions of grammar occur here and nowhere else.

Publishing.   The work is completed and can be turned in for rubric evaluation, self-evaluation, or conferencing. Students can also read their work one more time to ensure that it is complete. The students' writing can also be combined into a classroom journal and used during parent–teacher conferences so that caregivers can see the progress that their child has made throughout the term. Polished items can also become part of a class magazine, journal, or other presentation to be shared among classmates or students in other classes or grades.

Content Area Eleven: The Research Process

With the basics of the writing process behind us, let's look at how the research process is conducted.

The research process is complex, and it is important to break it down into manageable parts for students. Making the process as systematic as possible with clearly defined goals will enable students to stay on task, to develop skills that they can transfer to future projects, and to work independently. The process parallels the writing process with some important additions and considerations, which are discussed below.

Teaching Student Researchers.   What is the goal of instruction? Answering this question will help the teacher determines what items are most important to include in the classroom for research projects.

The most effective way to teach the research process is to use the skill-to-strategy approach. This means that students will have had the research process modeled for them in steps, along with an immediate opportunity to apply these steps in context as a learning strategy. For example, if the students are to locate information in a journal, the teacher must first model the process. Next, have the students practice together and then independently to see if they can actually carry out the task alone. Linking what is taught in class with real life activities will increase the chances of their successfully acquiring the skill.

The Research Process.   The following information will be helpful for both oral and written reports, if you are asked about how to structure the research process for students:

- Pose the Question. One of the easiest ways to help students narrow their topics is to have them pose the topic as a question to be answered. In this way, students can learn to recognize whether the question is too broad or too narrow to answer. Because it is easier to answer a question, students can try to find and narrow a topic by posing an answerable question. The question, *Why are there so many poor people in the world?* is not as answerable a question as *Why is the poverty rate in South Minneapolis so high?* Teaching students to refine their research questions is an important part of the research process.
- Identify the Focus of Research. Students are asked what specific steps they will take to research the answer to their question. If they are going to answer questions about poverty in South Minneapolis, they need to look at job, education, and other data to investigate their questions. Library and Internet resources must be identified and roles that define who will find the information must also be stated if the students are working in a group.
- Identify the Resources. Students also need to decide about what kinds of resources they will consult (e.g., living people, books, journals, Internet, etc.). Learning how to create categories is an extremely important aspect of this stage of the research process. Higher order thinking skills are required to arrange the information logically and to decide on what to include. Furthermore, students must learn how to draw relationships between categories and to synthesize the information into an assembled, coherent whole. They must also learn how to summarize the main points from the materials they read.
- Ensure that there is a multiplicity of materials. If students are to complete a research project, having multiple copies of popular journals will ensure that students have better access to resources in the classroom to meet the expectations of the assignment. Students can be asked to conduct opinion surveys in class about various subjects and to then write up their findings in a report. After finding, reading, and noting the information, they present their findings to the small group or whole class.
- Gather the information. To help students locate information for research projects, students need to plan their research strategies carefully. This includes listing all of the key terms and ideas related to their topic. Doing so will enable them to search the Internet and other databases more efficiently, which will provide them with a wealth of resources related to their topic.
- Develop the outline. Once the information has been gathered, it is time for the students to synthesize it into an outline. The outline will force the group to decide upon the ideas to be kept or excluded. For example, if the students are researching "Ocean Life," they can compare and contrast their outlines to ensure that they are on task (see Table 6.4):

TABLE 6.4

GROUP ONE	GROUP TWO
I. Sea Mammals	I. Coral Reefs
II. Crustaceans	II. Algae
III. ~~Fresh Water Perch~~	III. ~~Tourist Places~~

Items one and two from both groups would be kept; the extraneous items would be excluded.

- Students should also learn how to use graphics in their reports. Separate activities can be conducted to teach them this process. For example, students can conduct their own classroom research, collect data, and then present it in the form of a table. They can learn how to label and caption the table and how to incorporate the graphic into a written report. Other activities for tables include whole-class activities where the teacher and students generate lists of characteristics and categories of the subject they are studying (birds, mammals, and fish, for example), and the categories become part of a table's headings. Other considerations include text density, use of verbs, and use of bullet or numbered lists.

Because research projects rely heavily on sources, students need to know how to avoid plagiarism. To do so, they need to know what plagiarism is, how to quote and source, and reference materials in bibliographies and work cited lists. Let's look at each of these elements now.

Plagiarism. Plagiarism is wholesale copying of text out of books, newspapers, and so forth, and dropping the copied material into a paper without indicating that it is a quote and without citing the source. Even if you change a few words here and there, it is still plagiarism because the ideas are not truly yours. Here is an example of plagiarism:

> Plagiarism includes wholesale copying of text out of books, newspapers, and so forth, and dropping the copied material into your paper without indicating that it is a quote and without citing the source.

Here, only one change was made (*is* to *includes*) and no reference is given. Basically, you must cite the source when using the ideas, opinions, theories, actual spoken or written words, or data that are not part of common knowledge. Common knowledge includes any facts that any reasonable person would know; proprietary knowledge pertains to facts that are revealed through research or other hard work. For example:

1. There are twelve months in a year. (common knowledge)
2. There are five essay formats that you must know for NES exams. (proprietary knowledge)

The first item is something that everyone knows; the second item is not something that the average person would know. Once you can recognize the difference between common and proprietary knowledge, you have to know how to use sources in your writing. Quoting material correctly is the only acceptable way to avoid plagiarism. This is accomplished through direct and indirect quotations. The way that one cites direct and indirect quotations depends on two factors:

- Is the source primary or secondary?
- Are you using APA or MLA style?

Let's deal with primary and secondary sources first. Primary sources are the original documents from which you draw the quote; secondary sources are books, analyses, and so forth from which you draw a quotation that *they used in their book from an original source.* If you are writing a paper on the U.S. Constitution and you have a copy of it in front of you, then you are using a primary source and you would cite it as such.

Alternatively, if you are using a hypothetical book called *The Boosalis Guide to the U.S. Constitution* and you quote from the Constitution out of my sections that analyze it, then you are using a secondary source for your U.S. Constitution paper. Plus, you have to give my book and me a citation. Why? *Because I did the hard work in finding and dissecting portions of the Constitution for you and you have to give me credit for that!* Dictionaries, encyclopedias, CD-ROMS are often loaded with secondary source material, so you have to be very careful when quoting from them.

How you format in-text quotations and citations depends on the style you are using. There are a number of different styles: Chicago, Turabian, APA, and MLA. APA stands for the American Psychological Association, and MLA stands for Modern Language Association. The registration bulletins do not state which type of style you need to know for the test, so let's use the most popular ones: APA and MLA (most likely MLA, by the way). Table 6.5 shows comparative APA and MLA in-text quotations:

TABLE 6.5   Comparative Sources

APA IN-TEXT CITATIONS (OWL, 2004A)	MLA IN-TEXT CITATIONS (OWL, 2004B)
Primary Sources Boosalis (2004) provides an overview of APA and MLA style.	**Primary Sources** Boosalis's *"Beating Them All!"* provides an overview of APA and MLA style.
There are two primary ways to cite sources: APA and MLA (Boosalis, 2004).	There are two primary ways to cite sources: APA and MLA (Boosalis).
Secondary Sources According to Chris Boosalis, "There are two primary ways to cite sources: APA and MLA" (as quoted in Johnson, 2004, p. 23).	**Secondary Sources** According to Chris Boosalis, "There are two primary ways to cite sources: APA and MLA" (qtd. in Johnson 23).

When referencing a quotation in APA, you simply give the single or primary author first and the year of publication. If there are multiple authors, then you list them:

Boosalis, Boosalis, Boosalis, and Boosalis (2004) state that…

If you use the multiple-authored work in other parts of your document, then you can shorten the reference by using *et al:*

Boosalis et al. (2004) state that…

The Latin phrase *et al.* simply stands for "and others." If there are other works with the same authors under different titles published in the same year, you cite them as follows:

Boosalis et al. (2004a) state that…
Boosalis et al. (2004b) state that…

Quoting secondary sources in APA style simply gives the quotation and cites the secondary source this way:

> According to Chris Boosalis, "There are two primary ways to cite sources: APA and MLA" (as quoted in Johnson, 2004, p. 23).

This means that the quote of mine that you are using in your paper was found in Johnson's 2004 work on page 23.

MLA style is different. Look at the table again and note the differences. You should see that no year is given—only the source and the page number at the end of the quote. Note how this is handled in both primary source examples. Secondary sources are handled in way that is similar to APA, but the abbreviation "qtd. in" is used instead of the whole phrase.

Developing a reference list also differs in APA and MLA. First of all, in APA the reference list of books and journals at the end of the paper is called References; however, in MLA style, it is called Works Cited. Second, the way that books, journals, and electronic media are cited differ, too. Table 6.6 offers a comparison.

APA bibliographies have the following general format for books:

> Last Name, First Initial, Middle Initial. (Year). Title in italics. City of Publication, State: Publisher.

TABLE 6.6   Comparative Bibliographies

APA BIBLIOGRAPHY (OWL, 2004A)	MLA WORKS CITED (OWL, 2004B)
Book, Single Author Boosalis, C. N. (2004). *Beating them all!* Boston: Allyn and Bacon.	**Book, Single Author** Boosalis, Chris N. *Beating Them All.* Boston, MA: Allyn and Bacon.
Book, Multiple Author Boosalis, C. N., Boosalis, C. N., & Boosalis, C. N. (2004). *Beating them all!* Boston: Allyn and Bacon.	**Book, Multiple Author** Boosalis, Chris N., Chris N. Boosalis, and Chris N. Boosalis. *Beating Them All.* Boston, MA: Allyn and Bacon.
Journal Article Boosalis, C. N., Taghavian, A., & Myrhe, O. (2003). The role of CBEST scores. *The California Reader, 37, 22–36.*	**Journal Article** Boosalis, Chris N., Alex Taghavian, and Oddmund Myrhe. (2003). "The role of CBEST scores." *The California Reader.* 37.1 (2003): 22–36.
Websites Boosalis, C. N. (2003). Beating them all. Retrieved January 1, 2004, from http://www.beatingtherica.com.	**Websites** Boosalis, Chris. Beating them all. 1 November 2003. 1 January 2004, http://www.beatingtherica.com.
CD-ROM *Dissertation Abstracts* (SilverPlatter, CD-ROM, September 2003 release).	**CD-ROM** *Dissertation Abstracts.* CD-ROM. SilverPlatter. Sept. 2003.

The book title is in italics and only the first letter in the title is capitalized. Proper nouns and words after colons are also capitalized, but the rest are lowercase:

> Beating them all: Thirty days to success on English literature.

Journal articles follow roughly the same format, but the title is not italicized—*but the name of the journal is.* Furthermore, the volume number of the journal is given and so are the page numbers at the very end.

Websites are cited by offering the date of retrieval, along with the URL. Because websites change rapidly, it is important to state the date that you visited and extracted the material from the cite.

MLA bibliographies, on the other hand, have a number of distinguishing characteristics. Books are cited as follows:

> Last name, First Name, Middle Initial. <u>Title Underlined.</u> City, State of Publication: Publisher, Year.

Journal articles in MLA are referenced as follows:

> Last name, First Name, First Initial. "Title in Quotation Marks. <u>Journal Title Underlined.</u> Volume, Number (Year): Pages.

Websites in MLA are cited like this:

> Last Name, First Name (if any). Title of Page. Date Created—Day Month Year. Date Visited—Day—Month—Year. URL

Evaluating Sources.   As a teacher, you need to teach your students how to select and evaluate sources. Understanding selection criteria does appear in the registration bulletins, so we will cover this topic here.

An easy-to-recall method for evaluating sources is what I term ACTS. It stands for *accurate, credible, timeliness,* and *sources.* Each element of the acronym is discussed below.

- *Accurate.* The sources that you choose should be unbiased. A test of reasonability means looking for slanted or propagandized information and then maybe rejecting it. For example, when writing an article on the dangers of obesity, information provided to you from *Living the Fried Life* might not present the same type of information that *Cholesterol Today* might. Therefore, checking for political or other biases is important when determining reasonability.

- *Credible.* You have to judge whether the source is a credible one. To do so, you have to check the author's credentials and understand how the journal, paper, or editors select items to include in their publication. For example, articles in *Newsweek* are probably more reliable than articles found in *The National Enquirer.* The reputations of both journals are different, the selection criteria are different, and so are the motivations. In academia, the most respected journals are those that use peer-review processes, where an author submits a work, and the editor sends it out for review by leading figures in the field. Those "peers" determine whether the article will be published.

- *Timeliness.* Timeliness means that the information hasn't gone stale. For example, if you are writing an essay on effective diets for students and your sources are from

1900, then your information will miss over 100 years of new information on the topic. In short, you have to ensure that your information is current.

- *Sources.* The final element is to look for where your source gets its information. Just because an article appears in a leading journal does not mean that it is unbiased or completely factual. One must look at the sources listed to see if they are outdated, biased, or problematic in some way. Furthermore, one must be careful not to mistake an editorial (deliberately opinionated) with a news report (deliberately unopinionated). This is a common classroom activity: Photocopy five editorials and five news items without the titles and ask students to judge whether they are factual or opinionated. This exercise will help students to develop their evaluative reading skills. In any case, the sources one uses in a research report should use objective data to present a credible, accurate, and reasonable article.

Content Area Twelve: The Editing Process

Editing and revising occur before publishing a work. Editing involves organizing paragraphs, supporting ideas, and clarifying ideas, and providing transitions between paragraphs. Revising addresses sentence structure (grammar), mechanics (punctuation), and spelling. Only the major ideas that appear in the registration bulletins are discussed in this section (see Table 6.7).

TABLE 6.7

ORGANIZATION	Introduction
	Thesis
	Body paragraphs
	Conclusion
STYLE	Parallelism
	Redundancy
	Passives
	Transitions
GRAMMAR	Subject/verb agreement
	Comma splices
	Run-on sentences
	Sentence fragments

Organization.   When reviewing student essay data, look for organizational patterns in the essay and within each paragraph. What you are looking for is the basic five-paragraph essay that uses an introduction, thesis, body paragraphs, and conclusion. Within each paragraph, you are looking for topic sentences, sequenced supporting details, and a concluding sentence. Table 6.8 shows a generic five-part essay on spelling development.

When you review student data on the test, look for the five essay components and look at the structure of the body paragraphs, since they may reveal needs that you will have

TABLE 6.8 The Five-Paragraph Essay

Introduction	There are three stages in spelling development.
Thesis	The stages are prephonetic, phonetic, and transitional. Each one has different characteristics and activities.
Body Paragraph	Prephonetic spelling is the first and earliest stage of spelling. It is characterized by scribbling lines or using symbols arbitrarily to represent letters. Letter/sound activities help students move to the second phase of spelling development.
Body Paragraph	Phonetic spelling is the second stage of spelling development. A child's spelling of the dominant sounds heard at the beginnings and endings of words typify this stage. Learning to encode medial sounds through letter-box activities are common at this developmental level.
Body Paragraph	Transitional spelling is a later stage of spelling development. Here, the child encodes all of the major sounds heard in the word, but may need additional work in spelling patterns. This will help the child move into the conventional stage of spelling.
Conclusion	The prephonetic, phonetic, and transitional stages are part of spelling development, and each one has its own characteristics and required activities.

to identify in multiple-choice or short-answer questions (essay outlines or paragraph frames would be appropriate for developing organizational skills).

Editing Paragraphs.   Internal paragraph structure, paragraph organization, and transitional phrases between paragraphs will be covered on the exam. You will certainly be asked multiple-choice questions on some aspects of paragraph editing, and you may even be asked to write an essay about it. The data set might look something like this:

MY FAVORITE MEMORY

My best memery are about last chrismas. When I got a brant new bicicle. I rode it every day. When the snow melted. I saw it at ericks bike shop it was really cool, like the one that evel kenevels got. its biger than my old bike. My freind mike jumped it at taft park and he skined his knee. My dad told me that I'd havto be real carefull on my bike cause santa isn't enshured. I wanto jump my bike real high to like evel. Thats why I like this memery the best.

During the revising stage, you would ignore the sentence, style, and spelling problems and focus only on the paragraph's internal structure. Clearly, there is a topic sentence *(My best memery is about last christmas)* and a concluding sentence *(Thats why I like this memery the best)*. There are problems with the order of the ideas and there are also extraneous details in the paragraph that would have to be taken care.

Story Frames.   As students become more and more proficient in writing single words, sentences, and lengthier writings, structure development writing activities are used. The most common tool used for this purpose is the paragraph frame (Lewis, Wray, & Rospigli-osi, 1994). Story frames provide a scaffold to transition students from simple ideas about writing words and sentences to writing full paragraphs. The frames provide an outline that the teacher creates and the students complete (see Figure 6.2).

FIGURE 6.2

My favorite memory is _____. It is about _____. Also, _____. Thus, _____is my favorite memory.

Transitions between paragraphs might also be areas of instruction using either paragraph or story frames. Consider the following adverbs and how and when they are used (see Table 6.9):

TABLE 6.9

LINKING ADVERBS	COMPARATIVE ADVERBS	CONTINUATION ADVERBS	SUBSTITUTION ADVERBS
■ alternatively ■ on the other hand	■ similarly ■ likewise	■ furthermore ■ in addition	■ instead ■ rather

Transitions serve the following purpose: They explicitly link ideas within and between paragraphs. For example, they link ideas, compare idea, continue ideas, and substitute ideas. Space will not permit a full list of all of the available transitional phrases, and it would probably be unnecessary and prohibitive if you tried to memorize a list of them any-way. Therefore, your best approach is to remember the elements in the table above and then transfer these concepts to the exam.

Revision of Grammar and Mechanics.   You may also be asked to review student writing for style. Table 6.10 reflects examples of the major stylistic considerations that you should know for the test.

TABLE 6.10

Parallelism	*Swimming and to run are my favorite activities. Swimming and running are my favorite activities.
Redundancy	*Students need to write. Students need to study. Students need to learn. Students need to write, study, and learn.
Passives	*The book was read by the boy. The boy read the book.

If the organizational pattern of the sample data looks okay and the paragraphs are sequenced properly, then you may have to look at the style. Problems with parallelism are easy to identify In the examples above, the writer has not used the same forms of the words that are in the subject. Redundancies are also easy to spot, since the data may show a student who is writing the same words or phrases over and over again throughout the paragraph. Passive voice sentences are pretty simple to find, too. Look for the characteristic *was* + verb and a *by* phrase: "The dog **was walked by his owner.**"

Grammar.   Space will not permit a full review of English grammar. However, Table 6.11 shows common grammar errors that you can spot in data sets.

TABLE 6.11

Subject/Verb Agreement	*He walk to his house.
	He walks to his house.
Comma Splices	*He walked to his house yesterday, he had dinner with his family.
	He walked to his house yesterday, **and** he had dinner with his family.
Run-Ons	*He walked to his house yesterday he had dinner with his family.
	He walked to his house yesterday. He had dinner with his family.
	*He walked to his house yesterday and had dinner with his family and walked his dog and then went to bed.
	He walked to his house yesterday and had dinner with his family. Then he walked his dog and went to bed.
Fragments	*When he walked home yesterday. He had dinner with his family.
	When he walked home yesterday, he had dinner with his family.

In brief, look at the verbs in the data. If the verbs do not agree with the subject in number or tense, then they show areas of need. Comma splices, too, might be present. A comma splice occurs when a student "staples" two complete sentences together, instead of using a period to end one sentence before beginning another or joining them together with a conjunction. Run-on sentences are similar to comma splices, only lazier. Here, the writer not only leaves off a conjunction, but also forgets to supply a comma. Run-on sentences can also be too large a group of connected or unconnected thoughts. Sentence fragments usually begin with what's called a subordinating conjunction. You'll will recognize them because the thought seems incomplete.

Now go back to the sample paragraph, "My Favorite Memory." Using the above examples, try to find the agreement, splice, run-on, and fragment problems in the paragraph. You should be able to identify at lest one of each variety quite easily.

Mechanics.   Mechanics (punctuation) is listed as an area of assessment on the exam. You will most likely see data sets to be analyzed for the major areas of mechanics, so let's apply some of the principles to our sample paragraph:

My best memery are about last chrismas. when I got a brant new bicicle. I rode it every day. When the snow melted. I saw it at ericks bike shop it was really cool, like the one that evel kenevels got. its biger than my old bike. My freind mike jumped it at taft park and he skined his knee. My dad told me that I'd havto be real carefull on my bike cause santa isn't enshured. I wanto jump my bike real high to like evel. Thats why I like this memery the best.

Capitalization. In English, we capitalize the first word of each sentence. Clearly, this student is having difficulty with this as seen in sentence two. Proper nouns are also capitalized in English; and the student missed Christmas, Erick's Bike Shop, and Evel Knievel.

Punctuation. Commas are used in the following instances. In a series of three or more nouns or adjectives:

- Use commas

  The flag of the United States is red, white, and blue.

- Use commas to link independent clauses before *and, but, nor, for,* and *or:*

  I saw it at Erick's Bike Shop, **and** it was really cool.

- Use semicolons instead of *and, but, nor, for,* and *or* to join independent clauses:

  I saw it at Erick's Bike Shop; it was really cool.

- Use semicolons before words like *however, therefore,* and *thus:*

  I want to finish this section on grammar; however, I have lots more to type.

- Use apostrophes to show possession and contraction:

  Evel Knievel's   (possession).
  That's (contraction of *that is*).
  It's (contraction of *it is*).

Word Choice. Like mechanics, word choice might also be on the exam. There are two types of words to be aware of: those that are easily confused and those that are gender biased.

CONFUSING WORDS. Many lists of easily confused words exist. They include words like accept/except, affect/effect, borrow/lend, can/may, two/to/too, their/there/they're, its/it's, sit/set, and data/datum.

In the sample paragraph above, the student has several word confusions. Its and it's are confused: *It's bigger than my old bike* reflects the proper form, because the child is contracting "it is." The student is also contracting words erroneously: *Have to* is contracted as *havto,* and *want to* is contracted as *wanto.*

AVOIDING GENDER BIAS. No gender biases are present in the sample paragraph. However, for the test, you should know how to read for and how to amend instances of gender bias. In the first place, it is best to write in nonspecific terms:

A. Any lawyer who is worth **his** fee must be honest.
B. Any lawyers who are worth their fees must be honest.

Sentence A is biased, because it sounds as if all lawyers are men. The problem is corrected in sentence B by using the plural form, which renders the sentence gender neutral.

Words like *weathermen, mailmen, policemen,* and *firemen* are also outdated. Use these types of words instead:

Forecasters, mail carriers, police officers, firefighters.

Content Area Thirteen: Interpersonal Communications and Public Speaking

This final content area is about nonwritten communications. The bulk of the material covers preparing and delivering and evaluating informational, persuasive, and dramatic speeches. There may be general questions on the exam about human communications (interpersonal and mass), but the emphasis is on your understanding of the basic elements of public speaking.

Oral and Written Language Differences.   Similarities and differences between oral and written communications exist (Akinnaso, 1982). Both types of communication must consider the audience and its level of knowledge, experience, and expectations. Both also employ descriptions, main ideas, supporting details, and organizational principles and transitions. However, they differ in how much latitude one has in expressing complex ideas. Writing can be read and reread for clarification, but spoken language disappears the moment the utterance leaves one's lips. This plays a role in how we use short, powerful examples, summative graphics, and even body language when we speak.

Elements of Oral Communication.   Communication involves a sender who encodes a message for a receiver who hears the message and decodes (Barker, 1990). We decode messages for *etic* information (what is said on the surface), and *emic* information (what is said beneath the surface). The balance of this section describes how we encode and send information. We will discuss information on types of interaction between senders and receivers and the role of listeners.

Types of Interaction.   Interpersonal, small group, public, and mass communications affect the level of interaction and feedback that a receiver may offer to the speaker (Luft, 1984). In all instances, both etic and emic information and nonverbal signals will influence how the listener decodes the message. Following are different sender/receive configurations to know for the test.

Dyadic Communication.   Dyadic communication is basic two-person, interpersonal communication. The amount of feedback is high, and the sender can tailor her message for the listener and adapt her communicative style based on how well the listener seems to receive the information. Now is a good time to describe active listening and the role of the receiver during dyadic interactions. Active (participatory) listening includes analytic, supportive, reflective, and evaluative listening. Here are the descriptions of each that apply to the exam (Boone, Kurtz, & Block, 1997; DeVito, 2002; Lesikar, Petit, & Flatley, 1999):

- *Analytic listening* is hearing and understanding the message that one receives. Questions are for clarification and the interaction is straightforward. Participation is to ensure that misunderstandings are few and clarification requests are common.
- *Supportive listening* is different from pure analytic listening. Although clarification questions will occur here, the listener shows solidarity with the speaker and encouragement to validate what the speaker is saying. In short, the feedback one offers to the speaker is supportive and encouraging.
- *Reflective listening* combines analytic and supportive listening. Here, the listener clarifies both verbal and nonverbal cues to ensure understanding, and the listener may also interact and restate ideas back to the speaker to demonstrate understanding. The reflective listening may be either supportive or nonsupportive, depending on whether one agrees with what one is hearing.
- *Evaluative listening* is the most critical listening of all. One listens carefully for opinions stated as facts, inconsistencies, or flaws in logic. Feedback can be highly critical, and respondents may need to learn how to offer critical feedback in a way that is nonjudgmental and impersonal, yet honest and straightforward. Learning about when to offer evaluative criticism to a speaker may also be necessary, as certain times for criticism may not be as favorable as other times. For example, telling a speaker that he is not doing well *during* the speech may not be well received.

Small Group Communication. Small group communication relies on the same types of listening (analytic, supportive, reflective, evaluative), but it can be less interpersonal because one must take cues from more than just one person as one speaks (Beebe & Masterson, 2000). In addition, this type of communication may differ from dyadic communication because the roles may be assigned externally (Benne & Sheats, 1948). For example, the leader may have the responsibility of keeping the discussion on task. In the classroom, students will need to learn how to use summary statements to move from one point of discussion to the next and how to build consensus among all members of the group. Listeners, too, play a role in the interaction, because they need to have the opportunity to ask clarifying questions during the small group discussion. The teacher's role in this instance is to ensure that all ideas will be entertained without criticism, until the students are asked to evaluate and select their best ideas for presentation to the class.

Public and Mass Communications. Public and mass communications are less interpersonal, as you know, and there are fewer opportunities for providing feedback or for seeking clarification directly from the source. The speaker must take this fact into consideration to ensure that messages are clear and not lost by nonverbal and other interference that can distract the listener or reduce the impact of the speech. Because the test focuses on public speaking, we will spend more time on that topic in the final parts of this section.

Types of Speeches. There are four types of speeches to know for the exam: extemporaneous, informational, persuasive, and interpretive. Each type is described below.

- *Extemporaneous speeches* can be either informational or persuasive, but they tend to be brief, on-the-spot deliveries that can be word-for-word reading from one's notes to a group of listeners or a speech invented off the top of one's head. The key to the success of speeches of this nature is knowing how to select and present information succinctly in a summative format for a specific audience.

■ *Informational speeches* follow the same format that you learned about in written communications. These speeches can describe cause and effect, problems and solutions, details and demonstrations, and so forth. Facts are presented and summarized, and the goal is to inform the audience about a subject rather than to persuade people to take one position or another.

■ *Persuasive speeches* are delivered to move an audience to act or to take a particular position on a subject. Knowing the audience is very important because the speaker must tailor the message to audience members. The message must be adapted to their level of knowledge, to their belief systems, and to their logical or emotional hot buttons. The format is to first gain their attention and to establish a connection with them. The body of the speech moves from one compelling point to the final, most compelling point. Then, the speaker makes a final request for action. We will discuss persuasive techniques under the section on *preparing speeches*.

■ *Dramatic interpretations* are soliloquies taken from dramatic plays. Shakespeare's plays are obvious selections. The expectation of the audience is different from what one finds in informational or persuasive speeches. Since the delivery of the dialogue is what will carry the speech, the words must be delivered powerfully and vividly. The presentation itself becomes its own adjective and verb. Furthermore, the passage that one selects must be one that can be delivered in this manner, since the effectiveness of the rendition will be conveyed in large part through physical reactions and demonstrations.

Preparing Speeches.   The formula for preparing speeches is the same as what you saw in the writing process. There is brainstorming, drafting, editing, revising, and presenting. Outlines are essential during drafting. Main ideas and summaries are extracted and organized in an informational pattern (cause and effect, problem solution, etc.) or in a persuasive format.

Knowing the audience is paramount (Boon, Kurtz, & Block, 1997). If you do not consider what they already know, then the speech may come off as either condescending or over their heads. The message must be tailored to their logical or emotional expectations. This will help you get the audience to accept what you are asking them to consider (e.g., multiple points of view or a singular call to action).

If the speech is persuasive, one can make an argument using either inductive or deductive reasoning (Lesikar et al., 1999). Inductive reasoning presents the facts of a case to a person first with the hope that the author and reader arrive at the same conclusion together. On the other hand, deductive reasoning presents the author's conclusion first and then shows the reader the points that make such a conclusion plausible. In either case, the speaker has to make a choice about which type of reasoning will be used in order to organize the body of the speech effectively.

The level of objectivity is another important consideration. The least subjective evidence often comes from statistical data that shows why something is numerically true. Each statement that the speaker makes can be bolstered by objective data to make the case factually powerful. Using quotes from authority figures is another way to support arguments because the reputation of the source will provide support to one's argument (DeVito,

2002). Listeners do take a person's credibility into account when hearing a speech, so authoritative quotes can be very helpful.

Common ground and "bandwagoning" are the most emotional techniques that one can use to influence people (Cialdini, 1984). Here, the speaker tries to get the listeners to buy into the position by showing that the speaker and the audience are on the same page. This technique can be effective if the audience might be repelled by a pro or con position on a issue. Testimonials are common parts of these techniques. Quotations from people who are "just like you" are used to support ideas and to move the audience from a position of resistance to acceptance before they are asked to "join the crowd." Again, the audience's expectations and level of sophistication must be considered, because people do not like to be manipulated.

Delivering Speeches.   There are a number of considerations for delivering a speech, including volume, rate, and tone (Boone et al., 1997; DeVito, 2002; Lesikar et al., 1999):

- Volume is good for emphasizing and distinguishing main ideas from supporting ideas.
- Rate can be varied, too. Obviously, a normal rate of speech is expected but speaking more quickly or slowly at selected points in the speech can increase the dramatic aspects of the presentation and make them more compelling.
- Tone is also very important. It, too, can be varied for effect, though a speech can be rendered incoherent or frivolous if the wrong tone is selected. If the topic is serious, then the tone should also be serious—the audience takes its cue for how to receive the information from the speaker, and they might not know what to think if the tone does not match the topic.

From your own experience, you know that speeches delivered in a monotone voice might help some members of the audience sleep but do nothing for the message that one is trying to communicate to them.

Because nonverbal information is also communicated during speeches, it must also be considered carefully (Knapp & Hall, 1997).

- Gestures can be used for emphasis, though too many gesticulations or nervous tics can be highly distracting for the audience.
- Proxemics (social distance) is another important nonverbal consideration. Moving closer to the audience connotes intimacy, whereas moving away from the audience increases coldness and standoffishness. One must be careful to use the appropriate proxemics when delivering a speech to an audience or when speaking interpersonally.
- Finally, eye contact is important and can be cultural. Generally, maintaining eye contact is the way one conveys forthrightness and certainty in Western culture, so it must be used for a Western audience.

The discussion of nonverbal behaviors leads us to cultural considerations. For many cultures, certain gestures that Westerners use for nonverbal politesse are offensive to other groups (Lesikar et al., 1999).

- Pointing with one's index finger during the speech, for example, might be used for emphasis in one culture but may constitute an offensive gesture in another.

- Proxemics is another cultural variable. Some cultures may favor intimate distances, but others may favor space.
- Eye contact, too, cannot be assumed to be the same cross-culturally. Looking down or away from a speaker may be an indication of deep respect rather than disinterest.

In short, misunderstandings may arise if one does not consider the impact that nonverbal communication may have on a culturally diverse audience.

Evaluating Speeches.   The role of the audience is to interpret and evaluate a speaker's message. The audience can listen critically to detect any contradictions or gaps in logic found in a speech. The following are common rhetorical problems with speeches (Carrol, 2003, Carrol & Salazar, 2000):

- Relying on cliches to carry a message: *The early bird catches the worm.*
- Begging the question (assuming facts without first establishing them): *If you don't send in your entry, you won't win!*
- Including non sequiturs (connecting unrelated ideas together): *Preparing for exams is difficult, and I need to feed my dog.*
- Overgeneralizing (extending facts beyond their boundaries): *All lawyers are crooks.*
- Associating cause and effect erroneously (post hoc ergo procter hoc): *Crimes increase with every full moon!*

The audience must also separate fact from opinion: Were the statements supported with logic or emotion? Were facts drawn from reliable and unbiased sources? Finally, effectiveness is judged by the effect of the speech. If it was an informational speech, did it inform? If it was a persuasive speech, did it persuade? If neither of these goals were achieved, then the speech can be said to have failed in its purpose.

CONCLUSION

This chapter presented the final domain concerning written and oral language development. You learned about the writing process, the research process, editing, and public speaking. The Epilogue will offer you some important suggestions for your preparation for test day.

Your next step in preparing for—and passing—CSET Multiple Subjects exam is to take a practice exam. The *only* practice exam materials that can be endorsed at this time are the ones that come directly from the test maker itself. A practice exam was deliberately excluded from this text because practicing on contrived materials can lead one to grow accustomed to questions that do not mirror what one finds on the actual test. Thus, the *essential* ingredient in your studies will be the official multiple-choice questions and practice essays that are available at the Official CSET website. Please see your registration bulletin for the Internet address. Additional support may also be found at *http://www.ablongman.com/ boosalis* in the form of CSET workshops and distance tutoring. Please visit the site for the latest information on these topics.

TEST DAY

In addition to the obvious considerations of getting enough nourishment and sleep prior to test day, there are several things you need to keep in mind.

1. *Know the real scores.* Be sure that you know what score you are aiming for on each subtest. Review chapter one and be sure to memorize the tally tables for each of the subtests, so that you can apply them with ease.
2. *Know how to manage your time.* Be sure that you understand the procedures for managing your time on the test. It is recommended that you register for all of the subtests and take them all at one time. That way, you will have a good idea about the content tested on all the tests, and you will be better able to prepare should have to take the tests a second time. If you are taking only one or two subtests, then review the specific plans for each combination of subtest.
3. *Use written and multiple-choice strategies.* Be sure that you know the strategies for the written and multiple-choice sections and that you have practiced them on the study guides. Note: In all cases, complete the essays, even if you run out of time on the multiple-choice questions. That way, you can get feedback on your writing and level of content knowledge from the score report that you receive after the exam.
4. *Dress comfortably and bring earplugs.* Since you can neither control the location of the exam nor its environment, be sure to dress for test success. That means wearing comfortable clothes. A layer or two is a good idea, depending on the season, since you can more easily remove a sweater than ask the test proctor to turn the thermostat either up or down. Foam earplugs are another good idea. They can be purchased at your local pharmacy. One candidate reported that the person next to her sighed constantly during the exam. So, it may be a good idea for you to use earplugs during the

exam in order to ensure that you are able to focus on the task at hand. Try them out prior to test day.

5. *Be confident!* If you have studied the content and practiced the strategies, then you are in an excellent position to do well on the exam. Take pride in that…and beat the exam!

REFERENCES

Adams, D. (1995). *The hitchhiker's guide to the galaxy.* New York: Ballantine Books.

Adams, M. J. (1990). *Beginning to read: Thinking and learning about print.* Cambridge, MA: MIT Press.

Akinnaso, F. N. (1982). On the differences between spoken and written language. *Language and Speech, 25 (Part 2),* 97–125.

Anderson, P. (1985). Explaining intercultural differences in nonverbal communication. In Larry A. Samovar & Richard E. Porter (eds.), *Intercultural communication: A reader* (6th ed., pp. 286–296). Belmont, CA: Wadsworth.

Armbruster, B. B., & Nagy, W. E. (1992). Vocabulary in content area lessons. *The Reading Teacher, 45,* 550–551.

Armstrong, T. (2000). *Multiple intelligences in the classroom* (2nd ed.). Alexandria, VA: Association for Supervision and Curriculum Development.

Asher, J. (1982). *Learning another language through actions: The complete teachers' guidebook.* Los Gatos, CA: Sky Oaks.

Asher, J. L. (1969). The total physical response to second language learning. *The Modern Language Journal, 53,* 1–17.

Asher, J. J., & Garcia, R. (1969). The optimal age to learn a foreign language. *Modern Language Journal, 53,* 334–341.

Babbs, P. J., & Moe, A. J. (1983). Metacognition: A key for independent learning from text. *The Reading Teacher, 37,* 422–426.

Ball, E. W., & Blachman, B. A. (1991). Does phoneme awareness training in kindergarten make a difference in early word recognition and developmental spelling? *Reading Research Quarterly, 26,* 49–66.

Barker, L. (1990). *Communications* (5th ed.). Englewood Cliffs, NJ: Prentice-Hall.

Barnitz, J. G. (1998). Revising grammar instruction for authentic composing and comprehending. *The Reading Teacher, 51,* 608–611.

Barnlund, D. (1989). *Communicative styles of Japanese and Americans: Images and realities.* Belmont, CA: Wadsworth.

Bates, E., & MacWhinney, B. (1981). Second language acquisition from a functionalist perspective: Pragmatics, semantics, and perceptual strategies. In H. Winitz (ed.), *Annals of New York Academy of Science conference on native language and foreign language acquisition* (pp. 190–214), New York: New York Academy of Science.

Baum, L. F. (2000). *The wonderful wizard of oz: 100th anniversary edition.* New York: Harper Collins.

Baumann, J. F., Jones, L. A., & Seifert-Kessell, N. (1993). Using think alouds to enhance children's comprehension monitoring abilities. *The Reading Teacher, 47,* 184–193.

Baumann, J. F., Seifert-Kessell, N., Jones, L. A. (1992). Effect of think aloud instruction on elementary students' comprehension monitoring ability. *Journal of Reading Behavior, 25,* 407–438.

Bear, D., & Barone, D. (1989). Using children's spellings to group for word study and directed reading in the primary classroom. *Reading Psychology, 10,* 275–292.

Bear, D., Invernizzi, M., Templeton, S., Johnston, F. (2000). *Words their way: Word study for phonics, vocabulary, and spelling instruction.* Upper Saddle River, NJ: Merrill.

Bear, D., & Templeton, S. (1998). Explorations in developmental spelling: Foundations for learning and teaching phonics, spelling, and vocabulary. *The Reading Teacher, 52,* 222–242.

Beebe, S., & Masterson, J. (2000). *Communicating in small groups: Principles and practices* (6th ed.). Boston: Allyn and Bacon.

Benne, K., & Sheats, P. (1948). Functional roles of group members. *Journal of Social Issues, 4,* 41–49.

Bernstein, B. (1964). Elaborated and restricted codes: Their social origins and some consequences. *American Anthropologist, 66,* 55–69.

Bley-Vroman, R. (1986). Hypothesis testing in second language acquisition. *Language Learning, 36,* 353–376.

Bloom, P. (Ed.). (1994). *Language acquisition: Core readings.* Cambridge, MA: MIT Press.

Boone, L. E., Kurtz, D. L., & Block, J. R. (1997). *Contemporary business communications.* Upper Saddle River, NJ: Prentice Hall.

Bottomley, D. M., Bottomley, W. A., & Melnick, S. A. (1997/1998). Assessing children's views about themselves as writers using the writer self-perception scale. *The Reading Teacher, 51,* 286–296.

Brown, R. (1973). *A first language: The early stages.* Cambridge, MA: Harvard University Press.

Bryan, J. (1998). KWWL: Questioning the known. *The Reading Teacher, 7,* 618–620.

Burns, P. C., Roe, B. D., & Ross, E. P. (1999). *Teaching reading in today's elementary schools.* Boston: Houghton Mifflin.

Burroway, J. (1999). *Writing fiction: A guide to narrative craft*. New York: Longman.

Cairns, H. S. (1996). *The acquisition of language*. (2nd ed.). Cambridge, MA: Harvard University Press.

Canale, M., & Swain, M. (1980). Theoretical bases of communicative approaches to second language teaching and testing. *Applied Linguistics, 1*, 1–47.

Carnine, D., Silbert, J., Kame'enui, E. J., & Tarver, S. (2004). *Direct instruction reading* (4th ed.). New York: Pearson Education.

Carrol, R. T. (2003). *The skeptic's dictionary: A collection of strange beliefs, amusing deceptions, and dangerous delusions*. Hoboken, NJ: John Wiley & Sons.

Carrol, R. T., & Salazar, K. (2000). *Becoming a critical thinker—A guide for the new millennium*. New York: Pearson.

Carr, K. S. (1983). The importance of inference skills in the primary grades. *The Reading Teacher, 36*, 518–522

Carr, K. S., Dewitz, P., & Patberg, J. (1989). Using cloze for inference training. *The Reading Teacher, 42*, 380–385.

Carr, K. S., & Ogle, D. (1987). KWl plus: A strategy for comprehension and summarization. *Journal of Reading, 30*, 626–631.

Carr, P. (1993). *Phonology*. New York: St. Martin's Press.

Chamot, A. U., & O'Malley, J. M. (1986). *A cognitive academic language learning approach: An ESL content based curriculum*. Washington, DC: National Clearinghouse for Bilingual Education.

Chapman, C. (1993). *If the shoe fits: How to develop multiple intelligences in the classroom*. Arlington Heights, IL: SkyLight.

Chomsky, C. (1969). *The acquisition of syntax in children from 5 to 10*. Cambridge, MA: MIT Press.

Chomsky, N., & Halle, M. (1968). *The sound patterns of English*. New York: Harper and Row.

Cialdini, R. T. (1984). *Influence: How and why people agree to things*. New York: Morrow.

Clay, M. M. (1993a). *An observation survey of early literacy achievement*. Portsmouth, NH: Heinemann.

Clay, M. M. (1993b). *Reading recovery: A guidebook for teachers*. Portsmouth, NH: Heinemann.

Cohen, A. D. (1996). Speech acts. In S. L. McKay & N. H. Hornberger (Eds.), *Sociolinguistics and language teaching* (pp. 383–420). New York: Press Syndicate of the University of Cambridge.

Cohen, D. H. (1968). The effect of literature on vocabulary and reading achievement. *Elementary English, 45*, 209–213, 217.

Cooper, J. D. (2003). *Literacy: Helping children construct meaning* (5th ed.). Boston: Houghton Mifflin.

Courtney, A. M., & Abodeeb, T. L. (1999). Diagnostic-reflective portfolios. *The Reading Teacher, 52*, 708–714.

Crane, S. (1898). The open boat: A tale intended to be after the fact of being the experience of four men from the sunk steamer Commodor. In P. Lauter (Ed.), *The Heath anthology of American literature* (Vol. Two). Lexington, MA: D. C. Heath.

CSET (2003–2004a). *Registration Bulletin*. California Commission on Teacher Credentialing and National Evaluation Systems, Inc.

CSET (2003–2004b). *Registration Bulletin* [and test information] retrieved March 23, 2004 from *http://www.cset.nesinc.com*.

Cummins, J. (1979). Cognitive/academic language proficiency, linguistics interdependence, the optimal age question and some other matters. *Working Papers on Bilingualism, 19*, 197–205.

Curtis, S. (1977). *Genie: A psycholinguistic study of a modern-day "wild child."* New York: Academic Press.

DeVito, J. A. (2002). *Essentials of human communication* (4th ed.). Boston: Allyn and Bacon.

Duffelmeyer, F. A. (1994). Effective anticipation guide statements for learning from expository text. *Journal of Reading, 37*, 452–457.

Duffelmeyer, F. A., & Baum, D. D. (1992). The extended anticipation guide. *Journal of Reading, 35*, 654–656.

Dunn, A. H., & Graves, M. F. (1987). Intensive vocabulary instruction as a prewriting technique. *Reading Research Quarterly, 22*, 311–329.

Ediger, M. (1999). Evaluation of reading progress. *Reading Improvement, 36*, 50–56.

Eimas, P. (1975). Developmental studies of speech perception. In L. Cohen & P. Salapatek (Eds.), *Infant perception*. New York: Academic Press.

Fassold, R. (1984). *The sociolinguistics of society*. New York: Blackwell.

Fassold, R. (1990). *The sociolinguistics of Language*. Rowley, MA: Newbury House.

Faulkner, W. (1991). *The sound and the fury* (reissue edition). New York: Vintage.

Gardner, R., & Lambert, W. (1959). Motivational variables in second language acquisition. *Canadian Journal of Psychology, 13*, 266–72

Gass, S. M., & Selinker, L. (1994). *Second language acquisition: An introductory course*. Hillsdale, NJ: Lawrence Erlbaum.

Gass, S., & Selinker, L. (1983). *Language transfer in language learning*. Rowley, MA: Newbury House.

Gass, S. (1984). A review of interlanguage syntax: Language transfer and language universals. *Language Learning, 34*, 115–132.

Giles, H., & Smith, P. (1979). Accomodation theory: Optimal levels of convergence. In H. Giles & R. St. Clair (Eds.), *Language and social psychology* (pp. 45–65). London: Basil Blackwell.

Goldstein, L. M. (1987). Standard English: The only target for nonnative speakers of English? *TESOL Quarterly, 21,* 417–436.

Gray-Schlegel, M. A., & King, Y. (1998). Introducing concepts about print to the preservice teacher: A hands-on experience. *The California Reader, 32,* 16–21.

Gunning, T. (2004a). *Creating literacy instruction for all children in grades pre-k to 4.* New York: Pearson Education.

Gunning, T. (2004b). *Creating literacy instruction for all children in grades 4 to 8.* New York: Pearson Education.

Hakuta, K. (1974). A preliminary report on the development of grammatical morphemes in a Japanese girl learning English as a second language. *Working Papers on Bilingualism, 3,* 18–43.

Halliday, M. A. K. (1978). *Language as social semiotic: The social interpretation of language and meaning.* Baltimore, MD: University Park Press.

Hemingway, E. (1995). *The old man and the sea* (Reissue Edition). New York: Scribner.

Hennings, D. G. (2002). *Communication in action: Teaching literature-based language arts.* Boston: Houghton Mifflin.

Hoffman, J. V. (1998). When bad things happen to good ideas in literacy education: Professional dilemmas, personal decisions, and political traps. *The Reading Teacher, 52,* 102–112.

Huang, J., & Hatch, E. (1978). A Chinese child's acquisition of English (pp. 118–131). In E. Hatch (Ed.), *Second language acquisition.* Rowley, MA: Newbury.

Hyman, L. M. (1975). *Phonology: Theory and analysis.* New York: Holt, Rinehart and Winston.

Hymes, D. (1972). On communicative competence. In J. Pride & J. Holmes (Eds.), *Sociolinguistics.* Harmondsworth, UK: Penguin Books.

Ingram, D. (1989). *First language acquisition.* Cambridge, MA: Academic Press.

Invernizzi, M. A., Abouzeid, M. P., & Bloodgood, J. W. (1997). Integrated word study: Spelling, grammar, and meaning in the language arts classroom. *Language Arts, 74,* 185–192.

Jipson, J., & Paley, N. (1991). The selective tradition in teachers' choice of children's literature. Does it exist in the elementary classroom? *English Education, 23,* 148–159.

Johnson, J., & Newport, E. (1989). Critical period effects in second language learning: The influence of maturational state on acquisition of ESL. *Cognitive Psychology, 21,* 60–99.

Joos, M. (1967). *The five clocks.* New York: Harcourt, Brace and World.

Katamba, F. (1993). *Morphology.* New York: St. Martin's Press.

Kellerman, E., & Sharwood-Smith, M. (1986). *Cross-linguistic influence in second language acquisition.* Elmsford: Pergamon.

Kemporson, R. (1977). *Semantic theory.* Cambridge, UK: Cambridge University Press.

Kesselman-Turkel, J., & Peterson, F. (1982). *Note-taking made easy.* Chicago: Contemporary Books.

Klima, E., & Bellugi, U. (1966). Syntactic regularities in the speech of children. In J. Lynons & R. Wales (Eds.), *Psycholinguistic papers.* Edinburgh, UK: Edinburgh University Press.

Knapp, M. L., & Hall, J. (1997). *Nonverbal communication in human interaction* (4th ed.). Fort Worth, TX: Harcourt Brace Jovanovich.

Knowles, J. (2003). *A separate peace.* New York: Scribner.

Krashen, S., & Terrell, T. (1983). *The natural approach.* New York: Pergamon.

Krashen, S. D. (1981). *Principles and practice in second language acquisition. English Language Teaching series.* London: Prentice-Hall International.

Krashen, S. (1982). Principles and practice in second language acquisition. Oxford, UK: Pergamon Press.

Krashen, S. (1983). Practical applications of research. *Psycholinguistic Research ACTFL Yearbook.* Lincolnwood, IL: National Textbook.

Krashen, S. (1985). *The input hypothesis: Issues and implications.* New York: Longman.

Krashen, S. (1993). The power of reading. Englewood, NJ: Libraries United.

Krashen, S., & Terrell, T. (1983). *The natural approach: Language acquisition in the classroom.* Oxford, UK: Pergamon Press.

Labov, W. (1972). *Language in the inner city: Studies in black English vernacular.* Philadelphia: University of Pennsylvania Press.

Langer, J. A. (1981). From theory to practice: A prereading plan. *Journal of Reading, 24,* 152–156.

Larson-Freeman, D. (1976). An explanation for the morpheme acquisition order of second language learners. *Language Learning, 26,* 125–34.

Larsen-Freeman, D., & Long, M. H. (1991). *An introduction to second language acquisition research.* New York: Longman.

Lazear, D. (1998). *The rubrics way: Using MI to assess understanding.* Tucson, AZ: Zephyr Press.

Lazear, D. (1999). *Eight ways of teaching: The artistry of teaching for multiple intelligences* (3rd ed.). Arlington Heights, IL: SkyLight.

Lee, D. M., & Allen, R. V. (1963). Learning to read through experience. (2nd ed.). New York: Meredith.

Lemke, J. *Talking science: Language, learning, and values.* New York: Ablex.

Lenneberg, E. H. (1967). The biological foundations of language. New York: Wiley.

Lesikar, R. V., Pettit, Jr., J. D., & Flatley, M. E. (1999). *Lesikar's basic business communication* (8th ed.), Boston: Irwin/McGraw Hill.

Lessow-Hurley, J. (1990). *The foundations of dual language instruction.* White Plains, NJ: Longman.

Levinson, S. (1983). *Pragmatics.* Cambridge, UK: Cambridge University Press.

Lewis, M., Wray, D., Rospigliosi, P. (1994). "…And I want it in your own words." *The Reading Teacher, 47,* 528–536.

Locke, J. (1983). *Phonological acquisition and change.* New York: Academic Press.

Luft, J. (1984). *Group processes: An introduction to group dynamics.* (3rd ed.). Palo Alto, CA: Mayfield.

Manzo, A. V. (1975). Guided reading procedure. *Journal of Reading, 19,* 287–291.

McCauley, J. K., & McCauley, D. S. (1992). Using choral reading to promote language learning for ESL students. *The Reading Teacher, 45,* 526–534.

McIntosh, M. E., & Draper, R. J. (1995). Applying the question–answer relationship strategy in mathematics. *Journal of Adolescent & Adult Literacy, 39,* 120–131.

Mesmer, H. A. (2001). Decodable text: A review of what we know. *Reading Research and Instruction, 40,* 121–142.

Mesmer, H. A., & Hutchins, E. J. (2002). Using QARs with charts and graphs. *The Reading Teacher, 56,* 20–29.

Mitchell, J. P., Abernathy, T. V., & Gowans, L. P. (1998). Making sense of literacy portfolios: A four step plan. *Journal of Adolescent & Adult Literacy, 41,* 384–389.

Newell, J. (1984). *Advance organizers: Their construction and use in instructional development.* ERIC Document ED 298908.

Newmark, L. (1966). How not to interfere with language learning. *Language Learning: The Individual and the Process. International Journal of American Linguistics, 40,* 77–83.

Odlin, T. (1989). Language transfer. Cross-linguistic influence in language learning. Cambridge, UK: Cambridge University Press.

Ogle, D. M. (1986). K-W-L: A teaching model that develops active reading of expository text. *The Reading Teacher, 39,* 564–571.

O'Grady, W., Dobrovolsky, M., & Aronoff, R.. (1993). *Contemporary linguistcs: An introduction.* New York: St. Martin's Press.

O'Mally, E. (Ed.). (1998). *Reading/language arts framework for California public schools, kindergarten through grade twelve.* Sacramento: California Department of Education.

Owens, R. (1984). *Language development: An introduction.* Columbus, OH: Charles E. Merril.

Owl. (2004a). Using American Psychological Association (APA) Format (Updated to 5th Edition). Retrieved March 23, 2004 from *http://owl.english. purdue.edu/handouts/research/r_apa.html.*

Owl. (2004b). Using Modern Language Association (MLA) Format. Retrieved March 23, 2004 from *http://owl.english.purdue.edu/handouts/research/ r_mla.html.*

Oyama, S. (1976). A sensitive period for the acquisition of nonnative phonological system. *Journal of Psycholinguistic Research, 5,* 261–284.

Park, B. (1982). The big book trend—A discussion with Don Holdaway. *Language Arts, 59,* 814–821.

Parker, D. B. (1994). The rise and fall of the wonderful wizard of oz as a "parable on populism." *Journal of the Georgia Association of Historians, 15,* 49–63.

Peregoy, S., & Boyle, O. (1993). *Reading, writing, and learning in ESL: A resource book for K–8 teachers.* White Plains, NJ: Longman.

Pfaff, C. (Ed.). (1987). First and second language acquisition processes. Cambridge, MA: Newbury House.

Potok, C. (1995). *The chosen.* New York: Fawcett Books.

Rasinski, T. V. (2000). Speed does matter in reading. *The Reading Teacher, 54,* 146–151.

Ruesch, H. (1991). *Top of the world: A novel.* New York: Pocket Books.

Salinger, J. D. (1991). *Catcher in the rye.* (reissue ed.). New York: Little, Brown.

Samuels, S. J. (1997). The method of repeated readings. *The Reading Teacher, 50,* 376–381.

Searle, J. R. (1969). *Speech acts.* Cambridge, UK: Cambridge University Press.

Selinker, L. (1969). Language transfer. *General Linguistics, 9,* 67–92.

Selinker, L. (1972). Interlanguage. *International Review of Applied Linguistics, 10,* 209–31.

Serafini, F. (2000/2001). Three paradigms of assessment: Measurement, procedure, and inquiry. *The Reading Teacher, 54,* 384–393.

Shanahan, T., & Shanahan, S. (1997). Character perspective charting: Helping children develop a more complete conception of story. *The Reading Teacher, 50,* 668–677.

Skinner, B. (1957). *Verbal behavior.* New York: Appleton-Century-Crofts.

Stahl, S. A., & Kuhn, M. R. (2002). Making it sounds like language: Developing fluency. *The Reading Teacher, 55,* 582–584.

Stahl, S. A., & Shiel, T. G. (1992). Teaching meaning vocabulary: Productive approaches for poor readers. *Reading and Writing Quarterly: Overcoming Learning Difficulties, 8,* 223–241.

Stauffer, R. (1980). *The language experience approach to the teaching of reading* (2nd ed.). New York: Harper.

Strickland, D., & Morrow, L. (1989). Environments rich in print promote literacy behavior during play. *Reading Teacher, 43,* 178–179.

Tadlock, D. F. (1978). SQ3R—Why it works, based on an information processing theory of learning. *Journal of Reading, 22,* 110–113.

Taylor, B. (1975). The use of overgeneralization and transfer learning strategies by elementary and intermediate students in ESL. *Language Learning, 25,* 73–107.

Taylor, M. (1992). The language experience approach and adult learners. National Centers for ESL instruction (ERIC Document Reproduction Service EDO-LE-92–01). *http://www.cal.org/ncle/digest/lang_exper. html (May, 21, 2003).*

Tompkins, G. (2003). *Literacy for the 21st century* (3rd ed.). Englewood Cliffs, NJ: Prentice-Hall.

Traxel, J. (1983). The American Revolution in children's fiction. *Research in the Teaching of English, 17,* 61–83.

Trelease, J. (1995). Sustained silent reading. *California English, 1,* 8–9.

Turner, D. (1978). *The effect of instruction on second language learning and second language acquisition.* Paper presented at 12th Annual TESOL Conference, Mexico City, April 1978.

Turner, E., & Rommetveit, R. (1967). The acquisition of sentence voice and reversibility. *Child Development, 38,* 650–660.

Vacca, R. T., & Vacca, J. L. (1989). *Content area reading.* (3rd ed.). Glenview, IL: Scott, Foresman.

Van Allen, R., & Allen, C. (1970). Language experience and reading. Chicago: Britanic Enciclopedic Press.

Walsh, T. (1996). *A short introduction to x-bar syntax and transformations.* Superior, WI: Parlay Enterprises.

White, L. (1989). *Universal grammar and second language acquisition.* Amsterdam: John Benjamins.

Whorf, B. L. (1956). *Language, thought and reality: The selected writings of Benjamin Lee Whorf.* Cambridge, MA: MIT Press.

Williams, J. P. (1980). Teaching decoding with an emphasis on phoneme analysis and phoneme blending. *Journal of Educational Psychology, 72,* 1–15.

Wolfram, W., & Johnson, R. (1982). *Phonological analysis: Focus on American English.* Washington, DC: Center for Applied Linguistics.

Wysocki, K., & Jenkins, J. R. (1987). Deriving word meanings through morphological generalization. *Reading Research Quarterly, 22,* 66–81.

Yopp, H., & Yopp, R. (2000). Supporting phonemic awareness development in the classroom. *The Reading Teacher, 54,* 130–143.

INDEX